Inhalt

Vorwort

Hinweise, Tipps und Übungsaufgaben zu den Kompetenzbereichen

1	Kompetenzbereich: Hörverstehen	1
1.1	Strategien zum Kompetenzbereich „Hörverstehen"	1
1.2	Übungsaufgaben zum Kompetenzbereich „Hörverstehen"	3
	Hörverstehen Test 1: The football game	3
	Hörverstehen Test 2: Hit Radio 100.50	6
	Hörverstehen Test 3: Flight 175	8
	Hörverstehen Test 4: At the shopping centre	11
2	Kompetenzbereich: Leseverstehen	13
2.1	Strategien zum Kompetenzbereich „Leseverstehen"	13
2.2	Übungsaufgaben zum Kompetenzbereich „Leseverstehen"	14
	Leseverstehen Test 1: Signs	14
	Leseverstehen Test 2: London attractions	17
	Leseverstehen Test 3: Cinema	21
	Leseverstehen Test 4: Very trendy!	24
	Leseverstehen Test 5: A dream come true	28
3	Kompetenzbereich: Schreiben	30
3.1	Strategien zum Kompetenzbereich „Schreiben"	30
3.2	Hilfreiche Wendungen zur Textproduktion	32
3.3	Übungsaufgaben zum Kompetenzbereich „Schreiben"	35
4	Kompetenzbereich: Sprechen	45
4.1	Hinweise und Strategien zum Kompetenzbereich „Sprechen"	45
4.2	Hilfreiche Wendungen und Beispiele zum Kompetenzbereich „Sprechen"	47
4.3	Übungsaufgaben zum Kompetenzbereich „Sprechen"	51

Kurzgrammatik

1	Adverbien – *adverbs*	59
2	Bedingungssätze – *if-clauses*	60
3	Fürwörter – *pronouns*	61
4	Grundform – *infinitive*	62
5	Indirekte Rede – *reported speech*	62
6	Modale Hilfsverben – *modal auxiliaries*	64
7	Konjunktionen – *conjunctions*	65
8	Partizipien – *participles*	66
9	Passiv – *passive voice*	67

Fortsetzung siehe nächste Seite

Inhalt

10	Präpositionen – *prepositions*	68
11	Relativsätze – *relative clauses*	71
12	Steigerung und Vergleich – *comparisons*	72
13	Wortstellung – *word order*	73
14	Zeiten – *tenses*	74

Original-Abschlussprüfungsaufgaben

Hauptschulabschlussprüfung 2012

Hörverstehen	2012-1
Answer Sheet	2012-4
Leseverstehen	2012-5
Answer Sheet	2012-11
Schreiben	2012-12

Hauptschulabschlussprüfung 2013

Hörverstehen	2013-1
Answer Sheet	2013-4
Leseverstehen	2013-5
Answer Sheet	2013-11
Schreiben	2013-12

Hauptschulabschlussprüfung 2014

Hörverstehen	2014-1
Answer Sheet	2014-4
Leseverstehen	2014-5
Answer Sheet	2014-11
Schreiben	2014-12

Hauptschulabschlussprüfung 2015

Hörverstehen	2015-1
Answer Sheet	2015-4
Leseverstehen	2015-5
Answer Sheet	2015-11
Schreiben	2015-12

Hauptschulabschlussprüfung 2016

Hörverstehen	2016-1
Answer Sheet	2016-4
Leseverstehen	2016-5
Answer Sheet	2016-11
Schreiben	2016-12

Hauptschulabschlussprüfung 2017

Hörverstehen	2017-1
Answer Sheet	2017-4
Leseverstehen	2017-5
Answer Sheet	2017-11
Schreiben	2017-12

Original-Prüfungsaufgaben
und Training

HAUPTSCHULABSCHLUSS

Englisch

Baden-Württemberg

2012–2017

MP3-CD

Bildnachweis
S. 3: Fußball: © Judi Seiber/www.sxc.hu; Puck: © Snack Admiral/www.sxc.hu; Tennisball: © Jean Scheijen/www.sxc.hu; Football: © Penny Bubar/www.sxc.hu
S. 5: © H. Oestrich/www.sxc.hu
S. 7: © rhineline/www.photocase.de
S. 9: schiefer Turm: © Elvis Santana/www.sxc.hu; Eiffelturm: © Eric Weijers/www.sxc.hu
S. 10: Reichstag: © Martin T. Teubner/www.sxc.hu; Tower Bridge: © Nimalan Tharmalingam/www.sxc.hu
S. 14: Schild 1: © McKenna/www.sxc.hu; Schild 2: © Tom Fawles/www.sxc.hu; Schild 3: © Jeff Jones/www.sxc.hu
S. 15: Schild 1: © Dani Simmonds/www.sxc.hu; Schild 2: © Jeff Jones/www.sxc.hu; Schild 3: © Jeff Jones/www.sxc.hu
S. 18: © Foto 1 © Toranico. Shutterstock, Foto 2 © Can Stock Photo Inc./mimagephotography, Foto 3 © Andresr. Shutterstock, Foto 4 © CorelDraw Inc.
S.19: Foto 1: © www.freeimages.co.uk; Foto 2: © Maria Zmuda; Foto 3: © www.Pixel Quelle.de; Foto 4: © ddp images; Foto 5: © Adam Ciesielski; Foto 6: © Carin Araujo/www.sxc.hu
S. 21: Foto 1, 2 und 3: © Allstar Picture Library
S. 37/38: © Ales Vrtal, Kemmern
S. 39: © Bernd Wiedemann, Gauting
S. 51: © Keith Syvinski/www.sxc.hu
S. 52: © Mac Brown/www.sxc.hu
S. 70/71: © Paul Jenkinson

Deckblatt Hinweise, Tipps und Übungsaufgaben zu den Kompetenzbereichen:
© Willselarep, Image provided by Dreamstime.com
Deckblatt Kurzgrammatik: © www.gimmestock.com/shakif
Deckblatt Original-Aufgaben der Abschlussprüfung © James Moore

alle übrigen Bilder: Redaktion

© 2017 Stark Verlag GmbH
11. ergänzte Auflage
www.stark-verlag.de

Das Werk und alle seine Bestandteile sind urheberrechtlich geschützt. Jede vollständige oder teilweise Vervielfältigung, Verbreitung und Veröffentlichung bedarf der ausdrücklichen Genehmigung des Verlages. Dies gilt insbesondere für Vervielfältigungen, Mikroverfilmungen sowie die Speicherung und Verarbeitung in elektronischen Systemen.

Inhalt

MP3-CD

Text 1: The football game	Track 1
Text 2: Hit Radio 100.50	Track 2
Text 3: Flight 175	Track 3
Text 4: At the shopping centre	Track 4
Abschlussprüfung 2012	Track 5
Abschlussprüfung 2013	Track 6
Abschlussprüfung 2014	Track 7
Abschlussprüfung 2015	Track 8
Abschlussprüfung 2016	Track 9
Abschlussprüfung 2017	Track 10

*Die Hintergrundgeräusche auf der CD stammen aus folgenden Quellen:
pacdv, Partners in Rhyme und freesound*

Jeweils im Herbst erscheinen die neuen Ausgaben
der Hauptschulabschlussprüfungen an Werkrealschulen.

Lösungen der Prüfungsaufgaben:
Gabriele Steiner, Ariane Last (ab 2016)
Illustration Kurzgrammatik: Paul Jenkinson

Vorwort

Liebe Schülerinnen, liebe Schüler,

jeder, der in der Schule eine Fremdsprache lernt, kennt das Gefühl, dass es Bereiche gibt, in denen die Kenntnisse und Fähigkeiten noch verbessert werden können. Diese Unsicherheiten machen sich im Unterricht, aber auch bei Prüfungen bemerkbar. Die beste Methode, um Lücken zu schließen oder einfach nur mehr Sicherheit im Umgang mit der englischen Sprache zu gewinnen, ist eine langfristige Vorbereitung, im Laufe derer man sich solide Kenntnisse aneignet. Mit dem vorliegenden Buch kannst du deine Englischkenntnisse dauerhaft verbessern und dich so selbstständig und effektiv auf die Hauptschulabschlussprüfung im Fach Englisch vorbereiten oder einfach nur sicherstellen, dass du dem Englischunterricht gut folgen kannst.

- Jedes Kapitel widmet sich einem **Kompetenzbereich** der Prüfung. In den ersten Abschnitten erfährst du jeweils, welche Anforderungen auf dich zukommen können und wie du dich am besten darauf vorbereitest. Du kannst also gezielt bestimmte Bereiche herausgreifen, die du besonders trainieren möchtest.
- Anhand der **Übungen und der Abschlussprüfungsaufgaben 2012 bis 2017** kannst du trainieren, wie man mit verschiedenen Aufgabenstellungen in den einzelnen Fertigkeitsbereichen umgeht und wie man sie erfolgreich löst.
- Die beiliegende **MP3-CD** enthält alle Hörverstehenstexte. Sie hilft dir dabei, dein Hörverständnis gezielt zu verbessern.
- In der **Kurzgrammatik** werden alle wichtigen grammatischen Themen knapp erläutert und an Beispielsätzen veranschaulicht. Hier kannst du nachschlagen, wenn du in der Grammatik einmal unsicher sein solltest.
- Eine Auswahl **hilfreicher Wendungen**, die dir sicherlich in den unterschiedlichsten Bereichen nützlich sein werden, erleichtert dir das selbstständige Verfassen kleiner wie größerer Texte.
- Am Ende des Buches findest du ein **Lösungsheft** mit ausführlichen Lösungsvorschlägen und hilfreichen **Hinweisen** und **Tipps** zum Lösen der Aufgaben.

Sollten nach Erscheinen dieses Bandes noch wichtige Änderungen in der Abschlussprüfung 2018 vom Ministerium für Kultus, Jugend und Sport bekannt gegeben werden, findest du aktuelle Informationen dazu im Internet unter: www.stark-verlag.de/pruefung-aktuell

Wir wünschen dir viel Spaß beim Üben und viel Erfolg in deinen Prüfungen!

Dein Stark Verlag

Hinweise und Tipps zum Hauptschulabschluss

1 Ablauf der Prüfung

Der schriftliche Prüfungsteil wird zentral, die mündliche Prüfung von deiner Schule gestellt. Deine Abschlussprüfung besteht aus den folgenden Prüfungsteilen:

Prüfungsteil	Dauer	Prüfungsanteil
I. Hör- und Hör-/Sehverstehen	30 Min.	
	15 Minuten Pause	50 %
II. Leseverstehen	60 Min.	
III. Schreiben		
IV. Sprechen monologisch	5 Min.	
IV. Sprechen dialogisch	5 Min.	50 %
V. Sprachmittlung	5 Min.	

2 Inhalte und Themen

Die Prüfung hat kein aufgabenübergreifendes Thema. In den einzelnen Prüfungsteilen werden verschiedene Texte eingesetzt, die alle thematisch voneinander unabhängig sind. Es handelt sich hierbei um authentische Texte, die aus der Lebenswelt junger Menschen stammen.

3 Leistungsanforderungen

Allgemeine Kenntnisse und Fertigkeiten

Von dir wird erwartet, dass du geschriebene oder gesprochene Texte zu bekannten Themen verstehst, auch wenn darin unbekannte Worte enthalten sind. Das Ausfüllen von Formularen, das Schreiben von E-Mails oder einfachen Texten nach Vorgaben sollte dir auch keine Probleme bereiten.
Beim Sprechen kommt es darauf an, dass du in einfachen Alltagssituationen zwischen zwei Gesprächspartnern vermitteln kannst und dass du einen vorbereiteten Vortrag halten, Fragen stellen und auf Fragen reagieren kannst.

Hör- und Hör-/Sehverstehen

Dieser Prüfungsteil besteht aus verschiedenen Teilen. Nachdem du fünf Minuten Zeit hattest, dir die Aufgabenblätter anzusehen, hörst du in der Regel mehrere Texte von einer CD. Du hörst die Texte immer zweimal. Zu jedem Teil gibt es Aufgaben. Hier musst du z. B. die richtigen Bilder oder Aussagen ankreuzen, oder einzelne Wörter, die du hörst, in einen Lückentext eintragen. Selbst formulierte Sätze werden nicht gefordert. Dein Wortschatz muss natürlich groß genug sein, um auch schwierigere Anweisungen, Fragen und Aussagen zu verstehen, unbekannte Worte aus dem Kontext zu erschließen und die Kernaussage längerer Texte zu verstehen. Zum Schluss hast du noch einmal fünf Minuten Zeit, um deine Ergebnisse auf den Antwortbogen *(answer sheet)* zu übertragen.

Leseverstehen

Auch hier musst du die richtigen Antworten (A, B, C oder true/false) auf einem *answer sheet* ankreuzen. Du sollst zeigen, dass du beispielsweise Texte auf Hinweis- oder Verbotsschildern verstehst. Ein Lückentext mit Wörtern zum Auswählen überprüft ebenfalls dein Textverständnis. Es werden dir auch andere kurze Texte vorgelegt, deren zentrale Aussage du verstehen musst, um entscheiden zu können, welche der angegebenen Lösungen richtig oder falsch sind.

Schreiben

Die Arbeitsblätter für diesen Prüfungsteil erhältst du zusammen mit den Arbeitsblättern für den Teil Leseverstehen. Hier kannst du zeigen, dass du eigene Texte auf Englisch schreiben kannst.
Dieser Prüfungsteil besteht meist aus folgenden drei Teilen:
- einem Lückentext
- einem Formular, das ausgefüllt, oder einem Dialog, der ergänzt werden muss
- einer E-Mail

In den Prüfungsteilen Leseverstehen und Schreiben darfst du während der gesamten Prüfungszeit das Wörterbuch verwenden.

Sprechen

Dieser Prüfungsteil wird in der Regel als Tandemprüfung durchgeführt.

Monologisches Sprechen: Vor der Prüfung bereitest du ein Thema vor, über das du sprechen möchtest. Du berichtest über dich und deine Familie oder dein Hobby. Dazu bringst du geeignete Gegenstände (z. B. Bilder, Fotos, Postkarten) mit, über die du dann erzählst.

Dialogisches Sprechen: Der Prüfer/die Prüferin teilt an die Prüflinge „prompt cards" aus. Auf der einen Karte stehen Informationen, auf der anderen Karte stehen Stichworte für Fragen. Sind alle Fragen gestellt und beantwortet, wechselt ihr die Rollen. Hierfür bekommt ihr neue Karten.

Sprachmittlung: Hier sollst du in einer Situation, die dir auf Deutsch erklärt wird, zwischen zwei Personen vermitteln. Person A spricht nur Deutsch, Person B spricht nur Englisch. Du musst abwechselnd einmal ins Deutsche und einmal ins Englische übertragen. Es geht nicht darum, Wort für Wort zu übersetzen, sondern sinngemäß den Inhalt wiederzugeben.

4 Bewertung

Zur Bewertung der Prüfungsteile Hör- und Hör-/Sehverstehen und Lesen werden **nur** die *answer sheets* von den Prüfern kontrolliert. Beim Schreiben geht es vorrangig um Verständlichkeit: würde z. B. ein Engländer verstehen, was du geschrieben hast? Einen Punktabzug gibt es allerdings für Abschreibfehler.
Auch bei der mündlichen Prüfung gilt als Mindestanspruch: würde ein Engländer das verstehen? Darüber hinaus achten die Prüfer auch auf deine Aussprache und deine Flexibilität: Ist dein Wortschatz groß genug oder benutzt du immer die gleichen Worte? Kannst du ein Gespräch in Gang halten?

5 Hinweise und Tipps zur schriftlichen Prüfung

- Lies die Aufgaben und Anweisungen **genau** durch. Achte darauf, was von dir verlangt wird, z. B. eine Begründung, warum eine Antwort falsch ist.
- Übertrage deine Ergebnisse **sorgfältig** auf die *answer sheets*. Es ist schade, wenn du hier durch Übertragungsfehler Punkte vergibst.
- Versuche zunächst, unbekannte Worte aus dem Zusammenhang zu erschließen. Vielleicht verstehst du den Satz auch ohne dieses Wort. Das Nachschlagen im Wörterbuch braucht **viel Zeit** und muss gut geübt sein.
- Verwende nicht zu viel Zeit für Aufgaben, die dir schwierig erscheinen. Besser ist es, zuerst alle Aufgaben zu bearbeiten und am Schluss noch einmal zu den Aufgaben zurückzukehren, die dir Probleme bereitet haben.
- Für die Prüfungsteile Leseverstehen und Schreiben solltest du dir eine Uhr mit in die Prüfung nehmen. Es ist wichtig, dass du dir die Zeit sinnvoll einteilst.

6 Mündliche Prüfung

Die mündliche Prüfung wird dezentral durchgeführt. Die Aufgabentypen sind festgelegt. Sowohl die einzelnen Aufgaben als auch den Termin legt jede Schule selbst fest. Solltest du nach der schriftlichen Prüfung zwischen zwei Noten stehen, hast du die Möglichkeit, eine zusätzliche mündliche Prüfung abzulegen. Sprich mit deinem Fachlehrer über die Anforderungen einer freiwilligen mündlichen Prüfung.

▶ **Hinweise, Tipps und Übungsaufgaben zu den Kompetenzbereichen**

1 Kompetenzbereich: Hörverstehen

Hörverstehenstexte und die zugehörigen Aufgabenstellungen können sehr unterschiedlich sein. Die Texte, die du im Unterricht oder im Rahmen von Klassenarbeiten oder in der Abschlussprüfung zu hören bekommst, spiegeln meist **reale Sprechsituationen** wider, d. h. man kann solche oder ähnliche Texte im „wirklichen Leben" hören. Die Inhalte der Texte können von der Begrüßungsansprache eines Flugkapitäns über die Lautsprecheransagen an einem Bahnhof oder die Kommentierung eines Fußballspiels bis hin zu Gesprächen zwischen mehreren Personen reichen.

Genauso vielfältig wie die verschiedenen Arten von Hörtexten können auch die Aufgabenstellungen ausfallen. In diesem Kapitel werden dir die häufigsten Textarten und Aufgabenstellungen zum Kompetenzbereich „Listening" vorgestellt. Die Prüfung zum Hörverstehen in der Hauptschulabschlussprüfung dauert 30 Minuten.

1.1 Strategien zum Kompetenzbereich „Hörverstehen"

Vorgehen beim Üben

Zu Übungszwecken kannst du den Hörverstehenstext auf der Audio-CD ruhig so oft anhören, wie du möchtest. Lies ihn aber nicht durch! Versuche, die Arbeitsaufträge nur durch Zuhören zu beantworten. Nur wenn du überhaupt nicht auf die richtige Lösung kommst, solltest du den Hörverstehenstext im Lösungsteil dieses Buches lesen. Bei der Bearbeitung der Hörverstehensaufgaben solltest du wie folgt vorgehen:

- Höre den entsprechenden Text auf der CD einmal an, sodass du weißt, worum es darin geht.
- Lies die Aufgabenstellungen genau durch. Hast du sie alle verstanden? Kläre unbekannte Wörter mithilfe eines Wörterbuches.
- Höre die CD noch einmal an. Diesen Schritt kannst du so oft wiederholen, wie es für dich hilfreich ist.
- Höre die CD an und versuche dabei, die Aufgaben zu lösen.
- Wenn du alle Aufgaben bearbeitet hast, solltest du überprüfen, ob deine Lösungen richtig sind, indem du dir den Text ein weiteres Mal anhörst.
- Anschließend überprüfst du deine Antworten anhand der Lösungen am Ende des Buches. Wenn du viele Fehler gemacht hast, dann überlege genau, wie sie zustande gekommen sind. Hast du den Hörtext nicht genau verstanden? Hast du die Fragestellung falsch verstanden? Lies gegebenenfalls den Hörverstehenstext durch und wiederhole die gesamte Aufgabe in ein paar Wochen.
- Versuche, mit der Bearbeitung jeder weiteren Hörverstehensaufgabe in diesem Buch die Zahl der Hörsequenzen zu reduzieren, bis du bei der in der Hauptschulabschlussprüfung üblichen Anzahl angelangt bist.

Kompetenzbereich: Hörverstehen

Vorgehen in der Prüfung

In der Abschlussprüfung hörst du die Arbeitsanweisungen auf der CD **einmal**, die Texte zum Hörverstehen hörst du **zweimal**. Sie werden dir alle von einer CD vorgespielt. Für die Prüfung zum Hörverstehen gilt:

Arbeitsschritt 1

Nach dem Austeilen der Aufgabenblätter bekommst du fünf Minuten Zeit, in denen du die Aufgaben genau anschauen kannst. Lies dabei die Aufgabenstellungen sorgfältig durch und überlege genau, welche Informationen du bislang noch nicht verstanden hast. Du hörst die Hörverstehenstexte zweimal. Zu den Aufgaben, die du nach dem ersten Hören bereits beantworten kannst, kannst du gleich die **richtige Lösung aufschreiben**. Alle Lösungen musst du auf das dafür vorgesehene *answer sheet* schreiben. Korrekte Lösungen auf anderen Blättern werden nicht gewertet. Pass auf, dass du keine Fehler beim Übertragen der Lösungen von deinen Notizen auf das *answer sheet* machst.

Arbeitsschritt 2

Wenn überhaupt, dann solltest du dir erst während des zweiten Hördurchgangs **Notizen machen**. Das Anfertigen von Notizen kann dich vom Zuhören abhalten, daher solltest du dabei ganz gezielt vorgehen und wirklich nur die wichtigsten Dinge aufschreiben, die du dir so nicht merken kannst. Da du nach dem ersten Hören die Arbeitsaufträge kennst, weißt du, welche **Detailinformationen** gefragt sind. Solche Detailinformationen können beispielsweise Adressen sein oder es werden Eigennamen buchstabiert, die du zur Lösung einer Aufgabe exakt aufschreiben musst. In solchen Fällen lohnt es sich, Notizen zu machen.

Arbeitsschritt 3

Nach dem zweiten Hören bekommst du noch einmal fünf Minuten Zeit, um jede Aufgabe auf deinem Arbeitsblatt noch einmal gründlich durchzulesen und entsprechend zu lösen. Hast du nach dem ersten Hören bereits einige Aufgaben beantwortet, so überprüfe sie jetzt noch einmal auf ihre Richtigkeit. Bei Detailinformationen, die innerhalb von einzelnen Aufgaben gefragt sind, solltest du zur Beantwortung deine Notizen heranziehen.

Einen Punkt solltest du immer beachten: Die Fragen folgen in der Regel der Reihenfolge im Text. Wenn du die Lösung zu einer der mittleren Fragen nicht weißt, dann passe beim zweiten Hören in der Mitte des Textes besonders gut auf.

TIPP

- Höre genau zu. Worum geht es im Text?
- Nach dem ersten Hören: Lies die Aufgabenstellungen nochmals genau. Trage die Lösungen zu den Aufgaben ein, die du schon beantworten kannst. Welche Informationen fehlen dir noch?
- Mache dir während des zweiten Hörens Notizen über Details, die du für die Beantwortung der Fragen brauchst.
- Nach dem zweiten Hören: Löse nun die restlichen Aufgaben. Überprüfe auch noch einmal die Aufgaben, die du nach dem ersten Hören bereits gelöst hast.

1.2 Übungsaufgaben zum Kompetenzbereich „Hörverstehen"

Hörverstehen Test 1: The football game

season ticket	– *Dauerkarte*
(to) apologise	– *sich entschuldigen*
rude	– *unhöflich*
rather than	– *eher als*
old-fashioned	– *altmodisch*
appreciate	– *hier: es zu schätzen wissen*

> **Matching**
> Bei diesem Aufgabentyp musst du dem gehörten Text Bilder zuordnen. Das bedeutet, dass du ganz genau hinhören musst, damit du dir alle wesentlichen Informationen merken kannst, um dann das richtige Bild ankreuzen zu können.

1. Listen to the CD and look at the pictures. Which picture shows the piece of sports equipment of the sport event Mrs Warden wants to see at the weekend? Mark the right answer.

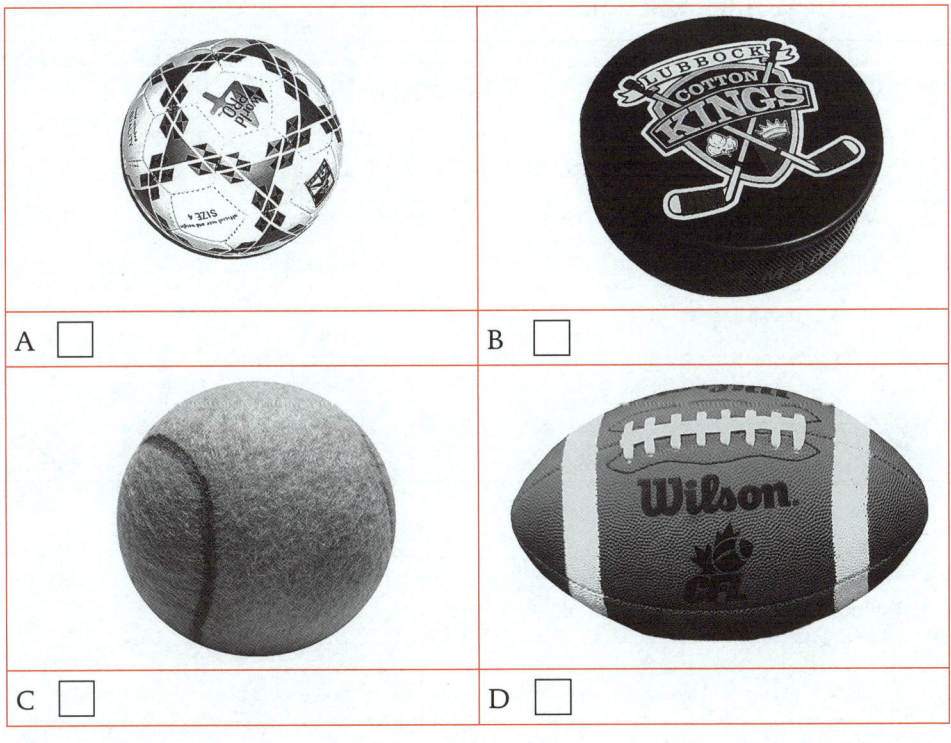

Kompetenzbereich: Hörverstehen

TIPP

Right or wrong
Diesen Aufgabentyp kennst du sicher schon lange aus dem Unterricht. Du sollst jeweils entscheiden, ob eine Aussage richtig oder falsch ist. Meist weicht dabei die Formulierung der Aussage in der Aufgabenstellung etwas von der im Text ab.

2. Listen to the CD and mark the right answer.

		right	wrong
a)	The woman's first name is Christina.	☐	☐
b)	She's interested in the game between Manchester United and Chelsea.	☐	☐
c)	Mr Warden doesn't like football.	☐	☐
d)	She wants to buy a ticket for her husband.	☐	☐
e)	The woman owns a season ticket.	☐	☐
f)	There are still a lot of tickets available for the game on Saturday.	☐	☐
g)	Tim Stone wants to accompany (*begleiten*) Mrs Warden to the game.	☐	☐
h)	Mrs Warden agrees to Tim Stone's suggestion (*Vorschlag*).	☐	☐
i)	Mrs Warden will watch the game on TV.	☐	☐

3. What does Mrs Warden want to buy? Mark the right ticket.

FA – THE HOME OF ENGLISH FOOTBALL

Manchester United : Arsenal London

15.30 h

Block D row 17, seat 7d

A ☐

FA – THE HOME OF ENGLISH FOOTBALL

Manchester United : Chelsea London

15.30 h

Block D row 17, seat 7d

B ☐

BRITISH NATIONAL ICE HOCKEY LEAGUE

Newcastle Vipers : Basingstoke Bisons

15.30 h

row 6 seat 86

C ☐

4. Fill in the missing information.

	Tim Stone	Mrs Warden
ticket	Tim Stone has a ticket for _____.	Mrs Warden normally has a _____.
game on Saturday	He will watch it _____.	She will watch it _____.

5. Fill in the missing words from the text.

Mrs Warden _____ the ticket hotline because she wants to buy a ticket for the _____ game on Saturday. Normally she has a season ticket but she gave it to her _____ as she was ill. Tim Stone, who _____ for Manchester Ticket Office, thinks she wants to buy a ticket for her _____. Mrs Warden is _____ about this misunderstanding. Tim Stone offers her _____ ticket for the _____ on Saturday as an apology. Mrs Warden refuses his offer and says she prefers to _____ the game on TV.

Kompetenzbereich: Hörverstehen

T2

Hörverstehen Test 2: Hit Radio 100.50

Vokabeln

Stay tuned!	– Bleibt dran!
available	– erhältlich
(to) dress up	– sich verkleiden
for free	– kostenlos
gift	– Geschenk
first come, first served	– „Wer zuerst kommt, mahlt zuerst."

TIPP

> *Multiple choice*
> Auch dieser Aufgabentyp ist dir bestimmt vertraut. Dir wird eine Frage mit mehreren möglichen Antworten vorgegeben und du musst entscheiden, welche Antwort am besten zum Inhalt des Textes passt. Auch hier wird die Formulierung in der Aufgabenstellung variiert.

Worksheet

1. Listen to the CD and mark the right answer.

   a) What is the presenter's name?
   - A ☐ Marc Anthony
   - B ☐ Marc Bent
   - C ☐ Marc Kent

   b) What is the name of the radio station?
   - A ☐ Hit Radio
   - B ☐ Hot Radio
   - C ☐ Hat Radio

   c) When will the "Four Top" concert start?
   - A ☐ at 9.30 in the evening
   - B ☐ at 9 o'clock in the morning
   - C ☐ at 9 o'clock in the evening

   d) What is on tonight in all the cocktail bars?
   - A ☐ Hawaiian night
   - B ☐ all the bars are closed
   - C ☐ a dance

   e) Where will the radio station party take place?
   - A ☐ at the Bluebird
   - B ☐ at the Blackbird
   - C ☐ at the cocktail bar

   f) How many tickets are they giving away for free?
   - A ☐ 30
   - B ☐ 20
   - C ☐ 10

Kompetenzbereich: Hörverstehen

2. Listen to the CD and mark the right answer.

                                                                                                  right wrong

   a) The Hawaiian Cocktail Night only takes place in three bars. ☐ ☐

   b) You get a cocktail for free when you dress up as if you were in Hawaii. ☐ ☐

   c) The DJ's name tonight is DJ Tim. ☐ ☐

   d) There are still tickets available for the party. ☐ ☐

   e) You can win tickets when you show up at the radio station. ☐ ☐

> **Vocabulary**
> Im Rahmen der Hörverstehensaufgaben wird gelegentlich auch dein Wortschatz geprüft. Dabei kommen die Vokabeln, nach denen gefragt wird, natürlich im Hörverstehenstext vor.

TIPP

3. Fill in the missing words from the CD.

   Marc is a _____. His radio station arranges a _____. There are no more tickets _____ for the party, but you can _____ the hotline and get tickets _____. You don't have to answer any questions – it's _____, _____. Marc also announces a _____ by "Four Top". It will take place at 9 o'clock in the evening at _____.

Hörverstehen Test 3: Flight 175

1. Listen to the CD and mark the right answer.

   a) What is the captain's name?
      - A ☐ Sandra Brown
      - B ☐ Sandy Brown
      - C ☐ Sandy Blue

   b) The flight goes from Hannover to
      - A ☐ London Heathrow.
      - B ☐ London Stansted.
      - C ☐ London Gatwick

   c) The flight will starts
      - A ☐ 5 minutes earlier.
      - B ☐ 30 minutes later.
      - C ☐ 20 minutes later.

   d) What does the captain say about the airspace in southern Britain?
      - A ☐ It is not overcrowded.
      - B ☐ It is overcrowded.
      - C ☐ Nothing.

   e) How long will the flight take?
      - A ☐ One hour.
      - B ☐ Two hours.
      - C ☐ 45 minutes.

   f) How high will they be flying?
      - A ☐ 15,000 feet
      - B ☐ 35,000 feet
      - C ☐ 25,000 feet

   g) What will be the average speed?
      - A ☐ 500 miles per hour
      - B ☐ 600 miles per hour
      - C ☐ 850 miles per hour

   h) The weather in London is
      - A ☐ nice and sunny.
      - B ☐ rainy.
      - C ☐ windy.

i) Temperatures in London will be at about
   A ☐ 20 degrees Fahrenheit.
   B ☐ 25 degrees Fahrenheit.
   C ☐ 25 degrees Celsius.

2. What describes the text you have heard the best?
   ☐ It is an announcement *(Durchsage)* by a flight captain.
   ☐ It is a speech delivered *(vorgetragen)* by a stewardess.
   ☐ One of the passengers is trying to entertain the other passengers.

3. Fill in the missing information.

numbers	We will be flying with an altitude of _____ feet.	Our flight will start _____ minutes later than scheduled.
names	This is your captain speaking. My name is _____.	We will land at _____-_____.
towns	I'd like to welcome you aboard on flight 175 from _____ to London Heathrow.	I hope you have a pleasant flight and that you enjoy your stay in _____.

4. In the pictures you see famous sights of European cities. Which City is the destination of the flight in the text? Mark the right picture.

A ☐

B ☐

C ☐

D ☐

Kompetenzbereich: Hörverstehen | 11

Hörverstehen Test 4: At the shopping centre　　T4

1. Listen to the CD and mark the right answer.　　right　wrong　　Worksheet
   a) Parents are searching for their daughter.　☐ ☐
   b) The missing girl's name is Maria.　☐ ☐
   c) Her dress is blue with red stripes.　☐ ☐
   d) The information desk is near the main entrance.　☐ ☐
   e) The car is standing in the emergency access road (Feuerwehrzufahrt).　☐ ☐
   f) The summer festival will take place in July.　☐ ☐
   g) There will be a lot of surprises during the summer festival.　☐ ☐
   h) It will last a whole month.　☐ ☐
   i) The speaker warns the customers of pickpockets.　☐ ☐
   j) The speaker closes the announcement with the words: "See you soon at our shopping centre."　☐ ☐

2. Fill in the missing words from the CD.

   The speaker asks the _____ in the shopping centre for their _____. A little girl has _____ her parents. They can pick her up at the _____. The speaker also calls for the _____ of the car identified to move it _____. In the end he mentions the _____, which will _____ at the shopping centre soon.

3. Which one is the number plate mentioned in the text? Mark the right answer.

H 555 BXG	R 467 NXG	5 HUG 67T
A	B	C

4. Which photo shows the girl from the story? Mark the right photo.

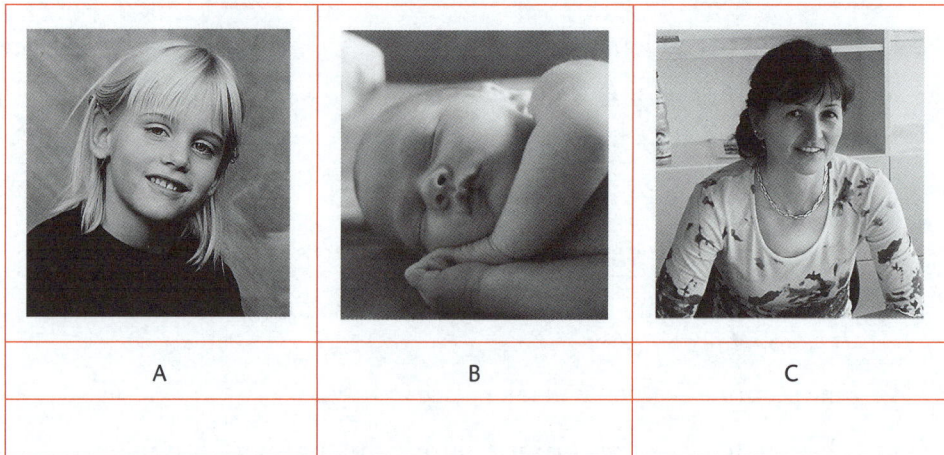

A	B	C

2 Kompetenzbereich: Leseverstehen

Es gibt viele verschiedene Arten von Lesetexten. Ebenso vielfältig können die Aufgabenstellungen dazu sein. Die Textsorten und Aufgabenstellungen, die am häufigsten im Unterricht, in Klassenarbeiten und in der Abschlussprüfung vorkommen, werden wir dir hier vorstellen.

Der Prüfungsteil zum Leseverstehen dauert zusammen mit dem Prüfungsteil „Schreiben" 60 Minuten.

2.1 Strategien zum Kompetenzbereich „Leseverstehen"

Ganz gleich, welche Art von Lesetext oder welche Art von Aufgabenstellung du bearbeiten musst, die Vorgehensweise ist dabei immer dieselbe.

Zunächst einmal ist es sinnvoll, den Text an sich ganz genau zu betrachten. Manchmal kannst du bereits am **Layout**, d. h. an der Gestaltung des Textes erkennen, um welche Textsorte es geht. Wenn du weißt, ob der dir vorliegende Text eine Werbeanzeige, ein Zeitungsartikel oder ein Interview ist, dann bist du schon einen Schritt weiter. — Arbeitsschritt 1

Nun solltest du die **Aufgabenstellungen genau lesen**, damit du weißt, unter welchen Aspekten du den Text bearbeiten sollst. Wenn du später den Lesetext liest, kannst du dabei ganz gezielt wichtige **Schlüsselwörter bzw. Textpassagen markieren**, damit du sie bei der Bearbeitung der Aufgaben schnell wiederfindest. — Arbeitsschritt 2

Jetzt solltest du den Text **genau lesen**. Suche dir gezielt die Informationen heraus, die du für das Bearbeiten der Aufgaben brauchst. Deswegen hast du bereits die Aufgabenstellungen gelesen, um genau zu wissen, worauf du bei dem Text achten musst. Unbekannte Wörter solltest du **im Wörterbuch nachschlagen**. Achte aber darauf, dass du nicht zu viele Wörter nachschaust, denn das kostet wertvolle Zeit. Manche Wörter kannst du außerdem ganz leicht aus dem **Sinnzusammenhang erschließen**. Ganz entscheidend ist, dass du dir bei diesem Arbeitsschritt einen guten Überblick über den Inhalt deines Textes verschaffst. — Arbeitsschritt 3

Nun bist du für die Beantwortung der Aufgaben gut gerüstet!

TIPP
- Schaue dir den Lesetext genau an. Kannst du vom „Layout" auf die Textsorte schließen?
- Lies den Text mehrmals genau durch. Schlage unbekannte Wörter im Wörterbuch nach. Verschaffe dir so einen guten Überblick über den Inhalt des Textes.
- Lies die Aufgabenstellungen genau. Markiere beim nochmaligen Lesen des Textes wichtige Textaussagen im Hinblick auf die Aufgabenstellungen.

2.2 Übungsaufgaben zum Kompetenzbereich „Leseverstehen"

Leseverstehen Test 1: Signs

1. Where can you see these signs? There is only one correct answer.

   a)

   A ☐ on a parking lot
   B ☐ in a restaurant
   C ☐ at the train station
   D ☐ in a supermarket

   b)

   A ☐ on the street
   B ☐ in the airport
   C ☐ in the bathroom
   D ☐ at an underground station

   c)

   A ☐ in a cafe
   B ☐ in a swimming pool
   C ☐ in a park
   D ☐ on a motorway

2. What do the signs say? There is only one correct answer.

a) **For Health Reasons PLEASE DO NOT FEED THE BIRDS**

- A ☐ You shall feed the birds.
- B ☐ Don't cross the street for safety reasons.
- C ☐ You shall not feed the birds.
- D ☐ Give only special food to the birds.

b) **HAVE A NICE DAY**

- A ☐ This is a free parking space.
- B ☐ Enjoy your day.
- C ☐ Parking is prohibited here.
- D ☐ No dogs are allowed here.

c) **CAUTION DUCK CROSSING**

- A ☐ Think of the speed limit.
- B ☐ This is a dangerous area.
- C ☐ Be careful because horses can be crossing the street.
- D ☐ Be careful because ducks can be crossing the street.

3. What do the signs say?

a)

Bill's Boats

▶ Rent a boat at Bill's Boats!
▶ Open from Monday to Sunday
▶ 9 a.m. to 7 p.m.
▶ Only 2 £ / hour.

(Closed in winter from November to March.)

A ☐ You get free advice lessons.
B ☐ You have to pay in advance.
C ☐ Bill's Boats is closed on Tuesdays.
D ☐ Bill's Boats is closed from November to March.

b)

▶ **ATTENTION** ◀

Don't leave your luggage unattended! Beware of pickpockets!

A ☐ Be careful because of the dog.
B ☐ Take care of your luggage.
C ☐ Don't cross the street here.
D ☐ Be careful.

c)

NEW: Gina's CD World

Buy two CDs – get one for free

Special offer – only this week

A ☐ The special offer is valid the whole year.
B ☐ When you buy two CDs you get two for free.
C ☐ When you buy two CDs you get one for free.
D ☐ The shop's name has changed.

Leseverstehen Test 2: London attractions

Bei dieser Aufgabe erhältst du die Beschreibungen von vier verschiedenen Sehenswürdigkeiten in und um London. Lies sie gut durch.

Hinweis

Text

The London Planetarium

- The Planetarium is over forty years old and offers star shows in the great green dome and two interactive zones.
- It is the only Planetarium in Europe which has Digistar 2, the world's most advanced star projector.
- The shows last 10–12 minutes with commentary.
- You can enjoy interactive exhibits before watching the star show. No pushchairs due to safety reasons.

Contact us: London Planetarium, Marylebone Road, London NW1

TATE MODERN

Tate Modern is Britain's newest national gallery of modern art. Tate Modern is home to the Tate's collection of international modern art from 1900 to the present day.
The major exhibition is:

> Collection 2000: which includes landscape, still life, body and history, exhibited in a completely new way.

Contact us: Sumner Street, Bankside, London, SE1 9TG

Phantom of the Opera

Lloyd Webber's romantic musical opera is based on Gaston Leroux's gothic novel of life beneath the stage of the Paris Opera House. A mysterious masked man falls in love with Christine, a singer who inspires "The Music of the Night".
"Phantom of the Opera" is held in Her Majesty's Theatre London. Built in 1897, this historic theatre has held many large productions including "Fiddler on the Roof" and "West Side Story". When Phantom first opened in London in 1986, Michael Crawford played the leading role.

Contact us: Her Majesty's Theatre, Haymarket, London, SW1Y 4QR

Legoland Windsor

Legoland Windsor offers something for everyone young and old with rides, buildings, interaction attractions and shows. Legoland park has a large number of restaurants and landscape to explore and the must see is a detailed reproduction of cities with people and landscape that will fascinate the whole family.

Contact us: Winkfield Road, Windsor, Berkshire, SL4 4AY

Kompetenzbereich: Leseverstehen

TIPP

Labelling / ordering information
Bei diesem Aufgabentyp werden dir häufig mehrere kurze Texte vorgelegt, die du anderen Textabschnitten oder Bildern sinnvoll zuordnen musst. Auch hierbei wird überprüft, ob du englische Lesetexte verstehen kannst. Diese Art von Aufgabenstellung hat den Vorteil, dass du z. B. durch Rechtschreibfehler keine Punkte verlierst.

Worksheet

1. What do you think the following people want to visit when they are in London?

a)  Herr Maier is a manager. He is not married. He lives in Hamburg and works for an international company. In his free time he likes to read books and is especially interested in art. Whenever he has time to spare – at home or on a business trip – he visits galleries.

b)  Jenny and her husband met when they were in Scotland. He was working as a doctor in a small village hospital and she was teaching the children there. What both are interested in most is stars and space.

c)  The Smiths have two children. Aron is five years old and still goes to kindergarten. His older sister, Karen, is already at school. The Smiths live in their own house in a small village near London. They have two dogs and three cats. The whole family loves riding. The children aren't very interested in visiting museums – they like playing and having fun instead.

d)  Mike and Brenda love the weekends since they don't have to work anymore. They love working in their garden or just sitting in the sun and having tea. Twice a month they go to the theatre.

London Planetarium _____
Phantom of the Opera _____
Tate Modern _____
Legoland Windsor _____

2. Look at the photographs. Which photographs go with which London attraction? Write the number of the photograph under the name of the attraction. Some photographs are not needed.

The London Planetarium	Phantom of the Opera	Tate Modern	Legoland Windsor

3. Explain what each London attraction has to show.

The London Planetarium
_____
_____

Phantom of the Opera
_____
_____

Tate Modern
_____
_____

Legoland Windsor
_____
_____

TIPP

Right, wrong, not in the text
Meist wird dir eine Aussage vorgelegt und du musst entscheiden, ob sie richtig ist oder nicht oder ob dazu gar keine Informationen im Text vorhanden sind. Manchmal ist die Frage etwas anders ausgedrückt als der entsprechende Satz im Text.
Dieses Buch soll dir beim Üben helfen, rate also nicht einfach. Wenn du die Antwort nicht weißt, dann lass eine Lücke. Markiere die Fragen, bei denen du dir nicht sicher bist. Schaue im Lösungsteil erst dann nach, wenn du die ganze Übung bearbeitet hast, und versuche herauszufinden, warum die Antwort so und nicht anders lauten muss.

4. Right, wrong or not in the text? Mark the correct answer.   right wrong not in the text
   a) A show in the planetarium lasts 15 minutes
   b) Digistar 2 is the most advanced projector in the world.
   c) The projector was very expensive
   d) In Tate Modern you find pictures from 1900 up to present date.
   e) Michael Stipe plays the male leading part in "Phantom of the Opera".
   f) He played only at the premiere in London
   g) The main attraction of "Legoland Windsor" is the reproduction of cities with people and landscapes.

5. Your class is planning a day trip. You are taking some notes in order to prepare the discussion where you want to go. Fill in the grid.

where	what to do
	see a play
amusement park	
	make different sports courses
movies	
concert hall	

Leseverstehen Test 3: Cinema

Bei dieser Aufgabe erhältst du ein Kinoprogramm mit Filmbeschreibung, Preisen und Aktionen als Material. Lies es gut durch.

MOVIE ☆ STAR CINEMA

As you know, every month Movie Star Cinema presents 3 all-time favourites in addition to our regular programme – films that have already been shown in the cinema but were so popular that lots of people want to see them again. We would like to present our new programme of all-time favourites for the next month. All of the all-time favourites cost £ 3.50, no matter what day or time you choose. After seeing the film, you can give your vote on what you thought of the film. You can win two free tickets for the Movie Star Cinema.

Pixar Film Studios present a film for the whole family: funny, moving and exciting. The film is about the small clown fish Marlin and his son Nemo. On his first day of school, Nemo runs away and gets caught by a diver. Will Marlin find Nemo again?

- Monday – Thursday 2.30 p.m., 6.45 p.m., Friday, Saturday 2.30 p.m., 6.45 p.m., 8.30 p.m., Sunday 12.15 p.m., 2.30 p.m., 6.45 p.m., 8.30 p.m. Hall 3

The Matrix is one of the most popular and successful science fiction and action films – see for yourself!

- Actors: Keanu Reeves, Carrie-Ann Moss
- Monday – Sunday 5.30 p.m., 8.30 p.m., 10.45 p.m., Hall 1

Although the end is common knowledge, James Cameron directs a film with an intense storyline. The great actors pull you into the action until the tension becomes almost unbearable.

- Monday – Friday, 3.00 p.m. Hall 4, 5.15 p.m. Hall 2, 8.00 p.m. Hall 4, Saturday + Sunday 12.15 p.m. Hall 4, 3.00 p.m., Hall 2, 5.15 p.m. Hall 4, 8.00 p.m. Hall 2

- Sneak Preview: 1st Thursday every month ◆ May-Special: popcorn, soft drink 0.3l £ 2,00
- Don't miss the exclusive Lord of the Rings weekend in June! All three parts of the popular fantasy epos written by J. R. R. Tolkien shot in New Zealand will be shown. Sign up now – there's only limited space ◆

Kompetenzbereich: Leseverstehen

TIPP

Multiple choice
Du bekommst Fragen mit verschiedenen Antworten. Lies die Fragen und die möglichen Antworten genau. Beachte, dass sie häufig anders formuliert sind als im Text. Versuche, die Antwort herauszufinden, die am besten zum Text passt. Wenn du dir unsicher bist, dann versuche es andersherum: Suche zuerst die Antworten, die falsch sind. Dann findest du vielleicht die richtige Antwort leichter. Die Reihenfolge der Fragen entspricht normalerweise dem Textaufbau, sodass du abschätzen kannst, wo im Text die Antwort stehen muss.

Worksheet

1. Which film would each of these people or families go to:
   A Finding Nemo, B The Matrix, C Titanic, D Lord of the Rings?
   Sometimes there is more than one correct answer.
   Mark the right answer to each question.   A B C D

   a) Emily and John love fantasy films.   ☐ ☐ ☐ ☐

   b) The Suttons want to go to the cinema with their
      three children (aged 4, 7, 10).   ☐ ☐ ☐ ☐

   c) Mr and Mrs Williams have a 16-year-old daughter.
      They all like to see love stories at the cinema. ☐ ☐ ☐ ☐

   d) Mark and his friends want to see a film that is excit-
      ing, and has a lot of action and famous actors in it. ☐ ☐ ☐ ☐

   e) Mr Smith wants to go to the cinema with his 6-year-
      old daughter. His daughter loves animals.   ☐ ☐ ☐ ☐

   f) Kelly and Ryan want to see a romantic film. ☐ ☐ ☐ ☐

   g) Mr and Mrs Lawson like beautiful landscapes and
      travelled all over New Zealand last year.   ☐ ☐ ☐ ☐

   h) Kathryn wants to take her brother to the cinema.
      But they can only go on a Friday afternoon. ☐ ☐ ☐ ☐

   i) Henry's favourite writer is J. R. R. Tolkien. ☐ ☐ ☐ ☐

2. Answer the following questions about the films.
   a) Who directed Titanic?
      A ☐ Clint Eastwood
      B ☐ James Cameron
      C ☐ Steven Spielberg

   b) Where does Monday's 5.15 p.m. performance of "Titanic" take place?
      B ☐ Hall 1
      C ☐ Hall 2
      D ☐ Hall 4

c) What is the special offer at the Movie Star Cinema?
- A ☐ popcorn and a 0.3 l soft drink
- B ☐ popcorn and a 0.5 l soft drink
- C ☐ popcorn and a ticket

d) Which film can you see at 10.45 p.m.?
- A ☐ The Matrix
- B ☐ Finding Nemo
- C ☐ Titanic

e) Which film will be shown as a special event in June?
- A ☐ Lord of the Rings I–III
- B ☐ The Matrix I–III
- C ☐ Finding Nemo

f) Who is the famous male actor in The Matrix?
- A ☐ Sean Connery
- B ☐ Keanu Reeves
- C ☐ James Cameron

g) What kind of fish is Nemo?
- A ☐ a shark
- B ☐ a goldfish
- C ☐ a clown fish

3. Right, wrong or not in the text? Mark the correct answer.

	right	wrong	not in the text
a) All films shown in this cinema were very popular.	☐	☐	☐
b) They have never been shown before.	☐	☐	☐
c) After the film you can vote how you liked it and win free tickets.	☐	☐	☐
d) The votings are also very popular.	☐	☐	☐
e) "Finding Nemo" was produced in the Pixar Film Studios.	☐	☐	☐
f) You have to sign up early for the Lord-of-the-Rings-Special.	☐	☐	☐

Leseverstehen Test 4: Very trendy!

Im Folgenden siehst du verschiedene Internetseiten einer englischen Firma. Du möchtest unbedingt neue Sneakers haben und bestellst sie dir über diese Homepage in England, weil sie dort günstiger sind. Lies zunächst die Internetseiten aufmerksam durch. Die Aufgaben findest du im Anschluss.

---

trendshoes.com

SEARCH:

female | male | register | basket

▶▶▶ 10 YEARS jubilee ◀◀◀
free delivery in Europe

UK's cheapest online-store
N E W   C O L L E C T I O N

FEMALE CATEGORIES
- Clothing
- Shoes
- Accessories

MALE CATEGORIES
- Clothing
- Shoes
- Accessories

SIGN IN *for our newsletter*
including: new collection, fashion news, specials

---

trendshoes.com

SEARCH:

female | male | register | basket

Art. No: **4317**

The American Classic retro styled sneakers popular for decades
£ 29,-

FEMALE CATEGORIES
- Clothing
- Shoes
- Accessories

MALE CATEGORIES
- Clothing
- Shoes
- Accessories

▶ **SPECIAL** free delivery in Europe

ORDER NOW!

trendshoes.com

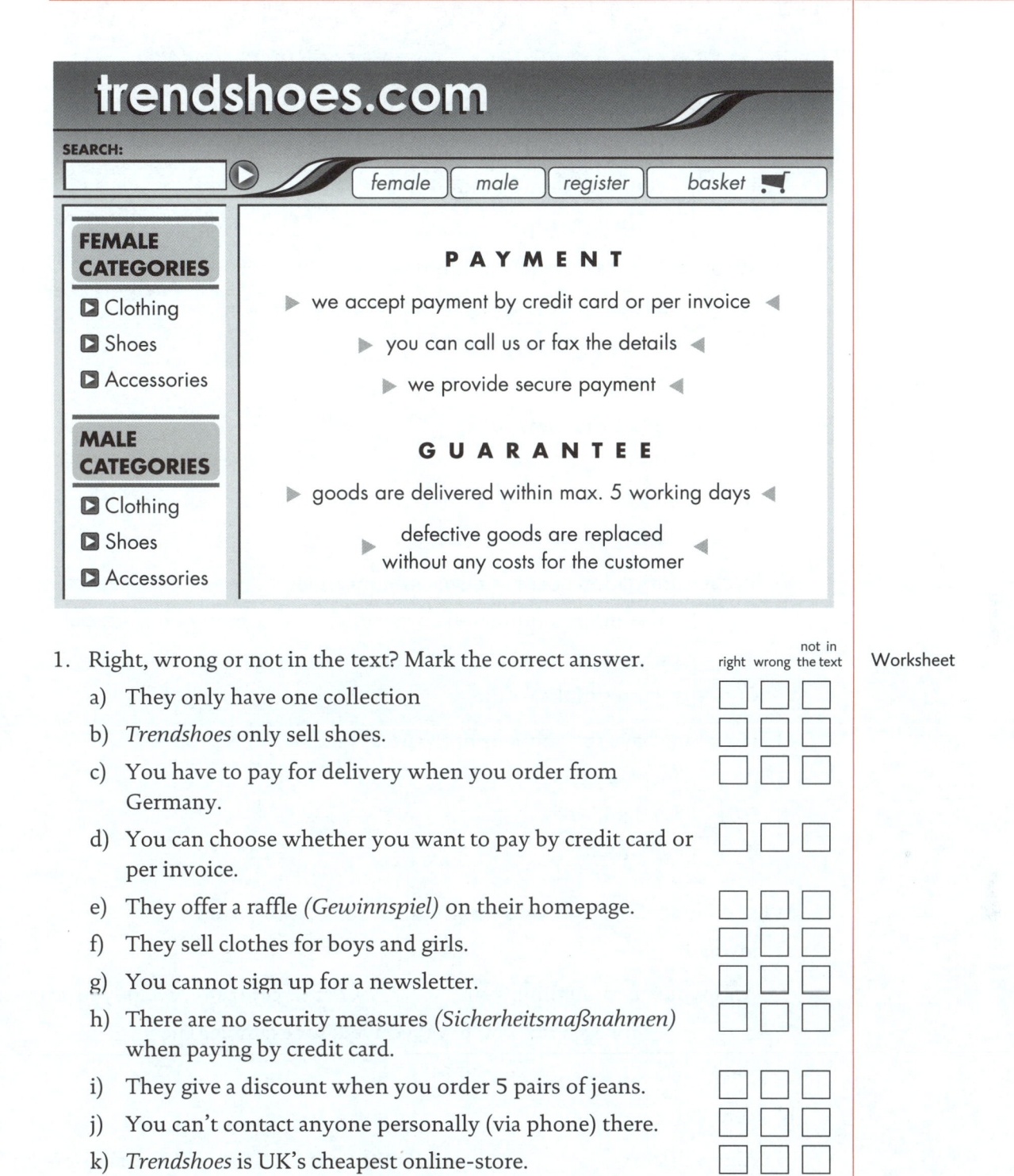

SEARCH:

female | male | register | basket

FEMALE CATEGORIES
- Clothing
- Shoes
- Accessories

MALE CATEGORIES
- Clothing
- Shoes
- Accessories

PAYMENT
- we accept payment by credit card or per invoice
- you can call us or fax the details
- we provide secure payment

GUARANTEE
- goods are delivered within max. 5 working days
- defective goods are replaced without any costs for the customer

---

1. Right, wrong or not in the text? Mark the correct answer. *(right / wrong / not in the text)*

   a) They only have one collection. ☐ ☐ ☐
   b) *Trendshoes* only sell shoes. ☐ ☐ ☐
   c) You have to pay for delivery when you order from Germany. ☐ ☐ ☐
   d) You can choose whether you want to pay by credit card or per invoice. ☐ ☐ ☐
   e) They offer a raffle *(Gewinnspiel)* on their homepage. ☐ ☐ ☐
   f) They sell clothes for boys and girls. ☐ ☐ ☐
   g) You cannot sign up for a newsletter. ☐ ☐ ☐
   h) There are no security measures *(Sicherheitsmaßnahmen)* when paying by credit card. ☐ ☐ ☐
   i) They give a discount when you order 5 pairs of jeans. ☐ ☐ ☐
   j) You can't contact anyone personally (via phone) there. ☐ ☐ ☐
   k) *Trendshoes* is UK's cheapest online-store. ☐ ☐ ☐

2. Mark the correct answer.
   a) Why is the delivery in Europe free this month?
      A ☐ Because of the 15th anniversary.
      B ☐ Because of the 10th anniversary.
      C ☐ It is always free.
   b) What articles does trendshoes.com sell?
      A ☐ clothes for boys and girls, shoes and accessories
      B ☐ clothes for boys and girls
      C ☐ shoes
   c) How much are the sneakers?
      A ☐ 19 £
      B ☐ 35 £
      C ☐ 29 £
   d) What information does the newsletter include?
      A ☐ latest information on the new collection, fashion news, specials
      B ☐ only prices
      C ☐ pictures of the clothes
   e) How long have the Sneakers been successful?
      A ☐ for two years
      B ☐ for decades
      C ☐ not yet

3. What do the following words mean? Fill in the missing words.
   a) invoice

   An invoice is something you _____ when a company wants you to _____ for a service you have received, for example. The _____ shows _____ what you have to pay.

   b) newsletter

   A newsletter _____ you about the latest _____ of a company or an institution. Normally you have to _____ in order to get a _____.

   c) free delivery

   Free delivery _____ that you don't have to _____ shipping fees when you have _____ something. to be sent to your _____.

4. Complete the form with your personal details.

trendshoes.com

SEARCH:

female | male | register | basket

FEMALE CATEGORIES
- Clothing
- Shoes
- Accessories

MALE CATEGORIES
- Clothing
- Shoes
- Accessories

ORDER FORM

NAME:
ADDRESS:
TEL.:
E-MAIL:
DATE OF BIRTH:
ARTICLE NUMBER:
COLOUR:

Leseverstehen Test 5: A dream come true

Hinweis

Teenprint is a newspaper for young people which gives them the opportunity to publish their own texts on topics they are interested in. The following text was written by Becky Miller, 19, who travelled through Australia before starting her apprenticeship in a hotel.

Text

TeenPrint — Travel
A Dream Come True

A It had always been one of my major dreams to travel through Australia for half a year. After I had finished school, it was time to let my dream come true. My parents, grandparents, aunt and uncle – everyone wanted to give me a present for passing my exams. That's where I was lucky: I asked everyone to give me money and together with my savings from the job I took the summer before, I was able to step into the travel agent's and book a flight to Sydney. There was a special offer that included two inland Australian flights. My parents weren't as excited as I was when I told them about my plans, but I promised to send them an e-mail as often as possible and that it would be a great chance for me to improve my English and to get experience in a foreign country. They gave in finally. I planned the trip on my own, but an Australian exchange student at our school helped me.

B I wanted to spend some time in Sydney because it is such a beautiful city. I wanted to go surfing at Bondi Beach, spend some time in Melbourne and Perth and of course I wanted to spend some time in the outback.

C The start of my journey was in Sydney. When I arrived, it was a beautiful, sunny day. I took a taxi to the youth hostel, as I was very tired because of the long journey. I chose a youth hostel in Sydney which was especially for backpackers, as it was cheaper than the usual ones. That was definitely the right choice: there were so many young people at the hostel that I felt comfortable there from the moment I arrived. For the rest of my journey I stayed in a backpacker hostel whenever it was possible. The backpackers were from all over the world and we had an exciting time there together. I met a girl named Marie from France who also wanted to travel on her own, and after two weeks in Sydney together we chose to do the rest of our journey together – a decision my parents appreciated very much.

D There isn't enough space here to tell you all the things I experienced during my time in Australia, but spending six months abroad was the best idea I ever had and I wouldn't have missed it for the world. I found so many new friends, I got to know Australia in so many different ways, I learned to look after myself and I improved my English a lot. During the months in Australia I decided to spend one year of my apprenticeship down under as well. It is a wonderful feeling to make a dream come true!

Kompetenzbereich: Leseverstehen

Worksheet

1. Right, wrong or not in the text? Mark the correct answer.

	right	wrong	not in the text
a) Becky went to Australia after finishing university.	☐	☐	☐
b) She had to pay for the trip on her own.	☐	☐	☐
c) Her friends were very jealous *(eifersüchtig)*.	☐	☐	☐
d) She flew to Perth.	☐	☐	☐
e) She got sick on the flight.	☐	☐	☐
f) Becky got a special flight offer.	☐	☐	☐
g) It was sunny when she arrived in Sydney.	☐	☐	☐
h) In Sydney she stayed in a youth hostel.	☐	☐	☐
i) She fell in love with a boy from Sweden.	☐	☐	☐
j) At the hostel in Sydney there were only Australian tourists.	☐	☐	☐
k) She travelled on her own for the whole time.	☐	☐	☐
l) Becky never regretted *(bereuen)* having made this trip.	☐	☐	☐
m) She plans to do part of her apprenticeship abroad.	☐	☐	☐

2. Which place names from the text can you find in the following word grid?

B	O	N	D	I	B	E	A	C	H
A	R	U	E	T	F	H	J	L	J
Y	F	R	K	S	J	Z	T	S	R
S	G	A	H	Y	G	U	N	B	F
F	G	J	R	D	W	Q	E	R	G
A	Z	Q	F	N	T	R	D	K	U
T	V	A	P	E	R	T	H	E	I
K	B	N	M	Y	F	G	T	U	H
R	Z	U	J	F	V	R	P	K	P
M	E	L	B	O	U	R	N	E	U

3. Which headline matches best which paragraph?
   Write the letter in the box next to the heading.

   a) Places to visit ☐
   b) How to make the dream reality ☐
   c) A conclusion ☐
   d) The trip ☐

3 Kompetenzbereich: Schreiben

Viele Schüler sind der Meinung, dass sie sich auf den Bereich „Schreiben" nicht vorbereiten können, da die Aufgabenformen sehr stark variieren und die Note – wie im Deutschunterricht – ohnehin ganz von der individuellen Einschätzung des Lehrers abhängt. Erschwerend kommen im Fach Englisch noch die Fremdsprache und die damit verbundenen möglichen Fehler hinzu. Aus diesen Gründen beschäftigen sich die meisten Schüler im Vorfeld einer Klassenarbeit oder der Hauptschulabschlussprüfung gar nicht erst mit diesem Kompetenzbereich, was von Nachteil ist, denn auch in diesem Bereich werden viele Punkte vergeben.

Mache nicht den gleichen Fehler! Lies die folgenden Seiten gut durch. Du wirst sehen: Eine sinnvolle und erfolgreiche Vorbereitung auf das Schreiben kleiner Aufsätze in Englisch ist möglich.

3.1 Strategien zum Kompetenzbereich „Schreiben"

Langfristige Vorbereitung

Auf die Textproduktion in Klassenarbeiten und in der Hauptschulabschlussprüfung kannst du dich nur langfristig gut vorbereiten. Wenn du dir erst zwei Tage vor der Prüfung überlegst, dass du in diesem Bereich noch Schwächen hast, dann ist das für eine sinnvolle Beschäftigung mit diesem Thema definitiv zu spät.
Schaue bzw. höre dir englischsprachige Interviews mit deinen Lieblingsstars im Fernsehen oder im Radio an, gehe in Kinofilme, die im englischen Originalton vorgeführt werden, lies viel in englischer Sprache. Es gibt auch englischsprachige Jugendzeitschriften in Deutschland. Wenn du sie dir nicht kaufen möchtest, kannst du sie dir in der Bücherei ausleihen. Wenn du dir eine DVD ansiehst, kannst du bei Filmen, die im Original englisch sind, zu Beginn die Sprache auswählen und dir dann den Film einfach auf Englisch (evtl. auch mit deutschen Untertiteln) anschauen. Du wirst sehen: Mit der Zeit verstehst du immer mehr und Redewendungen kommen dir immer vertrauter vor. Eine gute Übung ist es auch, sich viel in der Fremdsprache zu unterhalten. Sprich doch hin und wieder einmal mit deinen Freunden oder deinen Geschwistern englisch. So wird dir das eigenständige Formulieren von Mal zu Mal leichter fallen.

Das Schreiben des Textes

Ganz gleich, welche Art von Text du schreiben musst – egal ob es ein kurzer Text oder ein Brief ist – die Vorgehensweise ist dabei immer dieselbe.

▶ Lies die Aufgabenstellung gut durch und überlege genau, was darin von dir verlangt wird. Erhältst du mit der Aufgabenstellung irgendwelche Vorgaben (z. B. eine Ausgangssituation, Stichwörter, den Anfang oder das Ende einer Geschichte), die du in deinen Text einbringen musst? Oder sollst du einen „freien" Text schreiben? Wenn du einen Brief oder eine E-Mail schreiben sollst, überlege dir, wer der Empfänger ist und wie du mit ihm/ihr sprechen würdest. In einem Brief an einen Freund verwendest du eine andere Anrede als z. B. in einem Bewerbungsschreiben. **Arbeitsschritt 1**

▶ Wenn du mehrere Themen zur Auswahl hast, dann suche dir dasjenige aus, in dem du dich am besten auskennst. Es hat keinen Sinn, einem Freund in einem Brief von den Abenteuern beim Snowboarden zu erzählen, wenn man sich mit Snowboarden gar nicht auskennt. **Arbeitsschritt 2**

▶ Hast du dich für ein Thema entschieden, dann solltest du dir genau überlegen, was du dazu schreiben könntest. Es kann sehr hilfreich sein, wenn du dir Stichpunkte notierst, die du später in deinem Text verwenden möchtest. Beachte dabei genau die Vorgaben aus der Aufgabenstellung (z. B. in Form von Bildern oder Stichworten) und überlege dann, was du noch hinzufügen musst. Nimm dazu ein großes Stück Papier und notiere alles, was dir zum Thema einfällt und worauf du in deinem Text eingehen könntest. **Arbeitsschritt 3**

▶ Nun musst du den Text ausarbeiten. Achte dabei darauf, dass du Abhängigkeiten, Folgen etc. durch entsprechende Bindewörter (Konjunktionen) deutlich machst. Greife auf Redewendungen zurück, die du gelernt hast. Schreibe kurze, überschaubare Sätze – so kannst du Grammatikfehlern leichter vorbeugen.
Auf den Seiten 32–34 haben wir einige Redewendungen zusammengestellt, die dir beim Aufsatzschreiben helfen werden. Lerne sie auswendig. Du wirst sie immer wieder einsetzen können. **Arbeitsschritt 4**

▶ Nimm dir auf jeden Fall die Zeit, am Ende alles noch einmal in Ruhe durchzulesen. Ist alles logisch aufgebaut? Gibt es keine Gedankensprünge?
Wichtig ist aber auch, dass du noch einmal gezielt nach Rechtschreib- und Grammatikfehlern suchst und diese entsprechend verbesserst. **Arbeitsschritt 5**

> **TIPP**
> - Lies die Aufgabenstellung genau.
> - Wähle das für dich geeignete Thema aus.
> - Erstelle eine Stoffsammlung.
> - Arbeite deinen Text sorgfältig aus.
> - Lies deinen Text abschließend noch einmal genau durch und überprüfe dabei, ob alles logisch aufgebaut und verständlich geschrieben ist. Verbessere Rechtschreib- und Grammatikfehler.

3.2 Hilfreiche Wendungen zur Textproduktion

Anrede und Schlussformeln

Persönlicher Brief

Liebe Jane,	Dear Jane,
Viele Grüße / Liebe Grüße	Best wishes
	Love *(nur bei sehr guten Freunden, aber nicht unter Männern)*

Geschäftsbrief / Anfrage

wenn du den Namen des Ansprechpartners nicht kennst

Sehr geehrte Damen und Herren,	Dear Sir / Madam,
Mit freundlichen Grüßen	Yours faithfully

wenn du den Namen des Ansprechpartners kennst

Sehr geehrte Frau Roberts,	Dear Mrs Roberts,
Sehr geehrter Herr James,	Dear Mr James,
bei einer unverheirateten Frau	Dear Miss Berry,
wenn du nicht weißt, ob die Frau verheiratet ist oder nicht	Dear Ms Bell,
Mit freundlichen Grüßen	Yours sincerely

Einleitung und Schluss des Briefes

Danke für …	Thank you for …
Ich habe … erhalten.	I received …
Ich hoffe, dass …	I hope that …
Wie geht es dir?	How are you?
Im letzten Brief hast du mir über … erzählt.	In your last letter you told me about …
Im letzten Brief hast du mir erzählt, dass …	In your last letter you told me that …
Entschuldige, dass ich … vergessen habe, aber …	Sorry that I forgot to …, but …
Sage bitte … / Richte … bitte aus	Please tell …
Es wäre schön, wenn wir uns treffen könnten.	It would be nice if we could meet.
Bitte richte … Grüße aus.	Best wishes to … (Please) give my regards to …
Bitte schreibe mir bald zurück.	Write soon.
Ich freue mich darauf, bald von dir zu hören.	I'm looking forward to hearing from you. I hope I'll hear from you soon.

Ich freue mich auf deinen Brief.	I'm looking forward to your letter.
Ich werde dich anrufen.	I'll call you.

Häufig vorkommende Redewendungen/Ausdrücke

sich entschuldigen	I'm sorry
etwas bedauern	It's a pity that … / I'm disappointed that …
an etwas erinnern	Please remember to …
Überraschung äußern	I was surprised that …
eine Bitte äußern	Could you/would you …, please?
einen Wunsch äußern	I'd like to …
einen Entschluss mitteilen	I've decided to … I've made up my mind to … I'm going to …
eine Absicht mitteilen	I intend to / I'm planning to … I want to / I will …
Interesse ausdrücken	I'm interested in …
Freude ausdrücken	I'm happy/glad about
Überzeugung ausdrücken	I'm convinced that … I'm sure that …
nach dem Preis fragen	How much is it/ How much does it cost?
Ich hoffe, dir hat … gefallen.	I hope you liked/enjoyed …
Ich muss jetzt …	I have to …
Ich denke, es ist besser …	I think it's better to …

Auskunft geben über sich selbst

Ich wohne in …	I live in …
Ich wurde am … in … geboren.	I was born on … in …
Ich interessiere mich für …	I'm interested in …
Ich war schon in …	I've (already) been in …/to …
Ich möchte gerne … werden.	I'd like to be a/an …
Mir geht es gut.	I'm fine.
Mir geht es nicht gut.	I'm not well.
Ich mag …	I like … / I enjoy …
Ich mag … lieber (als…).	I prefer to … / I like … better (than …)
Ich weiß … noch nicht genau.	I still don't know exactly …
Ich plane, … zu tun.	I plan to …
Ich freue mich (sehr) auf …	I'm looking forward to … I'm excited about …

Ich konnte … nicht … I wasn't able to … / I couldn't …

In meiner Freizeit In my free time/spare time

Ich nehme regelmäßig an … teil. I take part in …

Layout eines Geschäftsbriefes

	24 Castle Street — writer's address
	Blackburn
	Lancashire
	LK6 5TQ
	6th March 2007 — date
Mrs J. Fox — recipient's name and address *(formal letters only)*	
Dane Cleaners	
3 Arthur Road	
Doddington	
NE3 6LD	
Dear Mrs Fox, — salutation	
Thank you for your letter … — letter	
Yours sincerely, — closing	
Adam Smith — signature	
Adam Smith — name	

3.3 Übungsaufgaben zum Kompetenzbereich „Schreiben"

Hier findest du zahlreiche Aufgaben zum Bereich „Schreiben". In den Übersichtskästen vor den verschiedenen Aufgabentypen kannst du jeweils nachlesen, worauf es in den folgenden Aufgaben ankommt bzw. was von dir erwartet wird.

> **Sprachliche Ausdrucksfähigkeit**
> - Beim Schreiben von Aufsätzen kommt es darauf an, dass du die von dir verfassten Sätze **sprachlich variieren** kannst. Dauernde Wiederholungen wirken auf den Leser mit der Zeit ermüdend.
> - Außerdem ist es wichtig, die einzelnen Sätze miteinander zu verknüpfen, um dem Leser Auswirkungen oder Folgen klarzumachen. Diese Verknüpfungen können durch entsprechende **Bindewörter** (Konjunktionen) hergestellt werden.
>
> In den folgenden beiden Übungen kannst du diese Punkte gezielt üben. Versuche aber auch bei allen anderen Schreibübungen, auf sprachliche Variationsmöglichkeiten bzw. auf die Verknüpfung von Sätzen durch Konjunktionen zu achten.

TIPP

1. Improve the following sentences by adding the words listed below to the words underlined.

    The _____ (1) house at the end of the street belongs to my parents.

    Grandma told me to throw the _____ (2) carpet away.

    James loves sitting in his room and listening to _____ (3) music.

    Take off your _____ (4) shoes!

    I live in a _____ (5) village.

    I got a _____ (6) blue coat for my birthday.

    We travelled a lot during our _____ (7) holidays.

1	mine	beautiful	pleased
2	old	too	well
3	tiny	yours	loud
4	clean	silent	dirty
5	small	shiny	up
6	red	dark	old
7	long	tiny	summer

2. Fill in the correct words.

I took an umbrella with me this morning _____ (1) it was raining.

_____ (2) I'm 18 years old I will leave home.

I'd love to visit New York, _____ (3) I don't have enough money.

Jack moved to another town _____ (4) become independent.

Clara washes the dishes _____ (5) she's talking to her best friend on the phone.

1	when	because	in spite of
2	although	when	but
3	but	that's why	still
4	because	but	in order to
5	while	in order to	when

3. Fill in the correct word.

On Saturday morning Kelly and Sara met in town to do _____ (1) shopping. They were invited to a birthday party _____ (2) and wanted to buy a present. At first they couldn't _____ (3) decide _____ (4) to buy, but _____ (5) they saw the new Pink CD and were sure that that _____ (6) be the right present for Tina. Now they could take a look _____ (7) for some cheap and trendy clothes for the party. Kelly _____ (8) a new T-shirt, but Sara didn't find anything. Afterwards they went home to _____ (9) for the party.

1	my	some	any
2	in the morning	on the evening	in the evening
3	really	hardly	finally
4	what	who	which
5	then	now	in order to
6	was	would	were
7	down	in front	around
8	sold	bought	is buying
9	get dressed	get together	get along

TIPP

Bilder als Schreibanlässe

Bei den Aufgaben aus dem Bereich „Schreiben" können dir Bilder als Schreibanlässe vorgelegt werden. Hier kannst du unter Beweis stellen, wie gut du dich auf Englisch ausdrücken kannst. Wenn du befürchtest, dein Englisch könnte nicht gut genug sein, um einen Aufsatz zu verfassen, dann bleibe bei einfachen Formulierungen. So kannst du unnötige Fehler vermeiden.

- Manchmal werden dir Bilder als „**visuelle Impulse**", d. h. als optische Schreibanlässe vorgegeben. Dann sollst du das Bild (oder die Bilder) lediglich als „Aufhänger" für eine kleine Geschichte verwenden. In diesem Fall empfiehlt es sich, das Bild/die Bilder zuerst einmal genau zu betrachten. Eine detaillierte Bildbeschreibung ist allerdings selten nötig, du sollst vielmehr deiner Fantasie freien Lauf lassen.

- Immer wieder wirst du es aber auch mit einer ganzen Reihe von Bildern, d. h. mit einer **Bildergeschichte** zu tun bekommen. Deine Aufgabe besteht dann darin, die Geschichte aufzuschreiben, die dir die Bilder erzählen. Auch hierbei kannst du sehr fantasievoll sein und deine Geschichte ausschmücken.

4. Love Story. Write the dialogue to the pictures.

Ann's parents were serious. They told her that she either had to stop seeing Kevin or she had to leave school. Ann didn't know what to do. She still loved Kevin very much, but she knew that she had to concentrate on school again because she didn't want to fail her exams. She and Kevin talked things over and they agreed to stop seeing each other for a while. They agreed to wait until Ann's exams were over.

38 | Kompetenzbereich: Schreiben

Kompetenzbereich: Schreiben | 39

5. Look at this picture story. Write about 12–15 sentences using the picture story. Try to describe things well.

6. What would you say? Make each answer longer so that it is like a conversation. Think carefully about the situation.

   Example: "Do you like watching television?"
   "No, I don't. I like reading books."

   a) *(at school)* "Do you like maths?"
   _____
   _____
   _____
   _____

   b) *(at the butcher's)* "Can I help you?"
   _____
   _____
   _____
   _____

   c) "My name is John."
   _____
   _____
   _____
   _____

   d) "Do you like the theatre?"
   _____
   _____
   _____
   _____

   e) "Do you like ice skating?"
   _____
   _____
   _____
   _____

Kompetenzbereich: Schreiben | 41

TIPP

Letters and e-mails

Natürlich ist auch die Bandbreite an Aufgaben zum Verfassen von Briefen und E-Mails groß. Dabei können sowohl formelle als auch persönliche Briefe oder E-Mails verlangt sein. Hier wird überprüft, wie gut du in der Lage bist, dich in Alltagssituationen schriftlich auf Englisch auszudrücken. Außerdem kannst du unter Beweis stellen, dass du mit dem Layout eines englischen Briefes vertraut bist, dass du also weißt, an welchen Stellen Adresse, Datum, Anrede etc. angeordnet werden.

- **Formelle Briefe und E-Mails:** Achte darauf, dass du keine saloppen Ausdrücke und Formulierungen verwendest. Bleibe in deiner Ausdrucksweise sachlich und nüchtern.

- **Persönliche Briefe und E-Mails:** Wie beim Schreiben von Dialogen solltest du bei persönlichen Briefen oder E-Mails zunächst einmal überlegen, in welche Rolle du schlüpfen sollst. Meist musst du als „fiktive", d. h. erfundene Person einem fiktiven Freund einen Brief schreiben und ihn über bestimmte Geschehnisse informieren. Dabei müssen Sprache und Stil des Briefes natürlich zu der Person passen, in deren Namen du den Brief oder die E-Mail verfasst.

7. What is the right start and ending to use for each of these letters? You are writing to:

   a) your aunt Mary

   b) Mrs Smith at the bank

   c) letter to the editor of a magazine (*Leserbrief*)

   d) your friend Luke

   e) Mr O'Brien, your English teacher

   f) a postcard to your grandparents

   g) application for a job

   h) a woman at an office

8. Write to a friend. Tell him/her about the musical "West Side Story", which you saw at the weekend. You can use the notes and questions below to write the letter.

   ▶ address, date, salutation (Dear ...)
   ▶ Ask him/her how he/she is.
   ▶ When you have seen the musical.
   ▶ Where you have seen the musical.
   ▶ With whom have you been there?
   ▶ How did you like it?
   ▶ Were the tickets expensive
   ▶ The musical is very popular. You recommend to buy tickets soon.
   ▶ You will call him / her soon.
   ▶ appropriate ending for the letter (Best wishes, ...)

9. Du möchtest in deinen Sommerferien ein wenig Geld dazuverdienen und ins Ausland gehen. Zufällig siehst du eine Anzeige für einen Ferienjob in einem Hotel in St. Albans. Verfasse ein Bewerbungsschreiben. Lies dir die Anzeige sorgfältig durch. Die Fragen unten können dir helfen, den Brief zu verfassen. Denke an das Layout des Briefes.

HOTEL BELLEVUE

First-rate hotel looking for temporary personnel for the summer.

▶ **customer service skills necessary**

send a CV and a letter of application to Tom Leary
Hotel Bellevue, 63 London Road, St Albans, Hertfordshire, AL5 6 PH

▶ Working hours: hours/days?
▶ Detail information about the job?
▶ Payment?
▶ About yourself: Name? Why are you interested in the job? What do you want to learn there? Which skills can you use there? How long do you want to work there?

10. You receive an e-mail from your friend in Dublin. Write an e-mail back. You may use the notes below.

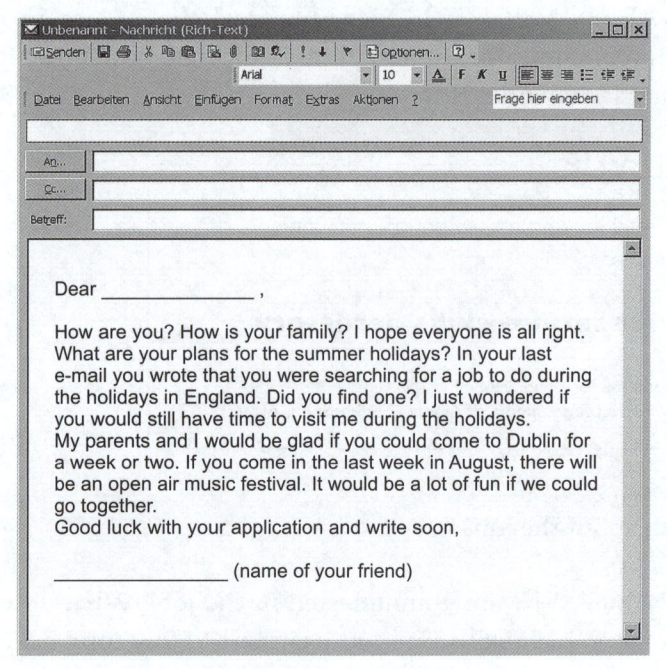

> Dear _____ ,
>
> How are you? How is your family? I hope everyone is all right. What are your plans for the summer holidays? In your last e-mail you wrote that you were searching for a job to do during the holidays in England. Did you find one? I just wondered if you would still have time to visit me during the holidays.
> My parents and I would be glad if you could come to Dublin for a week or two. If you come in the last week in August, there will be an open air music festival. It would be a lot of fun if we could go together.
> Good luck with your application and write soon,
>
> _____ (name of your friend)

- Tell him/her about your job at the hotel.
- You have one week left of your holidays.
- Tell him/her what you will do in your job: cleaning up rooms, support the staff at the reception desk, …
- You would love to come and visit last week of August and you are looking forward to the festival.
- Don't forget address and end of the e-mail.

4 Kompetenzbereich: Sprechen

Die mündliche Prüfung im Fach Englisch wird von der Schule gestellt, an der du deine Hauptschulabschlussprüfung ablegst. Aus diesem Grund kann die Prüfung von Schule zu Schule verschieden sein. Erkundige dich rechtzeitig bei der zuständigen Lehrkraft nach den Prüfungsanforderungen.

4.1 Hinweise und Strategien zum Kompetenzbereich „Sprechen"

Ablauf der Prüfung

- Es werden in der Regel zwei Schüler gleichzeitig geprüft. Du musst dich mit einem Mitschüler auf Englisch unterhalten. Wer mit wem zusammenkommt, wird per Los entschieden. Du brauchst aber keine Angst zu haben, denn auch wenn dein Partner vielleicht nicht so gut in Englisch ist, kannst du trotzdem die volle Punktzahl bekommen.

- Es sind immer zwei Lehrkräfte dabei. Eine Lehrkraft führt das Prüfungsgespräch mit dir und deinem Mitschüler, die andere Lehrkraft sitzt dabei und hört genau zu.

Prüfungsteile

Die mündliche Prüfung im Fach Englisch besteht aus zwei großen Teilen: **monologisches und dialogisches Sprechen**. Im ersten Teil (monologisches Sprechen) sprichst du alleine, im zweiten Teil (dialogisches Sprechen) musst du zeigen, wie gut du dich in einem Gespräch in der Fremdsprache Englisch ausdrücken kannst.

Den Prüfungsteil zum monologischen Sprechen bereitest du zu Hause vor.

Monologisches Sprechen

- Du erzählst etwas über dich selbst und kannst dazu Gegenstände wie Fotos oder Bücher mitbringen, um das, was du erzählst, zu illustrieren. Die Prüfer können einzelne Fragen nach deinem Vortrag stellen. Es soll aber kein Gespräch zwischen dir und dem Prüfer zustande kommen. Insgesamt dauert dieser Prüfungsteil 5 Minuten. Mögliche Themen könnten sein:
Familie, Freunde, Haustier, Urlaub, Hobby, Film

- Die Gegenstände, die du mitbringst, sollten zu deinem kleinen Vortrag passen, also Fotos deines Haustiers beispielsweise, wenn du darüber erzählen möchtest. Überlege dir am besten schon zu Hause, wie genau du die Gegenstände in deinen Vortrag einbauen möchtest. Je besser du vorbereitet bist, desto leichter wird dir dieser Prüfungsteil fallen.

TIPP

- Dein Referat sollte eine Einleitung, einen Hauptteil und einen Schluss haben.
- Nenne in der Einleitung das Thema des Referats und evtl. den Grund, warum du das Thema gewählt hast.
- Der Hauptteil soll alle wichtigen Informationen enthalten.
- Im Schluss fasst du den Inhalt deines Referats noch einmal kurz zusammen, äußerst deine Meinung oder ziehst ein Fazit.
- Schreibe dein Referat zu Hause zunächst einmal auf, um einen Überblick über den Umfang zu bekommen (ca. 300 Wörter). So fallen dir auch schnell Fehler oder Lücken im Wortschatz auf. Denke aber daran, dass du in der Prüfung nicht ablesen darfst.
- Formuliere dein Referat mit eigenen Worten. Natürlich kannst du zur Vorbereitung auf Bücher oder das Internet zurückgreifen; in der Prüfung solltest du aber deinen eigenen Text vortragen.
- Übe dein Referat mehrmals vor der Prüfung. Sprich laut und nicht zu hastig und achte auf eine deutliche Aussprache. Am besten hältst du dein Referat zunächst vor Freunden oder deinen Eltern. So gewöhnst du dich an das freie Sprechen.
- Beantworte die Fragen der Prüfer ausführlich und in englischer Sprache.
- Folgende Gesichtspunkte fließen in die Bewertung deines Vortrags ein:
Hatte dein Referat den vereinbarten Umfang? War der Vortrag inhaltlich vollständig, gut strukturiert und verständlich? Konntest du den Inhalt ohne zu stocken und sicher vortragen? Konntest du die Fragen der Prüfer verstehen und beantworten? Waren Wortschatz, Grammatik und Aussprache insgesamt angemessen?

Dialogisches Sprechen

Im Prüfungsteil zum dialogischen Sprechen sollst du mit deinem Mitschüler / deiner Mitschülerin ein kurzes Gespräch nach Vorgaben („prompts") führen.

▶ Dazu erhaltet ihr zu einem bestimmten **Thema** Kärtchen mit Vorgaben in Form von Stichpunkten, die euch als roter Faden für das folgende Gespräch dienen sollen.

▶ Auf diesen Karten werden euch Rollen vorgegeben, die ihr im folgenden Dialog einnehmen sollt. Einer von euch wird Fragen stellen, der andere wird diese beantworten. Die Details der Situation und der Rollen, die ihr einnehmen sollt, könnt ihr den Karten entnehmen. Mit einem neuen Paar *prompt cards* werden dann die Rollen getauscht. Dieser Prüfungsteil dauert wieder 5 Minuten.

Sprachmittlung

Der letzte Teil in der mündlichen Prüfung überprüft deine Fähigkeit in der „Sprachmittlung", also wie gut du zwischen deiner Muttersprache Deutsch und der Fremdsprache Englisch vermitteln kannst.

▶ Dazu machen die Prüfer mit dir ein Rollenspiel. Sie beschreiben dir, in welcher Situation sie sich befinden und welche Personen sie dabei spielen. Im Rollenspiel wird der eine nur Deutsch sprechen und der andere nur Englisch. Damit sie sich verständigen können, musst du zwischen ihnen dolmetschen.

▶ Falls du die Möglichkeit hast, solltet ihr euch zu Dritt auf das „Interpreting" vorbereiten. Zwei Mitschüler können dann den Dialog vortragen, während der Dritte dolmetscht. Falls du alleine übst, kannst du das Gespräch auf Band sprechen (denke an Pausen, die du zum Übersetzen brauchst) und anschließend dolmetschen. Vergleiche deine Lösung in einem zweiten Durchlauf Satz für Satz mit der Musterlösung. Beachte aber, dass es häufig mehrere richtige Lösungen gibt, die hier vielleicht nicht angegeben sind.

▶ Es ist in jedem Fall **hilfreich**, sich vorher **Szenarien zu überlegen**, in denen man dolmetschen müsste, wie z. B. beim Einkaufen oder im Hotel. So kann man sich schon einmal Vokabeln und Wendungen dazu überlegen.

TIPP

- Mit der Kurzgrammatik auf den Seiten 67–76 dieses Buches kannst du deine Kenntnis der englischen Grammatik noch einmal vertiefen und verbessern.
- Nutze das Fernsehprogramm in englischer Sprache. Es stellt eine Hilfe zum Hörverstehen dar, aber auch für das „Interpreting", da du Aussprache, Satzmelodie und Wendungen hörst.
- Bei der Bewertung in der Prüfung ist wichtig, ob du dem Gespräch folgen kannst, und schnell reagierst, ob deine Übersetzungen richtig und verständlich sind, wie sicher und gewandt du dich ausdrückst und wie du Verständigungsprobleme meisterst, etwa wie du den Faden wieder aufgreifst, wenn du nicht weiterweißt oder dir ein Wort nicht einfällt.

4.2 Hilfreiche Wendungen und Beispiele zum Kompetenzbereich „Sprechen"

Eine eigene Meinung ausdrücken *(Expressing an opinion)*

I (would) prefer... *Ich würde lieber...*	→ I would prefer not to... *Ich würde lieber nicht...*
I (would) like... *Ich würde / möchte gern...*	→ I don't like / I dislike... *Ich würde nicht gern...*
I think / believe / expect / imagine / suppose (that)... *Ich glaube (dass)...*	→ I don't think (...) (that)... *Ich glaube nicht (dass)...*
I doubt (that)... *Ich bezweifle (dass)...*	→ I don't doubt (that)... *Ich bezweifle nicht, dass...*
I'm for... *Ich bin für.../dafür, dass...*	→ I'm against... *Ich bin gegen.../dagegen, dass...*
I would... *Ich würde...*	→ I wouldn't... *Ich würde nicht...*
I'm sure / certain... *Ich bin sicher...*	→ I'm not sure / certain... *Ich bin nicht sicher...*
In my opinion... *Meiner Meinung nach...*	→ That's not my opinion. *Das ist nicht meine Meinung.*

Andere nach ihrer Meinung fragen (Asking other people for an opinion)

What's your opinion / view / reaction (about) …?	Was ist deine Meinung zu …? / Was denkst du über …?
How do you see / view the situation / this?	Wie siehst du die Situation?
Could you explain something / your ideas / your feelings / to me?	Könntest du mir etwas erklären?
What would you say about …?	Was würdest du über / zum Thema … sagen?
How do you feel about …?	Was hältst du persönlich von …?
(stark) *What about (for example: no smoking in public places)? Do you think that's right?*	Was denkst du über …? Glaubst du, dass das richtig / in Ordnung ist?
(stark, eine Antwort fordernd) *I don't suppose you'll / you would agree, will you / would you?*	Du wirst sicher nicht zustimmen, oder?

Du kannst auch Fragen mit Verneinungen stellen, um deinen Gesprächspartner zu einer Meinungsäußerung zu bringen:

Don't you think that …?	Glaubst du nicht, dass …?
Wouldn't you like to see …?	Hättest du nicht auch lieber …?
Shouldn't we …?	Sollten wir nicht …?

Zustimmen und widersprechen (Agreeing and disagreeing)

I agree (with you). *Ich bin deiner Meinung.*	→ (I'm sorry but) I disagree (with you). *Ich bin nicht deiner Meinung.*
Yes, of course. *Ja, natürlich.*	→ No, not at all. *Nein, ganz und gar nicht.*
That's a good idea. *Das ist ein guter Vorschlag.*	→ (Excuse me but I think) That's a bad idea. *Das ist kein guter Gedanke / keine gute Idee.*
I'm for that. *Ich bin dafür.*	→ (I'm afraid) I'm against that. *Ich bin dagegen.*
You're right (about / that …) *Du hast Recht (mit / wenn du sagst, dass …).*	→ (I'm sorry, but) you're wrong (about / that …). *Das stimmt nicht.*

Wenn du dir mit deiner Meinung nicht sicher bist, verwende Ausdrücke wie:

I'm not sure / certain
Ich bin nicht sicher.

Jemanden unterbrechen (Interrupting someone)

Can I ask you something?	*Kann ich dich etwas fragen?*
Can / May I (just) say something, please?	*Kann ich bitte etwas sagen?*
Excuse me, but …	*Entschuldigung, aber …*
I don't wish / I'm sorry to interrupt / stop you but …	*Ich möchte dich nicht unterbrechen, aber … / Ich unterbreche dich ungern, aber …*
I'm sorry, I don't agree with …	*Ich bin anderer Meinung (als) …*
I'm sorry, that's not right / fair.	*Das ist nicht richtig / fair.*
I'm sorry, but (I'd just like to say) …	*Es tut mir leid, aber …*

Darum bitten, dass etwas wiederholt wird (Asking for something to be repeated)

Excuse me, could you say that again, please?	*Kannst du das bitte noch einmal sagen?*
Sorry, could you repeat that / what you said about …?	*Kannst du das bitte wiederholen?*
I'm sorry / I'm afraid I didn't quite hear / catch / understand what you said. Could you say / repeat it again, please?	*Es tut mir leid, aber ich habe nicht genau verstanden, was du meinst / gesagt hast. Kannst du das bitte noch einmal sagen?*
I'm sorry / I'm afraid, I missed / forgot what you were saying (about …). Could you explain it again / once more, please?	*Es tut mir leid, ich habe nicht verstanden, was du (über …) gesagt hast. Kannst du mir das noch einmal erklären?*
I'm sorry / I'm afraid, you were talking a bit too fast for me – could you say it again a little bit slower / would you mind repeating what you said, please?	*Es tut mir leid, du hast für mich etwas zu schnell gesprochen. Könntest du das bitte etwas langsamer wiederholen? Es tut mir leid, das war ein wenig zu schnell für mich. Könntest du es bitte etwas langsamer wiederholen?*

Das Thema wechseln (Changing the subject)

We've talked a lot about … Could we look at … now?	*Wir haben viel über … geredet. Könnten wir jetzt über … sprechen?*
We should really talk about … too.	*Wir sollten wirklich auch über … reden.*
That's my opinion about (e.g. tennis). But what about (e.g. football)? What do you think about it?	*So denke ich über … Aber was meinst du zu …?*

Can we talk about ... now?	*Können wir jetzt über ... sprechen?*
Perhaps we should also talk about ...	*Vielleicht sollten wir auch über ... reden.*

Andere zum Reden bringen *(Making people talk)*

What do you think, (Anne)?	*Was meinst du ...?*

Entscheidungsfragen

Are you interested in ...?	*Interessierst du dich für ...?*

Bestätigungsfragen

The weather is terrible today, isn't it?	*Das Wetter ist schrecklich, oder?*

TIPP *Well, actually, I think ..., I guess ...* etc. sind hervorragende Pausenfüller. Verwende sie, wenn du einen Augenblick Zeit brauchst, um zu überlegen, was du als nächstes sagen möchtest.

Hier sind ein paar Beispiele für typische Alltagssituationen für den Prüfungsteil **„Sprachmittlung"**:

At the hotel	*Im Hotel*
At the souvenir shop	*Im Souvenirgeschäft*
On the telephone	*Am Telefon*
In a restaurant	*In einem Restaurant*
At the station	*Am Bahnhof*
Asking the way	*Nach dem Weg fragen*
At the tourist information centre	*Im Fremdenverkehrsamt / In der Touristeninformation*
At the travel agent's	*Im Reisebüro*

Hilfreiche Wendungen für den Prüfungsteil **„Sprachmittlung"**:

Sorry, I didn't understand you.	*Entschuldigung, ich habe Sie nicht verstanden.*
Could you please repeat that?	*Könnten Sie das bitte wiederholen?*
Could you please explain what a ... is?	*Könnten Sie mir bitte erklären, was ... ist?*
Could you please explain the word ... to me?	*Könnten Sie mir bitte das Wort ... erklären?*
What do you mean when you say ...?	*Was meinen Sie, wenn Sie ... sagen?*

Kompetenzbereich: Sprechen | 51

4.3 Übungsaufgaben zum Kompetenzbereich „Sprechen"

Monologisches Sprechen

> **Vortrag**
> Wähle unbedingt ein Thema, zu dem du etwas sagen kannst und sprich das Thema mit deinem Lehrer ab.
> Als Hilfestellung in der Prüfung darfst du meist einen Stichwortzettel verwenden, auf dem du üblicherweise 6–8 kurze Notizen zu deinem Referat vermerkt hast. Solltest du wirklich vor Aufregung einmal „den Faden" verlieren, wirst du froh über deine Aufzeichnungen sein. Eine gute Idee für die Prüfung ist es auch, ein Plakat anstelle des Stichwortzettels zu erstellen. Wenn du beispielsweise über eine Reise berichtest, kannst du einige Fotos aufkleben und diese beschriften. Du kannst auch passende Gegenstände (z. B. Souvenirs) mitbringen. So bekommt der Prüfer eine gute Vorstellung über deine Reiseeindrücke und du selbst hast eine gute Gedächtnisstütze.

TIPP

1. Das ist ein Beispiel für ein Foto, was du mit in die Prüfung nehmen könntest als Gesprächsanlass. Die Fragen, die du darunter findest sind Hilfestellungen zum Üben. In der Prüfung musst du selber etwas zu den mitgebrachten Fotos oder anderen Gegenständen sagen.

   a) Where is the boat?
   _____
   _____

   b) What is behind the boat?
   _____
   _____

   c) Who is in front of the boat?
   _____
   _____

d) What is the man doing?
_____
_____

2. Hier kannst du noch einmal üben, ein Bild zu beschreiben. Beantworte die Fragen.

   a) What is the man doing?
   _____
   _____
   _____
   _____

   b) Where is the man?
   _____
   _____
   _____

   c) Which instruments is the man playing?
   _____
   _____
   _____

   d) Describe the people who are listening to the man.
   _____
   _____
   _____

   e) Guess where the man may be from (have a look at his socks).
   _____
   _____

3. Vortrag: J. K. Rowling. Bereite ein Referat über J. K. Rowling, die Autorin der Harry-Potter-Bücher, vor.

4. Vortrag: „Summer Holiday". Bereite ein Referat über deinen letzten Sommerurlaub vor.

Kompetenzbereich: Sprechen

Dialogisches Sprechen

> **TIPP**
>
> *Reacting to prompts* (**Gesprächsführung nach Vorgaben**)
>
> Ihr erhaltet Kärtchen mit Gesprächsvorgaben. Auf der einen Karte stehen die Informationen zu einer bestimmten Situation, auf der anderen Karte Punkte, zu denen im Gespräch Fragen gestellt werden sollen. Eure Aufgabe ist nun, anhand der jeweiligen Vorgaben ein kurzes Gespräch zu führen, in das ihr die Vorgaben einbaut.
> - Verwende alle Vorgaben in dem Gespräch.
> - Sprich deutlich in ganzen Sätzen.
> - Bringe deine eigenen Ideen in das Gespräch ein.
> - Wecke das Interesse deines Gegenübers, indem du Fragen an ihn stellst.
> - Formuliere ganze, verständliche Sätze.
> - Verwende Redewendungen und achte auf die Aussprache und Grammatik.

5. Telling about a trip

   prompt A

   > BIKES FOR RENT IN BRISTOL
   > - rent a bike for your summer holiday
   > - 9 £ a day
   > - special rates for families: £ 60 for four persons for two weeks
   > - insurance covered in case of damage or thievery
   > - adresses of special bed and breakfast places available with storing positions for bikes
   > - we organise your bike trip completely on demand

   prompt B

   > - city?
   > - occasion?
   > - prices?
   > - special offers?
   > - insurance?
   > - additional information?
   > - complete trips?

Kompetenzbereich: Sprechen

6. At the cinema

   prompt A

   > NEW CINEMA IN TOWN
   > - new film: Harry Potter
   > - 8 auditoriums
   > - special prices for pupils: £ 4 per ticket
   > - soft drinks, popcorn, several snacks available
   > - film posters on sale
   > - special offer: tuesday's ticket plus snack and soft drink for £ 7,50

   prompt B

   > - about the cinema?
   > - new film?
   > - auditoriums?
   > - prices for pupils?
   > - snacks and drinks?
   > - posters on sale?
   > - special offer?

Sprachmittlung

TIPP

Die Prüfer nehmen ihre Gesprächsrollen ein. Der eine spricht nur Deutsch, der andere nur Englisch. Du hörst dem Gespräch der Prüfer aufmerksam zu. Anschließend wiederholen die Prüfer ihren Dialog. Dieses Mal ist es deine Aufgabe, ihre Fragen und Aussagen in die jeweils andere Sprache zu übersetzen. Das heißt, dass du die Gesprächsinhalte vom Englischen ins Deutsche und vom Deutschen ins Englische übertragen musst. Du erhältst keine schriftliche Vorlage des Gespräches, sondern musst die Inhalte dem Gespräch der Prüfer entnehmen.

- Beachte, dass du beim Übersetzen Aussagen häufig in die 3. Person übertragen musst.
  Beispiel: Sagt der deutsche Tourist: „Ich brauche ein Taxi zum Flughafen" übersetzt du "He/She needs a taxi to the airport".
- Versuche das Gesagte sinngemäß zu übertragen.
  Beispiel: "Here you are." → „Bitte schön."
- Umschreibe Wörter, die du nicht kennst, oder verwende ein ähnliches Wort.
  Beispiel: „Mein Pass ist weg"
  → "He can't find his passport. / He thinks he has lost his passport."
- Keinesfalls solltest du nichts sagen, wenn du eine Vorgabe nicht übersetzen kannst. Du solltest stattdessen versuchen, das Gespräch trotzdem fortzusetzen. Ist die Vorgabe zum Verständnis nicht unbedingt nötig, kannst du sie notfalls überspringen.
  Beispiel: Beim Einkaufen: „Nein, danke. Das ist mir zu teuer. Auf Wiedersehen."
  "No thanks. (…). Goodbye."
- Manchmal ist es auch möglich, die Körpersprache einzusetzen um einen Gegenstand/ Sachverhalt zu beschreiben.
  Beispiel: In der Apotheke: "Could you please give me something for/against …?"
  → Auf Brandblase, Schnittwunde etc. zeigen.

7. You want to go on a bike tour in Ireland next summer, so you go to a travel agent's for some information.

   TRAVEL AGENT: Hello, how can I help you?
   YOU: Du benötigst Informationen über Fahrradtouren in Irland.

   _____

   TRAVEL AGENT: When would you like to go?
   YOU: Ihr wollt in den nächsten Sommerferien dorthin fahren.

   _____

   TRAVEL AGENT: Would you like to rent bikes there or are you going to take your own bikes?
   YOU: Du bittest um Informationen für beide Möglichkeiten. Dann könnt ihr die Preise zu Hause vergleichen und euch entscheiden.

   _____

   TRAVEL AGENT: No problem. Here you are. Don't hesitate to come back if you have any questions.
   YOU: Du bedankst dich und verabschiedest dich.

   _____

8. At a hotel
   You're at a hotel in New York. A German tourist and his wife have just arrived and need help. You offer your help to the German tourist.

   RECEPTIONIST: Good afternoon. What can I do for you?

   _____

   GERMAN TOURIST: Schmidt, guten Tag. Ich habe eine Reservierung.

   _____

   RECEPTIONIST: Mr. Schmidt. Your reservation is from the fifteenth to the eighteenth of August. Could I have your passport and your credit card, please?

   _____

   GERMAN TOURIST: Hier, bitte. Können Sie uns morgen um 6:00 Uhr aufwecken?

   _____

RECEPTIONIST: Sure! Here's your key. Your room is number 223. Breakfast is served from 6 to 10 a.m. The breakfast room is on the first floor.

_____

GERMAN TOURIST: Können wir im Hotel auch Karten für das Musical „Lion King" kaufen?

_____

RECEPTIONIST: Sorry. We don't sell theatre tickets. You can buy them at the theatres on Broadway or at the ticket office on Times Square.

_____

GERMAN TOURIST: Danke. Auf Wiedersehen.

9. At the souvenir shop: You're at a souvenir shop in London. A German tourist needs help. You offer to help her.

ASSISTANT: Hello, can I help you?

_____

GERMAN TOURIST: Ja, bitte. Ich hätte dieses T-Shirt gerne in Blau.

_____

ASSISTANT: Here you are.

_____

GERMAN TOURIST: Wo kann ich es anprobieren?

_____

ASSISTANT: The changing rooms are over there.

GERMAN TOURIST: Dieses T-Shirt ist zu groß. Kann ich ein Kleineres haben?

_____

(Nach dem Anprobieren)
Jetzt passt es.

ASSISTANT: Would you like anything else?

_____

| | | **Kompetenzbereich: Sprechen** | **57** |

GERMAN TOURIST: Ich nehme auch diese beiden Postkarten. Verkaufen Sie auch Briefmarken?

ASSISTANT: No, I'm sorry. You have to buy them at the post office.

GERMAN TOURIST: Schade. Trotzdem Danke und auf Wiedersehen.

▶ **Kurzgrammatik**

Kurzgrammatik

Damit du wichtige Grammatikbereiche noch einmal wiederholen oder nachschlagen kannst, findest du hier die wichtigsten Grammatikregeln mit prägnanten Beispielen. Lies die Regeln genau durch und sieh dir die Beispiele an. Überlege dir zu jedem Beispiel ein eigenes Beispiel. Präge dir jeweils das Beispiel zu den Regeln ein. Wenn du eine Regel mit einem bestimmten Beispiel verknüpfen kannst, fällt es dir vielleicht leichter, dir die Regel zu merken. Auf jeden Fall aber gilt: Am Lernen dieser Regeln (und der Beispiele) führt kein Weg vorbei!

1 Adverbien – *adverbs*

Bildung
Adjektiv + *-ly*   glad → glad<u>ly</u>

Ausnahmen:
- *-y* am Wortende wird zu *-i*.   eas<u>y</u> → eas<u>i</u>ly
                                                          funn<u>y</u> → funn<u>i</u>ly

- auf einen Konsonanten folgendes   simp<u>le</u> → simp<u>ly</u>
  -le wird zu *-ly*.   horrib<u>le</u> → horrib<u>ly</u>
                                                          probab<u>le</u> → probab<u>ly</u>

- auf einen Konsonanten folgendes   fantast<u>ic</u> → fantast<u>ically</u>
  -ic wird zu *-ically*.

  Ausnahme: publ<u>ic</u> → publ<u>icly</u>

Beachte:
- In einigen Fällen haben Adjektiv und   daily, early, fast, hard, long, low, weekly, yearly
  Adverb dieselbe Form.

- Unregelmäßig gebildet wird: good → well

- Endet das Adjektiv auf *-ly*, so kannst du   friendly → in a friendly manner
  kein Adverb bilden und verwendest
  deshalb: *in a* + Adjektiv + *manner*

Verwendung
Adverbien bestimmen

- Verben,   She <u>easily</u> <u>found</u> her brother in the crowd.
                                                          Sie <u>fand</u> ihren Bruder <u>leicht</u> in der Menge.

- Adjektive oder   This band is <u>extremely</u> <u>famous</u>.
                                                          Diese Band ist <u>sehr</u> <u>berühmt</u>.

- andere Adverbien   He walks <u>extremely</u> <u>quickly</u>.
  näher.   *Er geht <u>äußerst</u> <u>schnell</u>.*

2 Bedingungssätze – *if-clauses*

Ein Bedingungssatz besteht aus zwei Teilen: Nebensatz (*if*-Satz) + Hauptsatz. Im **if-Satz** steht die **Bedingung**, unter der die im **Hauptsatz** genannte **Folge** eintritt.

Bedingungssatz Typ I

Bildung
- *if*-Satz (Bedingung): Gegenwart (*simple present*)
- Hauptsatz (Folge): Zukunft mit *will* (*will-future*)

Der *if*-Satz kann auch nach dem Hauptsatz stehen:
- Hauptsatz: *will-future*
- *if*-Satz: *simple present*

Im Hauptsatz kann statt *will-future* auch
- *can* + Grundform des Verbs oder
- *must* + Grundform des Verbs stehen.

If you <u>read</u> this book,
Wenn du dieses Buch liest,

you <u>will learn</u> a lot about Scotland.
erfährst du eine Menge über Schottland.

You <u>will learn</u> a lot about Scotland
Du erfährst eine Menge über Schottland,

<u>if</u> you <u>read</u> this book.
wenn du dieses Buch liest.

If you go to London, you <u>can see</u> Sandy.
Wenn du nach London gehst, kannst du Sandy treffen.

If you go to London, you <u>must visit</u> Big Ben.
Wenn du nach London gehst, musst du dir Big Ben ansehen.

Verwendung
Bedingungssätze vom Typ I verwendet man, wenn die **Bedingung erfüllbar** ist. Man gibt an, was unter bestimmten Bedingungen **geschieht, geschehen kann** oder was **geschehen sollte**.

If it's hot, we will go to the beach.
Wenn es heiß ist, gehen wir an den Strand.

If it's hot, we can go to the beach.
Wenn es heiß ist, können wir an den Strand gehen.

If it's hot, we must go to the beach.
Wenn es heiß ist, müssen wir an den Strand gehen.

Bedingungssatz Typ II

Bildung
- *if*-Satz (Bedingung): 1. Vergangenheit (*simple past*)
- Hauptsatz (Folge): Konditional I (*conditional I = would* + Grundform des Verbs)

<u>If</u> I <u>went</u> to London,
Wenn ich nach London ginge/gehen würde,

I <u>would visit</u> the Tower of London.
würde ich mir den Tower of London ansehen.

Verwendung
Bedingungssätze vom Typ II verwendet man, wenn die **Erfüllung der Bedingung unwahrscheinlich** ist.

3 Fürwörter – *pronouns*

Besitzanzeigende Fürwörter – *possessive pronouns*

Besitzanzeigende Fürwörter (*possessive pronouns*) verwendet man, um zu sagen, **was (zu) jemandem gehört**.
Steht ein besitzanzeigendes Fürwort allein, verwendest du eine andere Form, als wenn es bei einem Substantiv steht:

mit Substantiv	ohne Substantiv
my	mine
your	yours
his/her/its	his/hers/its
our	ours
your	yours
their	theirs

This is <u>my</u> bike. – This is <u>mine</u>.
This is <u>your</u> bike. – This is <u>yours</u>.
This is <u>her</u> bike. – This is <u>hers</u>.
This is <u>our</u> bike. – This is <u>ours</u>.
This is <u>your</u> bike. – This is <u>yours</u>.
This is <u>their</u> bike. – This is <u>theirs</u>.

Rückbezügliche Fürwörter – *reflexive pronouns*

Die rückbezüglichen Fürwörter (*reflexive pronouns*) **beziehen sich auf das Subjekt** des Satzes **zurück**:

myself
yourself
himself/herself/itself
ourselves
yourselves
themselves

<u>I</u> will buy <u>myself</u> a new car.
<u>You</u> will buy <u>yourself</u> a new car.
<u>He</u> will buy <u>himself</u> a new car.
<u>We</u> will buy <u>ourselves</u> a new car.
<u>You</u> will buy <u>yourselves</u> a new car.
<u>They</u> will buy <u>themselves</u> a new car.

each other / one another

each other / one another ist unveränderlich. Es bezieht sich auf **mehrere Personen** und wird mit „sich (gegenseitig), einander" übersetzt.

Beachte:
Einige Verben stehen ohne *each other*, obwohl sie im Deutschen mit „sich" übersetzt werden.

They looked at <u>each other</u> and laughed.
Sie schauten <u>sich</u> (gegenseitig) an und lachten.
oder: *Sie schauten <u>einander</u> an und lachten.*

to meet	*sich treffen*
to kiss	*sich küssen*
to fall in love	*sich verlieben*

4 Grundform – *infinitive*

Die Grundform mit *to* steht nach

- bestimmten Verben, z. B.:

to *agree*	zustimmen
to *attempt*	versuchen
to *choose*	wählen
to *decide*	entscheiden
to *expect*	erwarten
to *forget*	vergessen
to *hope*	hoffen
to *manage*	schaffen
to *offer*	anbieten
to *plan*	planen
to *promise*	versprechen
to *remember*	an etw. denken
to *seem*	scheinen
to *try*	versuchen
to *want*	wollen

  He decided to wait.
  Er beschloss zu warten.

- bestimmten Substantiven, z. B.:

attempt	Versuch
idea	Idee
plan	Plan
wish	Wunsch

  It was her wish to marry in November.
  Es war ihr Wunsch, im November zu heiraten.

- bestimmten Adjektiven, z. B.:

certain	sicher
difficult	schwer, schwierig
easy	leicht
hard	schwer, schwierig

  It was difficult to follow her.
  Es war schwierig, ihr zu folgen.

- den Fragewörtern *what, where, which, who, when, why, how.*

  We knew where to find her.
  Wir wussten, wo wir sie finden würden.

5 Indirekte Rede – *reported speech*

Die indirekte Rede verwendet man, um **wiederzugeben, was eine andere Person gesagt** oder **gefragt hat**.

Bildung

Um die indirekte Rede zu bilden, benötigt man ein **Einleitungsverb**. Häufig verwendete Einleitungsverben sind:

to add, to agree, to answer, to ask, to say, to tell, to think, to want to know

Kurzgrammatik

In der indirekten Rede verändern sich die **Fürwörter**, in bestimmten Fällen auch die **Zeiten** und die **Orts-** und **Zeitangaben**.

- Veränderung der **Fürwörter**
  persönliche Fürwörter:
  besitzanzeigende Fürwörter:
  hinweisende Fürwörter:

direkte Rede:	indirekte Rede:
I, you, we, you	he, she, they
my, your, our, your	his, her, their
this, these	that, those

- **Zeiten**
  Keine Veränderung, wenn das **Einleitungsverb** in der **Gegenwart**, der **2. Vergangenheit** oder der **Zukunft** steht.

direkte Rede:	indirekte Rede:
Jill says, "I love dancing."	Jill says (that) she loves dancing.
Jill sagt: „Ich tanze sehr gerne."	Jill sagt, sie tanzt sehr gerne.

Die Zeit der direkten Rede wird in der indirekten Rede **um eine Zeitstufe zurückversetzt**, wenn das **Einleitungsverb** in der **1. Vergangenheit** steht. Die Zeiten verändern sich dann folgendermaßen:

direkte Rede		indirekte Rede
simple present	→	simple past
simple past	→	past perfect
present perfect	→	past perfect
will-future	→	conditional I

Jill said, "I love dancing."	Jill said (that) she loved dancing.
Jill sagte: „Ich tanze sehr gerne."	Jill sagte, sie tanze sehr gerne.
Joe: "I like it."	Joe said he liked it.
Joe: "I liked it."	Joe said he had liked it.
Joe: "I've liked it."	Joe said he had liked it.
Joe: "I will like it."	Joe said he would like it.

- Veränderung der **Orts-** und **Zeitangaben**:

now	→	then
today	→	that day
yesterday	→	the day before
the day before yesterday	→	two days before
tomorrow	→	the next day
next week/year	→	the following week/year
here	→	there

Bildung der indirekten Frage

Häufige Einleitungsverben für die indirekte Frage sind *to ask, to want to know*.

- Enthält die direkte Frage ein **Fragewort**, **bleibt** dieses in der indirekten Frage **erhalten**. Die **Umschreibung** mit *do/does/did* **entfällt** in der indirekten Frage.

Tom: "When did they arrive in England?"	Tom asked when they had arrived in England.
Tom: „Wann sind sie in England angekommen?"	Tom fragte, wann sie in England angekommen seien.

- Enthält die direkte Frage **kein Fragewort**, wird die indirekte Frage mit **whether** oder **if** eingeleitet:

Tom: "Are they staying at the youth hostel?"	Tom asked if/whether they were staying at the youth hostel.
Tom: „Übernachten sie in der Jugendherberge?"	Tom fragte, ob sie in der Jugendherberge übernachteten.

> **Befehle/Aufforderungen in der indirekten Rede**
> Häufige Einleitungsverben sind *to tell*, *to order* (Befehl), *to ask* (Aufforderung). In der indirekten Rede steht bei Befehlen/Aufforderungen **Einleitungsverb + Objekt + (*not*) *to* + Grundform des Verbs** der direkten Rede.

Tom: "Leave the room."
Tom: „Verlass den Raum."

Tom told me to leave the room.
Tom forderte mich auf, den Raum zu verlassen.

6 Modale Hilfsverben – *modal auxiliaries*

Im Englischen gibt es zwei Arten von Hilfsverben: die vollständigen Hilfsverben *to be, to have, to do* und die modalen Hilfsverben *(modal auxiliaries)* can, may, must, shall, will.

> **Bildung**
> - Die modalen Hilfsverben haben für alle Personen **nur eine Form**, in der 3. Person Singular also kein -s.
> - Auf das modale Hilfsverb folgt die **Grundform** des Verbs **ohne *to***.
> - **Frage und Verneinung** werden **nicht** mit *do/does/did* **umschrieben**.
>
> Die modalen Hilfsverben können nicht alle Zeiten bilden. Deshalb benötigt man bestimmte **Ersatzformen**.
> - **can** (können)
>   simple past/conditional I: **could**
>   Ersatzform: *to be able to*
>
> - **may** (dürfen)
>   conditional: **might**
>   Ersatzform: *to be allowed to*
>
> - **must** (müssen)
>   Ersatzform: *to have to*
>
>   Beachte:
>   *must not/mustn't* = „nicht dürfen"
>
>   „nicht müssen" = *not* + *to have to*
>
> - **shall** (sollen)
>   conditional I: **should**
>   Ersatzform: *to be to, to want*

I, you, he/she/it
we, you, they } must

You must listen to my new CD.
Du musst dir meine neue CD anhören.

Can I have a cup of coffee, please?
Kann ich bitte eine Tasse Kaffee haben?

I can sing. / I am able to sing.
Ich kann singen.

You may go home early today. /
You are allowed to go home early today.
Du darfst heute früh nach Hause gehen.

He must be home by ten o'clock. /
He has to be home by ten o'clock.
Er muss um zehn Uhr zu Hause sein.

You must not eat all the cake.
Du darfst nicht den ganzen Kuchen essen.

You don't have to eat all the cake.
Du musst nicht den ganzen Kuchen essen.

Shall I help you? / Do you want me to help you?
Soll ich dir helfen?

7 Konjunktionen – *conjunctions*

Konjunktionen *(conjunctions)* verwendet man, um **zwei Hauptsätze oder Haupt- und Nebensatz miteinander zu verbinden**. Mit Konjunktionen lässt sich ein Text strukturieren, indem man z. B. Ursachen, Folgen oder zeitliche Abfolgen angibt.

after	– nachdem	What will you do <u>after</u> she's gone? *Was wirst du tun, <u>nachdem</u> sie gegangen ist?*
although	– obwohl	<u>Although</u> she was ill, she went to work. *<u>Obwohl</u> sie krank war, ging sie zur Arbeit.*
as	– als (zeitlich)	<u>As</u> he came into the room, the telephone rang. *<u>Als</u> er ins Zimmer kam, klingelte das Telefon.*
as soon as	– sobald	<u>As soon as</u> the band began to play, everybody started dancing. *<u>Sobald</u> die Band zu spielen begann, tanzten alle.*
because	– weil, da	I need a new bike <u>because</u> my old bike was stolen. *Ich brauche ein neues Rad, <u>weil</u> mein altes Rad gestohlen wurde.*
before	– bevor	<u>Before</u> he goes to work, he buys a newspaper. *<u>Bevor</u> er zur Arbeit geht, kauft er eine Zeitung.*
but	– aber	She likes football <u>but</u> she doesn't like skiing. *Sie mag Fußball, <u>aber</u> sie mag Skifahren nicht.*
either … or	– entweder … oder	We can <u>either</u> watch a film <u>or</u> go to a concert. *Wir können uns <u>entweder</u> einen Film ansehen <u>oder</u> in ein Konzert gehen.*
in order to	– um … zu, damit	Peter is in Scotland <u>in order to</u> visit his friend Malcolm. *Peter ist in Schottland, <u>um</u> seinen Freund Malcolm <u>zu</u> besuchen.*
neither … nor	– weder … noch	We can <u>neither</u> eat <u>nor</u> sleep outside. It's raining. *Wir können <u>weder</u> draußen essen <u>noch</u> draußen schlafen. Es regnet.*
so that	– sodass	She shut the door <u>so that</u> the dog couldn't go outside. *Sie machte die Tür zu, <u>sodass</u> der Hund nicht hinausgehen konnte.*
then	– dann	He bought an icecream, and <u>then</u> shared it with Sally. *Er kaufte ein Eis, (und) <u>dann</u> teilte er es mit Sally.*
when	– wenn (zeitlich), sobald	Have a break <u>when</u> you've finished painting. *Mache eine Pause, <u>sobald</u> du fertig gestrichen hast.*

while	– während, solange	While we were in London, we had very good weather. *Während wir in London waren, hatten wir sehr gutes Wetter.*

8 Partizipien – *participles*

Partizip Präsens – *present participle*

Bildung
Grundform des Verbs + *-ing*

read → read**ing**

Beachte:

- Stummes *-e* entfällt.

writ**e** → writ**ing**

- Nach kurzem betonten Vokal wird der Schlusskonsonant verdoppelt.

sto**p** → sto**pp**ing

- *-ie* wird zu *-y*.

l**ie** → l**y**ing

Verwendung
Das Partizip Präsens *(present participle)* verwendet man

- zur Bildung der Verlaufsform der Gegenwart,

Peter is reading.
Peter liest (gerade).

- zur Bildung der Verlaufsform der Vergangenheit,

Peter was reading when I came into the room.
Peter las (gerade), als ich in den Raum kam.

- zur Verkürzung eines Nebensatzes oder zur Verbindung von zwei Hauptsätzen mit demselben Subjekt.

Partizip Perfekt – *past participle*

Bildung
Grundform des Verbs + *-ed*

talk → talk**ed**

Beachte:

- Stummes *-e* entfällt.

liv**e** → liv**ed**

- Nach kurzem betonten Vokal wird der Schlusskonsonant verdoppelt.

sto**p** → sto**pp**ed

- *-y* wird zu *-ie*.

cr**y** → cr**ied**

- Unregelmäßige Verben: siehe die Liste in deinem Schulbuch. Die *past-participle*-Formen einiger wichtiger unregelmäßiger Verben sind hier angegeben.

be → been
have → had
give → given
go → gone
take → taken
write → written

Verwendung

Das Partizip Perfekt *(past participle)* verwendet man

- zur Bildung der zweiten Vergangenheit *(present perfect)*,

  He has talked to his father.
  Er hat mit seinem Vater gesprochen.

- zur Bildung der Vorvergangenheit *(past perfect)*,

  Before they went biking in France they had bought new bicycles.
  Bevor sie nach Frankreich zum Radfahren gingen, hatten sie neue Fahrräder gekauft.

- zur Bildung des Passivs,

  The fish was eaten by the cat.
  Der Fisch wurde von der Katze gefressen.

- zur Verkürzung eines Nebensatzes oder zur Verbindung von zwei Hauptsätzen mit demselben Subjekt.

9 Passiv – *passive voice*

Bildung

Form von *to be* + Partizip Perfekt

Tower Bridge was finished in 1894.
Die Tower Bridge wurde 1894 fertiggestellt.

Zeitform

- *simple present*

  Aktiv: Peter buys the milk.
  Passiv: The milk is bought by Peter.

- *simple past*

  Aktiv: Peter bought the milk.
  Passiv: The milk was bought by Peter.

- *present perfect*

  Aktiv: Peter has bought the milk.
  Passiv: The milk has been bought by Peter.

- *past perfect*

  Aktiv: Peter had bought the milk.
  Passiv: The milk had been bought by Peter.

- *future I*

  Aktiv: Peter will buy the milk.
  Passiv: The milk will be bought by Peter.

- *future II*

  Aktiv: Peter will have bought the milk.
  Passiv: The milk will have been bought by Peter.

- *conditional I*

  Aktiv: Peter would buy the milk.
  Passiv: The milk would be bought by Peter.

- *conditional II*

  Aktiv: Peter would have bought the milk.
  Passiv: The milk would have been bought by Peter.

Aktiv → Passiv

Beachte bei der Umwandlung vom Aktiv ins Passiv:

- Das Objekt des Aktivsatzes wird zum Subjekt des Passivsatzes.
- Das Subjekt des Aktivsatzes wird zum Objekt des Passivsatzes. Es wird mit *by* angeschlossen.
- Stehen im Aktivsatz zwei Objekte (direktes und indirektes Objekt), lassen sich zwei verschiedene Passivsätze bilden. Eines der Objekte wird zum Subjekt des Passivsatzes, während das zweite Objekt nicht verändert wird.

Beachte:
Das indirekte Objekt muss im Passivsatz mit *to* angeschlossen werden.

Aktiv: Peter (Subjekt) buys the milk (Objekt).
Passiv: The milk (Subjekt) is bought by Peter (Objekt).

Aktiv: They (Subjekt) gave her (ind. Obj.) a ball (dir. Obj.).
Passiv: She (Subjekt) was given a ball (dir. Obj.).

oder:
Aktiv: They (Subjekt) gave her (ind. Obj.) a ball (dir. Obj.).
Passiv: A ball (Subjekt) was given to her (ind. Obj.).

Passiv → Aktiv

Beachte bei der Umwandlung vom Passiv ins Aktiv:

- Das mit *by* angeschlossene Objekt des Passivsatzes wird zum Subjekt des Aktivsatzes; *by* entfällt.
- Das Subjekt des Passivsatzes wird zum Objekt des Aktivsatzes.
- Wenn im Passivsatz der mit *by* angeschlossene Handelnde fehlt, muss im Aktivsatz ein Handelnder als Subjekt ergänzt werden, z. B. durch *somebody, we, you, they*.

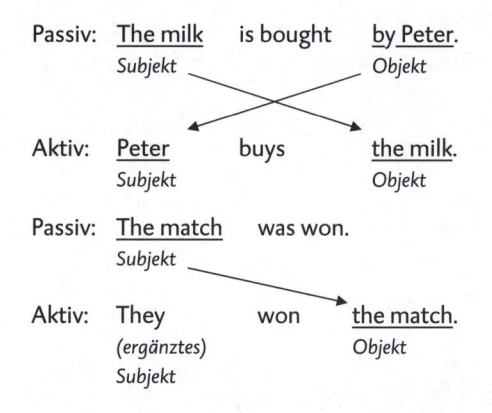

Passiv: The milk (Subjekt) is bought by Peter (Objekt).
Aktiv: Peter (Subjekt) buys the milk (Objekt).

Passiv: The match (Subjekt) was won.
Aktiv: They (ergänztes Subjekt) won the match (Objekt).

10 Präpositionen – *prepositions*

Präpositionen (*prepositions*) werden auch als Verhältniswörter bezeichnet. Sie drücken **räumliche, zeitliche oder andere Arten von Beziehungen** aus.

The ball is <u>under</u> the table.
Der Ball ist unter dem Tisch.

He came <u>after</u> six o'clock.
Er kam nach sechs Uhr.

I knew it <u>from</u> the start.
Ich wusste es von Anfang an.

Kurzgrammatik

Die wichtigsten Präpositionen mit Beispielen für ihre Verwendung:

- *at*

  Ortsangabe: *at home*

  I'm at home at the moment.
  Ich bin zurzeit zu Hause.

  Zeitangabe: *at three o'clock*

  He arrived at three o'clock.
  Er kam um drei Uhr an.

- *by*

  Angabe des Mittels: *to go by bike*

  She went to work by bike.
  Sie fuhr mit dem Rad zur Arbeit.

  Angabe der Ursache: *by mistake*

  He did it by mistake.
  Er hat es aus Versehen getan.

  Zeitangabe: *by tomorrow*

  You will get your DVD back by tomorrow.
  Du bekommst deine DVD bis morgen zurück.

- *for*

  Zeitdauer: *for hours*

  We waited for the bus for hours.
  Wir haben stundenlang auf den Bus gewartet.

- *from*

  Ortsangabe: *from Dublin*

  Ian comes from Dublin.
  Ian kommt aus Dublin.

  Zeitangabe: *from nine to five*

  We work from nine to five.
  Wir arbeiten von neun bis fünf Uhr.

- *in*

  Ortsangabe: *in England*

  In England, they drive on the left.
  In England herrscht Linksverkehr.

  Zeitangabe: *in the morning*

  They woke up early in the morning.
  Sie wachten am frühen Morgen auf.

- *of*

  Ortsangabe: *north of the city*

  The village lies north of the city.
  Das Dorf liegt nördlich der Stadt.

- *on*

  Ortsangabe: *on the left, on the floor*

  On the left you see the Empire State Building.
  Links sehen Sie das Empire State Building.

  Zeitangabe: *on Monday*

  On Monday she will buy the tickets.
  (Am) Montag kauft sie die Karten.

- *to*

  Richtungsangabe: *to turn to the left*

  Please turn to the left.
  Bitte wenden Sie sich nach links.

  Angabe des Ziels: *to London*

  He goes to London every year.
  Er fährt jedes Jahr nach London.

Kurzgrammatik

Präpositionen kommen häufig in **Orts- und Richtungsangaben** vor:

- behind — The ball is behind the chair.
- in front of — The apple is in front of the bottle.
- next to — Kim is next to Colin.
- near — Jenny is near the shop.
- outside — My car is outside my house.
- inside — Paula is inside the bank.
- under — The letter is under the book.
- on the left — My house is on the left.
- on the right — The door is on the right.
- in the middle (of) — My coat is in the middle.
  The bookshop is in the middle of the town.
- at — He is waiting at the bus stop.
- across — The café is across the street.
  She walks across the road.
- in — The cat is in the garden.
- into — Susan is putting the ball into the box.
- on — The milk is on the table.
- onto — The cat is climbing onto the garage roof.

- to

She drives to work.

- towards

Max is walking towards the cinema.

11 Relativsätze – *relative clauses*

Ein Relativsatz bezieht sich auf eine Person oder Sache des Hauptsatzes und beschreibt diese näher:

- Hauptsatz:
- Relativsatz:

The boy who looks like Jane is her brother.
Der Junge, der Jane ähnlich sieht, ist ihr Bruder.

The boy is her brother

who looks like Jane

Bildung

Haupt- und Nebensatz werden durch das Relativpronomen *(who, which, that)* verbunden.

- **who** bezieht sich auf **Personen**.

Peter, who lives in London, likes travelling.
Peter, der in London lebt, reist gerne.

- **which** bezieht sich auf **Sachen**.

The film "Dark Moon", which we saw yesterday, was far too long.
Der Film „Dark Moon", den wir gestern sahen, war viel zu lang.

- **that** bezieht sich ebenfalls auf **Sachen** und wird nur verwendet, wenn die **Information** im Relativsatz **notwendig** ist, um den ganzen Satz zu verstehen.

The film that we saw last week was much better.
Der Film, den wir letzte Woche sahen, war viel besser.

Verwendung

Mithilfe von Relativsätzen kannst du **zwei Sätze miteinander verbinden**, wenn sie dasselbe Subjekt haben.

London is England's biggest city. London has about 7.2 million inhabitants.
London ist die größte Stadt Englands. London hat etwa 7,2 Millionen Einwohner.

London, which is England's biggest city, has about 7.2 million inhabitants.
London, die größte Stadt Englands, hat etwa 7,2 Millionen Einwohner.

12 Steigerung und Vergleich – *comparisons*

Steigerung des Adjektivs – *comparisons of adjectives*

Bildung
Man unterscheidet:
- Grundform
- 1. Steigerungsform
- 2. Steigerungsform

Peter is y<u>oung</u>.
Jane is y<u>ounger</u>.
Paul is the y<u>oungest</u>.

Steigerung auf *-er, -est*
- einsilbige Adjektive

old, old<u>er</u>, old<u>est</u>
alt, älter, am ältesten

- zweisilbige Adjektive, die auf *-er, -le, -ow* oder *-y* enden

clever, clever<u>er</u>, clever<u>est</u>
klug, klüger, am klügsten

simple, simpl<u>er</u>, simpl<u>est</u>
einfach, einfacher, am einfachsten

narrow, narrow<u>er</u>, narrow<u>est</u>
eng, enger, am engsten

funny, funn<u>ier</u>, funn<u>iest</u>
lustig, lustiger, am lustigsten

Beachte:
- Stummes *-e* am Wortende entfällt.
- Nach einem Konsonanten wird *-y* am Wortende zu *-i-*.
- Nach kurzem Vokal wird ein Konsonant am Wortende verdoppelt.

simpl<u>e</u>, simpl<u>er</u>, simpl<u>est</u>

funn<u>y</u>, funn<u>ier</u>, funn<u>iest</u>

fi<u>t</u>, fi<u>tt</u>er, fi<u>tt</u>est

Steigerung mit *more …, most …*
- zweisilbige Adjektive, die nicht auf *-er, -le, -ow* oder *-y* enden

useful, <u>more</u> useful, <u>most</u> useful
nützlich, nützlicher, am nützlichsten

- Adjektive mit drei und mehr Silben

difficult, <u>more</u> difficult, <u>most</u> difficult
schwierig, schwieriger, am schwierigsten

Unregelmäßige Steigerung
Die unregelmäßig gesteigerten Adjektive solltest du lernen. Einige wichtige Adjektive sind hier angegeben.

good, better, best
gut, besser, am besten

bad, worse, worst
schlecht, schlechter, am schlechtesten

many, more, most
viele, mehr, am meisten

much, more, most
viel, mehr, am meisten

little, less, least
wenig, weniger, am wenigsten

Vergleich – *sentences with comparisons*

Bildung

- Wenn du sagen möchtest, dass **zwei Sachen gleich** sind:
  as + Grundform des Adjektivs + *as*

  Anne is <u>as</u> <u>tall</u> <u>as</u> John.
  Anne ist genauso groß wie John.

- Wenn du sagen möchtest, dass **zwei Sachen ungleich** sind:
  not as + Grundform des Adjektivs + *as*

  John is <u>not as</u> <u>tall</u> <u>as</u> Steve.
  John ist nicht so groß wie Steve.

- Wenn du sagen möchtest, dass **zwei Sachen verschieden** gut/schlecht/schön … sind:
  1. Steigerungsform des Adjektivs + *than*

  Steve is <u>taller</u> <u>than</u> Anne.
  Steve ist größer als Anne.

Steigerung des Adverbs – *comparison of adverbs of manner*

Adverbien können wie Adjektive auch gesteigert werden.

- Adverbien auf *-ly* werden mit **more, most** bzw. mit **less, least** gesteigert.

  She talks <u>more</u> <u>quickly</u> than John.
  Sie spricht schneller als John.

- Adverbien, die dieselbe Form wie das Adjektiv haben, werden mit **-er, -est** gesteigert.

  fast – fast<u>er</u> – fast<u>est</u>
  early – earli<u>er</u> – earli<u>est</u>

- Folgende Adverbien haben unregelmäßige Steigerungsformen:

  well – better – best
  badly – worse – worst

13 Wortstellung – *word order*

Im englischen Aussagesatz gilt die Wortstellung <u>Subjekt</u> – <u>Prädikat</u> – <u>Objekt</u> (*subject – verb – object*):

<u>The cat</u> <u>catches</u> <u>a mouse</u>.

- Das <u>Subjekt</u> gibt an, wer oder was etwas tut.

  <u>The cat</u>
  Die Katze

- Das <u>Prädikat</u> gibt an, was getan wird.

  <u>catches</u>
  fängt

- Das <u>Objekt</u> gibt an, worauf/auf wen sich die Tätigkeit bezieht.

  <u>a mouse</u>.
  eine Maus.

Beachte:

- Orts- und Zeitangaben stehen meist am Satzende.

  We will buy a new car <u>tomorrow</u>.
  Morgen werden wir ein neues Auto kaufen.

  Peter lives <u>in New York</u>.
  Peter wohnt in New York.

- Ortsangaben stehen vor Zeitangaben.

  He moved <u>to New York</u> in June.
  Er ist im Juni nach New York gezogen.

14 Zeiten – *tenses*

Gegenwart – *simple present*

Bildung
Grundform des Verbs, Ausnahme 3. Person Einzahl: Grundform des Verbs + *-s*

stand — he/she/it stan<u>ds</u>

Beachte:
- Bei Verben, die auf *-s, -sh, -ch, -x* enden, wird *-es* angefügt.

kis<u>s</u> — he/she/it kiss<u>es</u>
ru<u>sh</u> — he/she/it rush<u>es</u>
tea<u>ch</u> — he/she/it teach<u>es</u>
fi<u>x</u> — he/she/it fix<u>es</u>

- Bei Verben, die auf Konsonant + *-y* enden, wird *-es* angefügt; *-y* wird zu *-i-*.

car<u>ry</u> — he/she/it carr<u>ies</u>

Bildung von Fragen im *simple present*
Umschreibung mit Fragewort + *do/does* + Grundform des Verbs

Where does he live?
Wo lebt er?

Beachte:
Die Umschreibung wird nicht verwendet,
- wenn nach dem Subjekt gefragt wird (mit *who, what, which*).

<u>Who</u> <u>likes</u> pizza?
Wer mag Pizza?

<u>What</u> <u>happens</u> next?
Was passiert als Nächstes?

<u>Which</u> tree <u>has</u> more leaves?
Welcher Baum hat mehr Blätter?

- wenn die Frage mit *is/are* gebildet wird.

<u>Are</u> you happy?
Bist du glücklich?

Bildung der Verneinung im *simple present*
Umschreibung mit *don't/doesn't* + Grundform des Verbs

He <u>doesn't like</u> football.
Er mag Fußball nicht.

Verwendung
Das *simple present* beschreibt
- Tätigkeiten, die man gewohnheitsmäßig oder häufig ausführt,

Every morning John <u>buys</u> a newspaper.
Jeden Morgen kauft sich John eine Zeitung.

- allgemeingültige Aussagen.

London <u>is</u> a big city.
London ist eine große Stadt.

Signalwörter: *always, every morning, every afternoon, every day, often, never*

Verlaufsform der Gegenwart – *present progressive*

Bildung
am/is/are + Verb in der *-ing*-Form (Partizip Präsens)

read → *am/is/are* read**ing**

Bildung von Fragen im *present progressive*
am/is/are + Subjekt + Verb in der *-ing*-Form

<u>Is</u> Peter <u>reading</u>?
Liest Peter gerade?

Bildung der Verneinung im *present progressive*
am not/isn't/aren't + Verb in der *-ing*-Form

Peter <u>isn't</u> <u>reading</u>.
Peter liest gerade nicht.

Verwendung
Mit dem *present progressive* drückt man aus,

- dass etwas **gerade passiert** und **noch nicht abgeschlossen** ist.
  Signalwörter: *at the moment, now*

  At the moment, Peter <u>is drinking</u> a cup of tea.
  Im Augenblick trinkt Peter eine Tasse Tee.
  [Er hat damit angefangen und noch nicht aufgehört.]

- dass es um eine **zukünftige, bereits festgelegte Handlung** geht.

  We <u>are seeing</u> the match on Sunday.
  Am Sonntag sehen wir uns das Spiel an.

simple past – 1. Vergangenheit

Bildung
Regelmäßige Verben: Grundform des Verbs + *-ed*

walk → walk**ed**

Beachte:
- Stummes *-e* entfällt.

  hop<s>e</s> → hop**ed**

- Bei Verben, die auf Konsonant + *-y* enden, wird *-y* zu *-i-*.

  car**ry** → car**ried**

- Nach kurzem betonten Vokal wird der Schlusskonsonant verdoppelt.

  st**o**p → st**opped**

Unregelmäßige Verben: siehe die Liste in deinem Schulbuch. Die *simple-past*-Formen einiger wichtiger unregelmäßiger Verben sind hier angegeben.

be → was
have → had
give → gave
go → went
meet → met
say → said
see → saw
take → took
write → wrote

Bildung von Fragen im *simple past*
Umschreibung mit
Fragewort + *did* + Grundform des Verbs

<u>Why</u> <u>did</u> he <u>look</u> out of the window?
Warum sah er aus dem Fenster?

Beachte:
Die Umschreibung wird nicht verwendet,
- wenn nach dem Subjekt gefragt wird (mit *who, what, which*).

Who paid the bill?
Wer zahlte die Rechnung?

What happened to your friend?
Was ist mit deinem Freund passiert?

Which boy cooked the meal?
Welcher Junge hat das Essen gekocht?

- wenn die Frage mit *were* gebildet wird.

Were you happy?
Warst du glücklich?

Bildung der Verneinung im *simple past*
Umschreibung mit *didn't* + Grundform des Verbs

Why didn't you call me?
Warum hast du mich nicht angerufen?

Verwendung
Das *simple past* beschreibt Handlungen und Ereignisse, die **in der Vergangenheit geschehen** und **bereits abgeschlossen** sind.

Signalwörter: *yesterday, last week, last year, five years ago, in 1999*

Last week he helped me with my homework.
Letzte Woche half er mir bei meinen Hausaufgaben. [Das Helfen fand in der letzten Woche statt, ist also bereits abgeschlossen.]

Verlaufsform der 1. Vergangenheit – *past progressive*

Bildung:
was/were + Verb in der *-ing*-Form

watch → was/were watching

Verwendung
Das *past progressive* verwendet man, wenn zu einem bestimmten Zeitpunkt in der Vergangenheit eine Handlung abläuft.

Yesterday at 11 o'clock I was still sleeping.
Gestern um 11 Uhr habe ich noch geschlafen.

I was reading a book when he came into the room.
Ich las (gerade) ein Buch, als er ins Zimmer kam.

2. Vergangenheit – *present perfect simple*

Bildung
have/has + Partizip Perfekt des Verbs

write → has/have written

Verwendung
Das *present perfect simple* verwendet man, wenn
- ein Vorgang in der Vergangenheit begonnen hat und noch andauert,

He has lived in London since 2002.
Er lebt seit 2002 in London.
[Er lebt jetzt immer noch in London.]

- das Ergebnis einer vergangenen Handlung **Auswirkungen auf die Gegenwart** hat.

I <u>have finished</u> my work.
Ich bin mit meiner Arbeit fertig.

Beachte:
have/has können zu *'ve/'s* verkürzt werden.

I<u>'ve</u> eaten your lunch.
Ich habe dein Mittagessen gegessen.

He<u>'s</u> given me his umbrella.
Er hat mir seinen Regenschirm gegeben.

Signalwörter: *already, ever, just, how long, not … yet, since, for*

Beachte:
Das *present perfect simple* wird oft mit *since* und *for* verwendet (Deutsch: „seit").

- *since* gibt einen **Zeitpunkt** an:

Ron has lived in Sydney <u>since 1997</u>.
Ron lebt <u>seit 1997</u> in Sydney.

- *for* gibt einen **Zeitraum** an:

Sally has lived in Los Angeles <u>for five years</u>.
Sally lebt <u>seit fünf Jahren</u> in Los Angeles.

Verlaufsform der 2. Vergangenheit – *present perfect progressive*

Bildung
have/has + *been* + Partizip Präsens

write → <u>has/have been writing</u>

Verwendung
Das *present perfect progressive* verwendet man, um die **Dauer einer Handlung** zu **betonen**, die in der Vergangenheit begonnen hat und noch andauert.

She <u>has</u> <u>been</u> <u>sleeping</u> for ten hours.
Sie schläft seit zehn Stunden.

Vorvergangenheit – *past perfect*

Bildung
had + Partizip Perfekt

write → <u>had written</u>

Verwendung
Das *past perfect* verwendet man, wenn ein Vorgang vor einem anderen Vorgang in der Vergangenheit abgeschlossen wurde.

He <u>had bought</u> a ticket
Er hatte ein Ticket gekauft,

before he took the train to Manchester.
bevor er den Zug nach Manchester nahm.
[Beim Einsteigen war der Kauf abgeschlossen.]

Verlaufsform der Vorvergangenheit – *past perfect progressive*

Bildung
had + *been* + Partizip Präsens

write → had been writing

Verwendung
Das *past perfect progressive* verwendet man für Handlungen, die bis zu einem Zeitpunkt in der Vergangenheit andauern, zu dem eine neue Handlung einsetzt.

She had been sleeping for ten hours when the doorbell rang.
Sie hatte zehn Stunden geschlafen, als es an der Tür klingelte.
[Das Schlafen dauerte bis zu dem Zeitpunkt an, zu dem es an der Tür klingelte.]

Zukunft mit *will* – *will-future*

Bildung
will + Grundform des Verbs

buy → will buy

Bildung von Fragen im *will-future*
Fragewort + *will* + Grundform des Verbs

What will you buy?
Was wirst du kaufen?

Bildung der Verneinung im *will-future*
Fragewort + *won't* + Grundform des Verbs

Why won't you come to our party?
Warum kommst du nicht zu unserer Party?

Verwendung
Das *will-future* verwendet man, wenn ein Vorgang **in der Zukunft stattfinden** wird.

The holidays will start next week.
Nächste Woche beginnen die Ferien.

Signalwörter: *tomorrow, next week, next Monday, next year, in three years, soon*

Beachte:
Bei geplanten Handlungen verwendet man das *going-to-future*.

Zukunft mit *going to* – *going-to-future*

Bildung
am/is/are + *going to* + Grundform des Verbs

find → am/is/are going to find

Verwendung
Das *going-to-future* verwendet man, um auszudrücken, dass eine **Handlung geplant** ist.

I am going to work in England this summer.
Diesen Sommer werde ich in England arbeiten.

▶ **Prüfungsaufgaben**

Hauptschulabschlussprüfung in Baden-Württemberg
Englisch 2012

2012-1

I. Listening Comprehension

Part 1
You will hear five short conversations. You will hear each conversation twice. There is one question for each conversation. For questions 1–5 mark A, B or C.

1. When will Bob Hudson go to the restaurant?

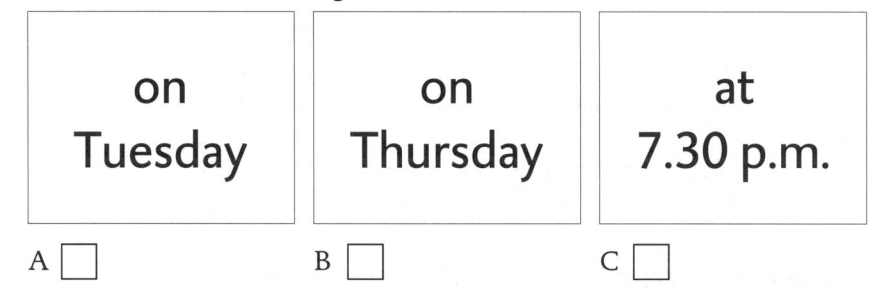

on Tuesday	on Thursday	at 7.30 p.m.
A ☐	B ☐	C ☐

2. How did Judy get to her appointment?

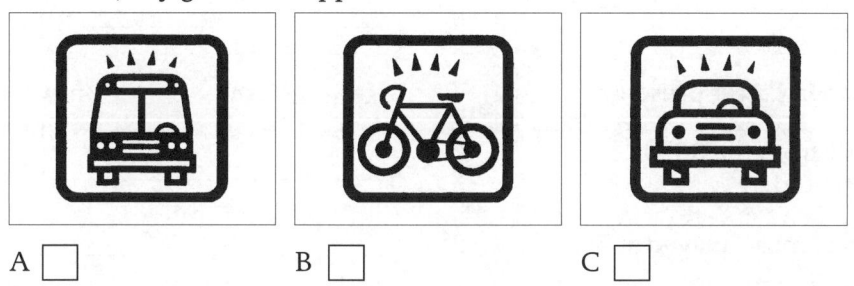

   A ☐   B ☐   C ☐

3. What type of vegetable isn't growing well this year?

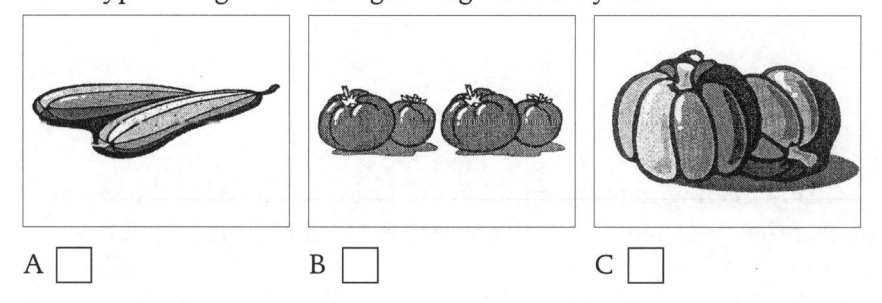

   A ☐   B ☐   C ☐

4. When will the girl be able to play volleyball again?

in 4 weeks	in 6 weeks	in 8 weeks
A ☐	B ☐	C ☐

5. Which train is the man going to take?

| 2 p.m. | 2.15 p.m. | 3.30 p.m. |

A ☐   B ☐   C ☐

Part 2

You will hear a radio presenter giving a preview of today's programmes. You will hear the preview twice. Listen and complete questions 6 to 10.

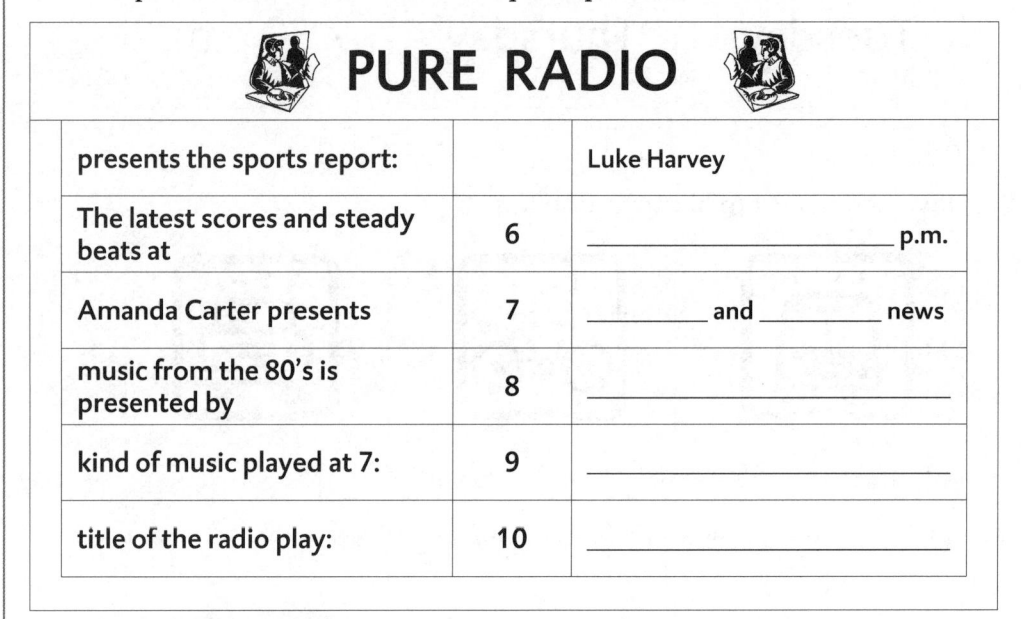

PURE RADIO

presents the sports report:		Luke Harvey
The latest scores and steady beats at	6	_____ p.m.
Amanda Carter presents	7	_____ and _____ news
music from the 80's is presented by	8	_____
kind of music played at 7:	9	_____
title of the radio play:	10	_____

Part 3

Listen to Chad Green who is having a job interview at a hotel at the moment. You will hear the interview twice. For questions 11 to 15 mark A, B or C.

11. Mrs Jones is the
    A ☐ hotel receptionist.
    B ☐ hotel owner.
    C ☐ hotel manager.

12. Chad Green wants to work in a hotel because
    A ☐ his grandma advised him to do so.
    B ☐ he didn't like working in an old people's home.
    C ☐ he liked his former work in a bed and breakfast place.

13. Chad's work experience in a restaurant was over
    A ☐ two weeks in summer.
    B ☐ three weeks in spring.
    C ☐ three weeks in summer.

14. What Chad liked best in the restaurant was
    A ☐ having a lot of colleagues there.
    B ☐ having some time for himself.
    C ☐ working in the kitchen.

15. If hotel guests are unfriendly,
    A ☐ it is necessary to tell them what you really think.
    B ☐ staying calm and respectful won't help.
    C ☐ good manners and patience will be expected from you.

Part 4

You will hear an interview with a professional female skateboarder. You will hear the interview twice. For questions 16 to 20 mark 'true' or 'false'.

	true	false
16. Ashley started skateboarding at the age of 14.	☐	☐
17. There are so many differences between women and men who skate.	☐	☐
18. There's a difference in the prize money for women and for men.	☐	☐
19. Ashley doesn't need any support.	☐	☐
20. The secret of success on the skateboard is to love it and have fun.	☐	☐

Part 5

You will hear a young couple talking about holiday plans. Where are the people going to spend their next summer holidays? You will hear this conversation twice.
For questions 21 to 25 write a letter, A–H, next to each person.

21. Jenny ☐
22. Ian ☐
23. Paul ☐
24. Mrs Stewart ☐
25. Mr and Mrs Brown ☐

A France
B USA
C Austria
D Germany
E China
F Australia
G The Canary Islands
H Norway

Listening – Answer Sheet

Part 1: Mark A, B or C.
Part 2: Fill in the correct answer.
Part 3: Mark A, B or C.
Part 4: Mark 'true' or 'false'.
Part 5: Fill in the correct letter.

Part 1

Number	A	B	C
1			
2			
3			
4			
5				/5

Part 2

Number	
6	/
7	
8	/
9	
10		/5

Part 3

Number	A	B	C
11			
12			
13			
14			
15				/5

Part 4

Number	true	false
16		
17		
18		
19		
20			/5

Part 5

Number	Letter
21	
22	
23	
24	
25		/5

_____/25

II. Reading Comprehension

Part 1 – Signs

Where can you see these notices? Mark A, B or C on the answer sheet.

Example

Return books here
- A ☐ in a post office
- B ☐ in a bank
- C ☒ in a library

1. **May contain traces of milk and nuts**
   - A ☐ on a bottle of lemonade
   - B ☐ on a cereal bar
   - C ☐ on a packet of ground coffee

2. **The use of mobiles is prohibited here.**
   - A ☐ in a park
   - B ☐ at the beach
   - C ☐ in the school yard

3. **Please rinse out your mugs after use! Thank you!**
   - A ☐ at the youth club
   - B ☐ in a restaurant
   - C ☐ at the library

4. **Buckle up! It's a law in this state.**
   - A ☐ at university
   - B ☐ in a bakery
   - C ☐ on an American motorway

5. **Warning! Some parts may have sharp edges. Assemble on a flat surface.**
   - A ☐ on instructions for use
   - B ☐ on a DVD player
   - C ☐ on a list of ingredients

6. **Protect from direct sunlight. Keep away from open flames or other hot items.**
   - A ☐ on a baking tray
   - B ☐ on a can of hair spray
   - C ☐ on a bottle of suntan lotion

Part 2 – Signs

What information do these signs give you?
Mark A, B, C or D on the answer sheet.

7.
Photocopies have been reduced in price!

(Black and white only – colour copies: no change)

- A ☐ There is no longer any colour photocopying here.
- B ☐ There are changes to the prices of all photocopies.
- C ☐ Some photocopies are now cheaper than they were.
- D ☐ Black and white copies are more expensive now.

8.
For sale

Educational software
(ages 6 and above)
Unwanted gift – box unopened
Fon: 183735

- A ☐ The software is for sale because the owner is too young.
- B ☐ The owner of the software has never used it.
- C ☐ The software is not suitable for children.
- D ☐ The person selling the software no longer wants to use it.

9.
LANGUAGE CLASSES

Tuesday: French 6 pm – 8 pm
Thursday: Italian 7 pm – 8 pm
Saturdays: Greek 4 pm – 5 pm
City College

- A ☐ There are no classes at the weekend.
- B ☐ The College is in a rural area.
- C ☐ The classes last one hour.
- D ☐ You can choose from three languages.

10.
Rollerblading / Skateboards

Please be careful and be aware of the public in this area.

Any damage to property or disturbance of the peace by night will be prosecuted.

Maximum fine up to £ 500.

- A ☐ Don't annoy the residents and don't smash up anything.
- B ☐ Rollerblading in this area won't disturb the peace by night.
- C ☐ You must pay at least £ 500 if you don't stick to the rules.
- D ☐ Inline skating will not be tolerated in this area.

Part 3 – Text

Are the statements 'true' or 'false' or 'not in the text'? Mark the correct answer on your answer sheet.

Crocodiles on Golf Courses

1. Crocodiles must like golf courses. One of them, Steve, has made himself at home on a course in Australia.

'Steve the croc' is 1.5 meters long and he lives in a lake on *The Willows Golf Resort* in Queensland, Australia. Golfers
5. call him the 'water hazard', but they're still not afraid of him. On most days Steve can be seen sunning himself, but whenever someone walks by, he hops back in the water. Freshwater crocodiles are shy and not as aggressive as their saltwater brothers. They usually feed on small animals like rats, chickens, rabbits and even
10. snails, so they are not really dangerous for humans. Of course the golfers try to stay away from the lake, but they know they are not going to get attacked if they leave Steve alone.

Crocodiles regularly visit Australia's golf courses, but unlike Steve they don't usually stay. Steve has become a tourist attraction.

© Adapted from: John Bilstein. In: Read on 06/2010, Carl Ed. Schünemann KG

Statements – 'true' or 'false' or 'not in the text'

	true	false	not in the text
11. A crocodile lives on a golf course in Australia.	☐	☐	☐
12. Golfers aren't frightened of Steve.	☐	☐	☐
13. Steve the croc avoids the players.	☐	☐	☐
14. Steve attacks golfers whenever they walk by.	☐	☐	☐
15. Freshwater crocodiles are less dangerous than saltwater crocodiles.	☐	☐	☐
16. Crocodiles enjoy playing with golf balls.	☐	☐	☐
17. In Australia all crocodiles live on golf courses.	☐	☐	☐
18. A lot of golf clubs try to attract tourists by keeping a crocodile.	☐	☐	☐

Part 4 – Text

Read the text and fill in the gaps. Mark A, B, C or D on the answer sheet.

Germany's Food Hotel

1 The food hotel in Neuwied, Germany, is a very special one – you can find rooms with furniture that looks _____ (19) cans in the lounges,
5 chairs made of beer crates and tables shaped like biscuits. 36 of Germany's most _____ (20) food companies such as crisp manufacturers, confectioners and brewers were asked to design and create unique bedrooms. "We have found sponsors _____ (21) industry for all our rooms,"
10 hotel manager Peter Grünhäuser told *reuters*. He said that companies could present their own product ideas in the bedrooms.
But not only your private room is _____ (22) in a special way. The restaurant, the public lounge and the bar, for instance, follow the same idea. So you can eat in a room furnished like a tea plantation; or a room is designed
15 like the TV advertisement for coconut candies with palm trees and photos of sandy beaches.
In keeping with the food and drink theme, the hotel runs _____ (23) own supermarket and the reception area invites guests to relax on chairs that look like shopping trolleys.
20 But there's one more thing to mention: the nights are not for _____ (24) – a double room costs 129 Euros per night!

© Adapted from: www.uk-reuters.com, 19.11.2010; writing by Michelle Martin, editing by Paul Casciato

	A	B	C	D
19	as	like	alike	how
20	popular	biggest	unknown	healthy
21	off	about	by	from
22	decorate	decorated	decorates	decorating
23	it's	his	its	their
24	something	nothing	somewhere	nowhere

Part 5 – Article

Complete the sentences by choosing the correct ending to each sentence.
Mark A, B or C on the answer sheet.

The Light of Liberty

1   On July 4th, 1884, France presented the United States with an incredible birthday gift: the Statue of Liberty! Without its pedestal it is as tall as a 15-story building. It represents the United States, but the world-famous
5   Statue of Liberty standing in New York Harbor was built in France. The statue was presented to some U.S. officials in France, taken apart, shipped across the Atlantic Ocean in crates and rebuilt in the U.S. It was France's gift to the American people.
10 It all started at dinner one night in a restaurant near Paris in 1865. A group of Frenchmen were discussing their dictator-like emperor and the democratic government of the U.S. They decided to build a monument to American freedom – and perhaps even strengthen French demands for democracy in their own country. They
15 agreed on a statue of a woman holding a torch – burning with the light of freedom. She was to stand on a broken chain to symbolize the end of slavery. On her head, they decided, should be a crown with seven rays, one for each continent and ocean.
    It took 21 years to turn their idea into reality. French supporters raised mon-
20 ey to build the statue, and the Americans only had to pay for the pedestal it would stand on. Finally, in 1886, the statue was dedicated to the American nation in a ceremonial act.

Adapted from: http://kids.nationalgeographic.com/kids/stories/history/statue-of-liberty/

25. The United States of America
    - A ☐ were given a statue by France.
    - B ☐ gave France a present.
    - C ☐ are incredibly big.

26. The Statue of Liberty
    - A ☐ was shipped in one piece.
    - B ☐ was shipped in pieces.
    - C ☐ wasn't shipped in peace.

27. In 1865
    - A ☐ some French people met for a meal.
    - B ☐ France was a democratic country.
    - C ☐ the gentlemen had a disgusting dinner.

28. They decided that the crown should symbolize
    A ☐ the end of slavery.
    B ☐ different parts of the earth.
    C ☐ seven rays.

29. The money was paid by
    A ☐ France.
    B ☐ America.
    C ☐ both countries.

Hauptschulabschlussprüfung Baden-Württemberg Englisch 2012

Reading – Answer Sheet

Part 1: Mark A, B or C.
Part 2: Mark A, B, C or D.
Part 3: Mark the correct answer.
Part 4: Mark A, B, C or D.
Part 5: Mark A, B or C.

Part 1

Number	A	B	C
1			
2			
3			
4			
5			
6			/6

Number	A	B	C	D
7				
8				
9				
10				/4

Part 3   correct answer: 0.5 pts

Number	true	false	not in the text
11			
12			
13			
14			
15			
16			
17			
18			/4

Part 4

Number	A	B	C	D
19				
20				
21				
22				
23				
24				/6

Part 5

Number	A	B	C
25			
26			
27			
28			
29			/5

_____/25

III. Writing

Part 1 – Letter

Sue is writing to a mail order firm.
Fill in the missing words.

> 4 Claremont Terrace
> Bath BA1 6EH
> phone: 0225-5557692
> 2nd April 2012
>
> Dear Sir, dear Madam,
>
> Thank you for _____ the T-shirt and the belt so promptly.
>
> The problem is I _____ a size 10 T-shirt and the one you sent me is size 14 which is unfortunately far too _____ for me.
>
> I am also not happy _____ the quality of the belt. In your catalogue it was described as a 'soft leather belt', but the leather is very _____ and not soft at all.
>
> Because of this I would like to _____ both items back to you. I'd be grateful if you could _____ my postage which comes to £ 5.30. Could you please deliver a size 10 T-shirt as soon _____ possible. I need it _____ the end of next week. Please _____ me if there is a problem with this date.
>
> Yours faithfully,
> Sue Ford

Part 2 – Text parts for presentation

7 pts

You have to prepare a presentation and introduce your favourite star (movie, music, sports, fashion etc.) to your class.
Fill in the mindmap with facts you know about him/her and information you want to give to the others.

Facts and highlights in his/her career:
_____
_____
_____

The way your star looks/dresses:
_____
_____
_____

My favourite star: _____

Additional information (at least 2):
- gender: _____
- age: _____
- nationality: _____
- marital status: _____

What do you like best about your star? Why?
_____
_____
_____

© Pavel Losevsky/Dreamstime.com

Write an introduction (which star? / why?) for your presentation (at least 2 sentences).

Good morning everybody, today ...
_____
_____
_____
_____
_____
_____
_____
_____
_____
_____
_____
_____
_____

Part 3 – Letter of application

8 pts

Here are two adverts you found on the internet.
You want to apply for a job abroad. You found the following advertisements on the internet. Choose the one that suits you best.
Write a letter of application:
- introduce yourself;
- tell about your qualities;
- ask for a job interview.

Write at least 60 words.

Sales Assistant
BASIC ELECTRONICS is looking for a reliable, friendly and flexible person with good computer skills who is good at serving customers. Good spoken and written English required.

Application letter to:
Mr Sam Doe, BASIC ELECTRONICS, 77 Masons Road, London

Gardener
You like being outside and working with your hands? You are physically fit and don't mind getting dirty? Then you're the right person for this job. No further experience required!

Application letter to:
Mrs Zoe Bricks, CITY GARDENS, 101 Park Lane, Dublin

___

Now please count your words: _____

Hauptschulabschlussprüfung in Baden-Württemberg
Englisch 2013

2013-1

I. **Listening Comprehension**

Part 1
You will hear five short conversations. You will hear each conversation twice. There is one question for each conversation. For questions 1–5 mark A, B or C.

1. What music will they have at the birthday party?

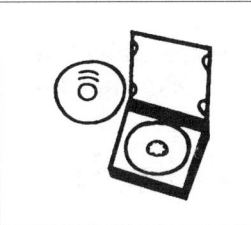

   A ☐   B ☐   C ☐

2. What is the daughter complaining about?

salty pizza	wrong topping	burnt pizza

   A ☐   B ☐   C ☐

3. Where does Georgia find her biology notes?

   A ☐   B ☐   C ☐

4. What does Finley say about his new job?

badly paid	not interesting	easy

   A ☐   B ☐   C ☐

5. How much does the customer pay for one ticket?

£56	£28	£76
A ☐	B ☐	C ☐

Part 2

You will hear a short biography of the singer Amy Winehouse. You will hear the biography twice. Listen and complete questions 6 to 10.

Amy Winehouse

Amy was born in:		London
complete date of birth:	6	_____
favourite kind of music in her childhood:	7	_____
name of 2006 album:	8	_____
earnings in Moscow:	9	$ _____
cause of death:	10	_____

© Fotograf: berlinfotos; http://en.wikipedia.org/wiki/File:AmyWinehouseBerlin2007.jpg; This file is licensed under the Creative Commons Attribution 2.0 Generic license.

Part 3

You will hear a conversation between a cab driver and her passenger in New York. You will hear the conversation twice.
For questions 11 to 15 mark A, B or C.

11. Getting to the museum will take them
    - A ☐ more than twenty minutes.
    - B ☐ probably not more than fifteen minutes.
    - C ☐ exactly twenty five minutes.

12. The cab ride will cost
    - A ☐ around $ 15.
    - B ☐ around $ 18 plus extra money for the driver.
    - C ☐ $ 18 at the most.

13. Today the museum closes
    A ☐ at 8 p.m.
    B ☐ at 6 p.m.
    C ☐ at 5.30 p.m.

14. The Chinese restaurant
    A ☐ offers small but cheap portions.
    B ☐ is luxuriously decorated and offers delicious duck.
    C ☐ offers large but not too expensive portions.

15. The passenger will get to the restaurant
    A ☐ by bus.
    B ☐ by subway.
    C ☐ by cab.

Part 4

You will hear an interview with a songwriter and guitarist from Tahiti. You will hear the interview twice. For questions 16 to 20 mark 'true' or 'false'.

	true	false
16. Right now Bob is on tour in Australia.	☐	☐
17. After an accident Bob started playing the guitar.	☐	☐
18. Bob stopped surfing in 1998.	☐	☐
19. Bob plays happy songs as well.	☐	☐
20. You can see Bob's bare toes during a concert.	☐	☐

Part 5

You will hear Harry and Donna talking about New Year's Resolutions. What are the people going to do next year? You will hear this conversation twice.
For questions 21 to 25 write a letter, A–H, next to each person.

21. Tony ☐
22. Harry ☐
23. Nelly ☐
24. Mr Stuart ☐
25. Donna ☐

A go to Spain
B learn Spanish
C eat healthier food
D learn to play an instrument
E stop smoking
F do more sports
G join a fitness club
H go scuba diving

Listening – Answer Sheet

Part 1: Mark A, B or C.
Part 2: Fill in the correct answer.
Part 3: Mark A, B or C.
Part 4: Mark 'true' or 'false'.
Part 5: Fill in the correct letter.

Part 1

Number	A	B	C
1			
2			
3			
4			
5			/5

Part 2

Number	
6	
7	
8	
9	
10	/5

Part 3

Number	A	B	C
11			
12			
13			
14			
15			/5

Part 4

Number	true	false
16		
17		
18		
19		
20		/5

Part 5

Number	Letter
21	
22	
23	
24	
25	/5

_____/25

II. Reading Comprehension

Part 1 – Signs

Where can you see these notices? Mark A, B or C on the answer sheet.

Example

Return books here

- A ☐ in a post office
- B ☐ in a bank
- C ☒ in a library

1. **Tickets sold out**
   - A ☐ at the train station
   - B ☐ at a bus stop
   - C ☐ at a concert hall

2. **Suitable for contact with food**
   - A ☐ on a pizza box
   - B ☐ on a price tag
   - C ☐ in a shoe shop

3. **Do not leave when door is closing**
   - A ☐ on a plane
   - B ☐ in a taxi
   - C ☐ on a train

4. **Diverted traffic ahead**
   - A ☐ at a tram stop
   - B ☐ in a shopping mall
   - C ☐ on a road

5. **No visitors beyond this point please!**
   - A ☐ in a supermarket
   - B ☐ in a book shop
   - C ☐ in a castle

6. **Hand wash only – sensitive fabric**
   - A ☐ in a factory's restroom
   - B ☐ on a pullover
   - C ☐ on a washing machine

Part 2 – Signs

What information do these signs give you?
Mark A, B, C or D on the answer sheet.

7.
Please clean up after your dog at all times

Thank you!

- A ☐ You mustn't walk your dog here.
- B ☐ Dogs are only allowed at special times.
- C ☐ Only clean dogs are allowed in here.
- D ☐ You should pick up your dog's droppings.

8.
Warning!

Video surveillance cameras in operation at **Warwick Castle**
Do not damage these old walls

- A ☐ You are allowed to use your camera and take photos here.
- B ☐ Any damage must be reported to the police.
- C ☐ You are being watched by cameras.
- D ☐ You can watch a video about the castle here.

9.
Old Chain Ferry

The last of its kind in Britain

Last crossing at 4 p.m.

50 p per person
buggies 20 p

- A ☐ No crossing later than 4 p.m.
- B ☐ Group prices are cheaper.
- C ☐ There are similar ferries in Britain.
- D ☐ No children allowed on the ferry.

10.
- ☞ Pay with coins
- ☞ Press ok
- ☞ Take ticket
- ☞ To cancel press black button
- ☞ Coins: 5p 10p 20p 50p £1
- ☞ No change given

- A ☐ You mustn't press the black button.
- B ☐ Pound notes are not accepted.
- C ☐ You have to press ok after taking the ticket.
- D ☐ You don't have to pay for the first 20 minutes.

Part 3 – Text

Are the statements 'true' or 'false' or 'not in the text'? Mark the correct answer on your answer sheet.

Skunk Ruins Christmas Presents

1. A skunk nearly ruined Christmas for 800 poor children in Purcell, a small town in Oklahoma (USA), last year. The animal got into a shed where toys worth thousands of dollars were kept and sprayed them with its terrible scent.
5. The toys had been collected by an organization called Operation Christmas to give to children from low-income families.

Volunteers tried to save as many of the presents as possible. They sprayed the smelly toys with a special fabric refresher many, many times and put
10. them out to air to get rid of the smell. But the skunk's scent was too strong, and only a few of the presents were rescued.

However, after they had heard about the skunk attack, people soon phoned Operation Christmas to ask what they could do to get new presents for the children.

15. Skunks don't normally spray their scent on Christmas presents; they use it to defend themselves against other animals and enemies. The spray is an oily liquid produced to frighten attackers away. The smell lasts for days and is very, very difficult to remove.

© Adapted from: "Skunk Ruins Christmas Presents" by Moya Irvine, in: Read On, January 2012, Nr. 658, 59. Jahrgang

Statements – 'true' or 'false' or 'not in the text'

	true	false	not in the text
11. The skunk made the presents smell horrible.	☐	☐	☐
12. Rich families donated a lot of presents.	☐	☐	☐
13. One of the presents was a toy skunk.	☐	☐	☐
14. Normally skunks use their scent against enemies.	☐	☐	☐
15. It's not a big problem to get rid of the smell.	☐	☐	☐

Part 4 – Text

Read the text and fill in the gaps. Mark A, B, C or D on the answer sheet.

Free Food for the "Dumpster Divers"

1. Some Americans who worry about the huge amount of food that is thrown away go "dumpster diving". They search _____ (16) bins outside supermarkets and restaurants to find food that's still good to eat. And
5. there's plenty of it. In the US, an estimated 27 per cent of food is thrown away.

This is hard to understand in a country where some poor people have difficulty in _____ (17) enough to eat. Some of these people go to soup kitchens for free meals and groceries. Stores often donate food that is not
10. perfect but still good to soup kitchens.

The dumpster divers are not always poor, _____ (18) many homeless people look for free food in this way, too. Some dumpster divers are Freegans, a group of people who campaign against waste of all kinds. Freegans believe that instead of throwing clothes and other things away and buying
15. new ones, we should repair them. And instead _____ (19) buying food, they use stuff that is good enough to eat but has been loaded into dumpsters.

Besides reducing waste, dumpster divers _____ (20) a lot of money. Some only eat waste food as part of their diet, while others never need to go
20. shopping at all.

© Adapted from: "Free Food for the 'Dumpster Divers'", by Moya Irvine, in: Read on, January 2012, Nr. 658, 59. Jahrgang

	A	B	C	D
16	through	threw	throughout	thought
17	buy	bought	buying	buys
18	although	moreover	because	while
19	from	off	of	for
20	safety	safely	safe	save

Part 5 – Article

Complete the sentences by choosing the correct ending to each sentence.
Mark A, B or C on the answer sheet.

A Rabbit in the Henhouse

1. On the surface, Otto seems like any other rabbit. He hops. He's fluffy. He lives on a farm. But he also eats the chickens' food, sits on chicken eggs and likes to hang out
5. with hens. He is a rabbit with the soul of a chicken! Otto lives with his owner, a farmer named Villee Kuusinen and his family on an island in the south of Finland. When Kuusinen bought 10 chickens, Otto came along as a bonus.

10. Kuusinen first thought something was odd when he noticed the rabbit sitting on chicken eggs in the henhouse. Then things got even stranger when Otto tried to join the hens on their perch[1]. Kuusinen explained: "I watched through the window how he jumped on the beam with the hens, failed, tried again and with a lot of practice eventually stayed up there."

15. Why does the rabbit seem to think he's a chicken? The chickens he lives with are called Silkie hens. This is a breed of chickens well-known for its fluffy feathers and strong parenting instincts. Otto has lived with these hens his whole life. He may simply feel he is one of them because he has never known anything else. Regardless, Otto has worked his way into the chickens' pecking
20. order[2]. "For the chickens, he is one of them," observes Kuusinen. "He often sits on the perch between the hens and under their wings."

© Alan & Sandy Carey/Science Source/Okapia

From JUNIOR SCHOLASTIC, December 9, 2011. Copyright © 2011 by Scholastic Inc. Reprinted by permissions of Scholastic Inc.

1 perch: Sitzstange
2 pecking order: Hackordnung, Rangordnung

21. Otto is a rabbit
    - A ☐ and lives with the chickens.
    - B ☐ and likes to eat chicken.
    - C ☐ and sits on chickens.

22. The farmer
    - A ☐ sold the rabbit.
    - B ☐ bought the rabbit.
    - C ☐ was given the rabbit for free.

23. He soon found out that
    - A ☐ the chickens were afraid of the rabbit.
    - B ☐ the rabbit was afraid of the chickens.
    - C ☐ Otto feels like a chicken himself.

24. Silkie hens
    A ☐ usually live with rabbits.
    B ☐ have special feathers.
    C ☐ sit on special perches.

25. This rabbit
    A ☐ likes sitting among the hens.
    B ☐ is head of the chickens' pecking order.
    C ☐ has strong parenting instincts.

Reading – Answer Sheet

Part 1: Mark A, B or C.
Part 2: Mark A, B, C or D.
Part 3: Mark the correct answer.
Part 4: Mark A, B, C or D.
Part 5: Mark A, B or C.

Part 1

Number	A	B	C
1			
2			
3			
4			
5			
6			/6

Part 2

Number	A	B	C	D
7				
8				
9				
10				/4

Part 3

Number	true	false	not in the text
11			
12			
13			
14			
15			/5

Part 4

Number	A	B	C	D
16				
17				
18				
19				
20				/5

Part 5

Number	A	B	C
21			
22			
23			
24			
25			/5

_____ /25

III. Writing

Part 1 – Letter

Linda has applied for a language school course in Ireland. A few weeks later she receives this letter from the language school.
Fill in the missing words.

Dublin, 15th April 2013
Course 28342013: "Learning by Speaking"
Phone: 00353-1-75846869

Dear Linda,

I am writing to _____ you that we have reserved you a place as a student in the above programme. This course runs _____ Monday, August 5th _____ Saturday, August 17th and has been confirmed as definitely running.

The _____ of this course is € 750 including schooling, host family accommodation and all organised free time _____ for the group in and around Dublin.

To confirm, please _____ this office. If you don't want to take part anymore, _____ your participation.

If you need any more _____, please do not hesitate to contact _____.

We look forward to _____ you in Dublin.

Yours sincerely,
Francis Green (francis.green@lsi.ie)

Part 2 – Dialogue

Dave hast lost his wallet and now he is talking to Mr Wood who works at the Lost Property Office in Hull. What does Mr Wood ask?
Complete the dialogue.
Fill in the missing questions.

7 pts

1. Mr Wood: _____

   Dave: "Hello. I have a problem: I've lost my wallet."

2. Mr Wood: _____

   Dave: "I lost it about an hour ago."

3. Mr Wood: _____

   Dave: "I think I was at the market."

4. Mr Wood: _____

   Dave: "The wallet is made of black leather and it looks brand new."

5. Mr Wood: _____

   Dave: "Two ten pound notes, some coins, my credit card, and there's also a photo of me with my dog in the inside flap."

6. Mr Wood: _____

   Dave: "Oh yes, that's my wallet. It's my lucky day."

7. Mr Wood: _____

   Dave: "Yes, of course. Where must I sign the form?"

Part 3 – E-mail

8 pts

You picked up this flyer in a sports shop.

> Win an American footballer's weekly wage with
>
> **Tiger's Sports & Clothes**
>
> What would you do with these $ 30,000?
> Simply write to us and let us know.
> The prize will be awarded to the best ideas.
> Send your text to:
> Janet@ti-sportsandclothes.com

- Write an e-mail to Janet
- Introduce yourself
- Describe at least two things you would do with the money and give reasons

Write at least 60 words.

From:	To:
Subject:	

Now please count your words: _____

Hauptschulabschlussprüfung in Baden-Württemberg
Englisch 2014

2014-1

I. **Listening Comprehension**

Part 1
You will hear five short conversations. You will hear each conversation twice. There is one question for each conversation. For questions 1–5 mark A, B or C.

1. What is the customer criticizing?

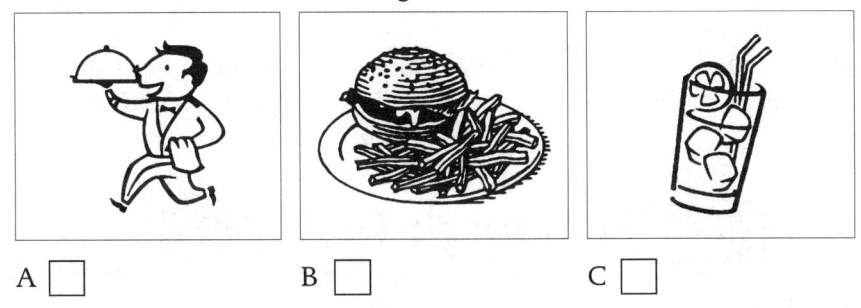

   A ☐   B ☐   C ☐

2. What couldn't be found after Tony's party?

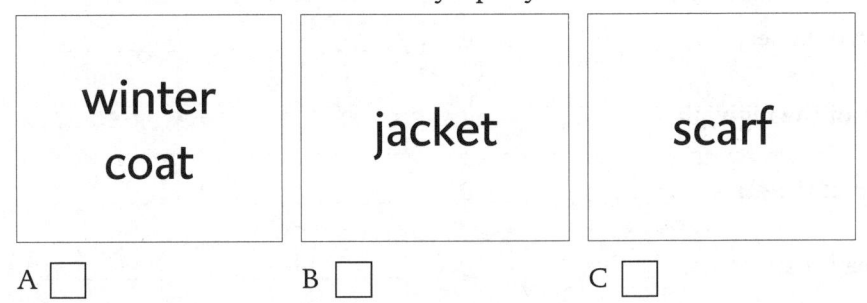

   | winter coat | jacket | scarf |

   A ☐   B ☐   C ☐

3. What time are they going to watch the film?

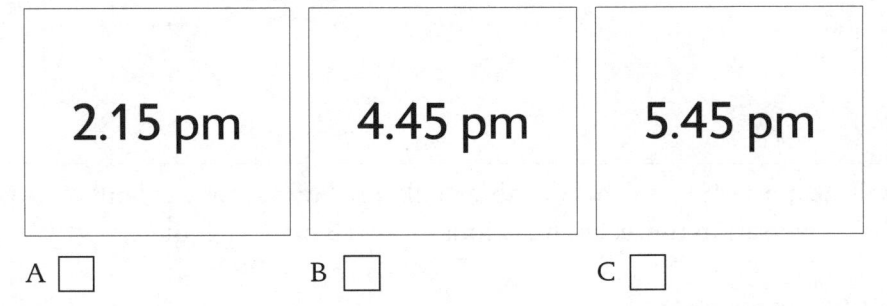

   | 2.15 pm | 4.45 pm | 5.45 pm |

   A ☐   B ☐   C ☐

4. What is the man having for dinner?

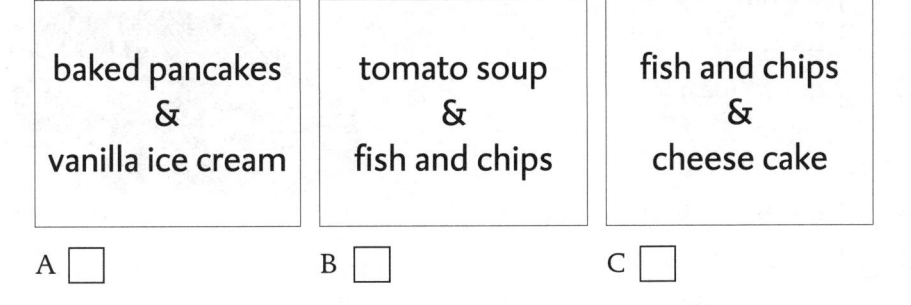

   | baked pancakes & vanilla ice cream | tomato soup & fish and chips | fish and chips & cheese cake |

   A ☐   B ☐   C ☐

5. Which homework needs to be done by tomorrow?

maths & geography	Spanish	English
A ☐	B ☐	C ☐

Part 2

You will hear some information and highlights about a guided bus tour in Edinburgh. You will hear the information twice. Listen and complete questions 6 to 10.

Edinburgh Tour

Edinburgh is:		The capital of Scotland
kind of buses:	6	_____
one of the highlights:	7	_____
kind of ticket:	8	_____
price for students:	9	_____
length of tour:	10	_____

Part 3

You will hear a father and his daughter talking about a car accident. You will hear the conversation twice. For questions 11 to 15 mark A, B or C.

11. Nothing happened to
    - A ☐ the car.
    - B ☐ the tree.
    - C ☐ the garage door.

12. There's too much dirt
    - A ☐ under the driver's seat.
    - B ☐ on the car windows.
    - C ☐ in the driveway.

13. The girl wants to
    A ☐ go on a weekend trip.
    B ☐ invite her friends for pizza.
    C ☐ drive to the cinema with the new Jeep.

14. At first the girl's father offers to
    A ☐ lend the girl his Jeep.
    B ☐ organise pizza for all.
    C ☐ pay for cinema tickets.

15. After the conversation with her dad the girl wants to
    A ☐ text her friends.
    B ☐ phone her friends.
    C ☐ visit her friends.

Part 4

You will hear an interview with Roseanne who has successfully completed her apprenticeship as a hairstylist. You will hear the interview twice. For questions 16 to 20 mark 'true' or 'false'.

	true	false
16. Roseanne has always dreamed of becoming a hairstylist.	☐	☐
17. Roseanne fell in love with a hairstylist.	☐	☐
18. Roseanne uses e-mail and Facebook as part of her job.	☐	☐
19. Yesterday Roseanne finished a course on sharpening hair scissors.	☐	☐
20. Roseanne has always made more money than other hairstylists.	☐	☐

Part 5

You will hear a teacher from a small school in Broadstairs talking to his students. He wants to know what the best and worst things about London are. What are the worst things in the students' opinion? You will hear this conversation twice.

For questions 21 to 25 write a letter, A–H, next to each person.

21. Bradley ☐
22. Aileen ☐
23. Gordon ☐
24. Judy ☐
25. Leona ☐

A bad working conditions
B the tube
C no speed limit
D high costs
E dirt
F British dishes
G hectic life
H unfriendly people on the tube

Listening – Answer Sheet

Part 1: Mark A, B or C.
Part 2: Fill in the correct answer.
Part 3: Mark A, B or C.
Part 4: Mark 'true' or 'false'.
Part 5: Fill in the correct letter.

Part 1

Number	A	B	C
1			
2			
3			
4			
5			

/5

Part 2

Number	
6	
7	
8	
9	
10	

/5

Part 3

Number	A	B	C
11			
12			
13			
14			
15			

/5

Part 4

Number	true	false
16		
17		
18		
19		
20		

/5

Part 5

Number	Letter
21	
22	
23	
24	
25	

/5

_____ /25

II. Reading Comprehension

Part 1 – Signs

Where can you see these notices? Mark A, B or C on the answer sheet.

Example

Return books here

- A ☐ in a post office
- B ☐ in a bank
- C ☒ in a library

1. **Do not use if seal is broken**
   - A ☐ on a jam jar
   - B ☐ on a DVD
   - C ☐ on a pullover

2. **Lifeguard on duty**
   - A ☐ at a hospital
   - B ☐ at a pool
   - C ☐ at a gym

3. **Do not chain bicycles to this gate. Access required at all times**
   - A ☐ on a train
   - B ☐ on a motorway
   - C ☐ at a construction site

4. **Water regularly**
   - A ☐ on a flowerpot
   - B ☐ on a package of tea
   - C ☐ on a piece of soap

5. **Make sure you have a valid ticket – Expect to be checked**
   - A ☐ at the DVD store
   - B ☐ at the cinema
   - C ☐ at the travel agency

6. **Please take some time during your visit for prayer and reflection**
   - A ☐ in a library
   - B ☐ in a museum
   - C ☐ in a church

Part 2 – Signs

What information do these signs give you?
Mark A, B, C or D on the answer sheet.

7. **Safety advice:**
   People must be at least 1.50 m to ride the bumper cars

   A ☐ You can ride the bumper cars when you're less than 1.50 m.
   B ☐ The bumper cars are only 1.50 m long.
   C ☐ You need to have a certain body height.
   D ☐ The bumper cars are safe for small people.

8. **Please stand clear of the doors**

   A ☐ Please use other doors.
   B ☐ Don't wait in front of the doors.
   C ☐ Stand in a queue in front of the doors.
   D ☐ The doors are made of clear glass.

9. **Please clean your hands with care before going to your workplace**

   A ☐ Wash your hands properly before you start working.
   B ☐ Your workplace must be handled with care.
   C ☐ You don't need to clean your hands.
   D ☐ Be careful with your hands at your workplace.

10. **No coins?**
    Park and pay by phone
    use your credit or debit card
    VISA MasterCard Maestro
    No need to display a voucher when using RingGo
    Number plate details will be checked by parking attendants

    A ☐ If you haven't got any coins, you can phone one of the attendants.
    B ☐ When using RingGo you have to display a voucher.
    C ☐ Parking attendants will check your credit card.
    D ☐ You can pay by phone if you have no coins.

© RingGo; Cobalt Telephone Technologies

Part 3 – Text

Are the statements 'true' or 'false' or 'not in the text'? Mark the correct answer on your answer sheet.

Teenager's Party out of Control after Facebook Posting

A teenager's sixteenth birthday party turned into a disaster after he posted it on Facebook and accidentally made it public for all users to see for about half an hour.

The teen, from Poole in Dorset, had planned 'the best party ever' for about 30 friends at his home. But after the event was seen on Facebook, about 400 young people turned up. According to the teenager at first a few people brought friends along, which didn't bother him. When a larger group came, he said no. The boy told a local newspaper: "After a while the street was full of people coming into the house and I kind of lost control of what happened."

The gatecrashers ruined the family home. They pulled the back door off, tore down curtains and damaged windows. The teen's father, who had left the house that evening, came back when a neighbour phoned him about what was going on. In the end, the police came with dogs and used megaphones to move the party 'guests' on. Everybody was gone within 25 minutes. The family said that the gatecrashers had done hundreds of pounds' worth of damage to their home.

© Adapted from: Moya Irvine, Read On June 2012, Nr. 6, 59. Jahrgang

Statements – 'true' or 'false' or 'not in the text'

11. Facebook users could see the teen's party posting for 30 minutes.
12. At first the boy wanted 40 people to come.
13. The teen told the newspaper that people just kept coming in through the side gate.
14. After being informed, the boy's father returned to the family home.
15. The police arrested some of the gatecrashers.

Part 4 – Text

Read the text and fill in the gaps. Mark A, B, C or D on the answer sheet.

It's Raining Frogs!

1. Nature can be unbelievably powerful. A major earthquake can destroy huge buildings and bring _____ (16) entire mountainsides. At Niagara Falls, more than 500,000 gallons (1,892,705 liters) of water crash
5. 18 stories down into the Niagara River every second – enough to fill nearly 50 Olympic-size swimming pools in a minute! And _____ (17) knows about hurricanes, blizzards, avalanches, forest fires, floods, tidal waves and even thunderstorms.

   But if you thought Mother Nature didn't have _____ (18) surprises,
10. think again. Nature has a load of other powers that, while less well-known, can only be described as freaky. _____ (19) you ever heard of animals falling from the sky? Read this:

   Small frogs rained on a town in Serbia, sending residents running for cover. "There were thousands of them," an inhabitant told a local newspaper. "I
15. thought maybe a plane carrying frogs had _____ (20) in the air," said another resident. Had the town gone crazy? Probably not. Scientists believe that tornadoes can suck up the surfaces of lakes, marshes and other bodies of water. When they do, they can take frogs and fish along for the ride. The tornadoes can then drop them miles away.

© Douglas E. Richards: Ten Freaky Forces of Nature. In: National Geographic Kids. © Douglas Richards/National Geographic Creative

	A	B	C	D
16	up	down	with	through
17	everyone	where	who	anyone
18	much	most	more	some
19	Will	Did	Can	Have
20	existed	experienced	exploded	excited

Part 5 – Article

Complete the sentences by choosing the correct ending to each sentence.
Mark A, B or C on the answer sheet.

The First FIFA World Cup in Brazil

1 The FIFA World Cup is the biggest soccer tournament in the world. Over a billion people tune in to watch teams from 32 countries
5 from all over the world. The competing teams battle it out at different venues in the host country. They all aim to receive the trophy as the new world champion at the
10 end of the final match.
   Although 19 tournaments have been held since 1930, only seven nations have won the prestigious World Cup. Brazil is at the top of the list with 5 wins, followed closely by Italy and Germany with 4 and 3 wins respectively. Argentina and Uruguay have 2 titles each and England, Spain and France one
15 each.
   After 1950, Brazil is hosting this tournament once again this year. 1950 was a special year in the history of the World Cup. India, for instance, who had qualified for the World Cup but withdrew when they found out that players had to wear football boots and would not be allowed to play barefoot. In the
20 end there were only 13 teams taking part.
   But there was also a tragic happening: The Italian team had had a plane crash just half a year before the World Cup 1950 started and half of the team died. Nevertheless they passed the qualification but unfortunately failed the finals. Finally Uruguay won the cup in the biggest stadium in Rio de Janeiro that
25 had been built for more than 180,000 people.

Adapted from: http://football.sporting99.com/trivia-on-the-fifa world-cup.html; Stand: 08. 04. 2013

21. Nowadays the tournament is played by
    - A ☐ 19 teams.
    - B ☐ 32 teams.
    - C ☐ 13 teams.

22. The 19 World Cups could only be won by teams from
    - A ☐ Europe and Africa.
    - B ☐ Africa and South America.
    - C ☐ South America and Europe.

23. The FIFA World Cup 2014
    A ☐ is the first to be played in Brazil.
    B ☐ is tournament number 18.
    C ☐ will take place in Brazil for the second time.

24. The Indian national team
    A ☐ cancelled their participation.
    B ☐ was banned from the tournament.
    C ☐ took part in the games.

25. Although the plane had crashed the Italian team
    A ☐ didn't take part in the tournament in Brazil.
    B ☐ could win the tournament in Brazil.
    C ☐ qualified for the tournament in Brazil.

Hauptschulabschlussprüfung Baden-Württemberg Englisch 2014   2014-11

Reading – Answer Sheet

Part 1: Mark A, B or C.
Part 2: Mark A, B, C or D.
Part 3: Mark the correct answer.
Part 4: Mark A, B, C or D.
Part 5: Mark A, B or C.

Part 1

Number	A	B	C
1			
2			
3			
4			
5			
6			/6

Part 2

Number	A	B	C	D
7				
8				
9				
10				/4

Part 3

Number	true	false	not in the text
11			
12			
13			
14			
15			/5

Part 4

Number	A	B	C	D
16				
17				
18				
19				
20				/5

Part 5

Number	A	B	C
21			
22			
23			
24			
25			/5

_____ /25

III. Writing

Part 1 – Letter

Devon Wildlife Trust advertise in a local newspaper about adopting an animal. Fill in the missing words.

Exeter, 12th June 2014
Devon Wildlife Trust

Dear animal lovers,

Devon Wildlife Trust enables you to adopt an animal in order to save our nature and wildlife. Would you _____ to adopt one of our species? You can choose _____ a bat, an otter and a beaver. The _____ for each animal is £ 20.

All you have to do is _____ in a form with your personal details like name, telephone _____ and address.

If you wish to pay _____ credit card you can find more _____ on our website. As soon _____ the money is transferred to us, you will get a letter with all the details about the animal you've chosen.

It is also _____ to have the adoption as a gift. In this case you can _____ a personal message to the person receiving your gift.

Thanks for **Trust**ing us!

Adapted from: http://www.devonwildlifetrust.org/adopt-a-species/

Part 2 – Dialogue

You are doing your work experience in a travel agency near Stuttgart. An English lady wants to make travel arrangements.
Complete the dialogue.
Fill in the missing questions.

7 pts

YOU: Guten Tag. Bitte setzen Sie sich. Wie kann ich Ihnen helfen?

MRS. F.: Good morning. My name is Lydia Fairbanks. I'd like to book a flight to Birmingham, please.

YOU: _____

(Frage, wann die Reise stattfinden soll.)

MRS. F.: I had planned to go at the beginning of September.

YOU: _____

(Sage, dass das schon sehr bald ist.)

MRS. F.: Yes, I know but we're having a family meeting there and first I didn't know whether I could go.

YOU: _____

(Frage, ob sie alleine reisen möchte.)

MRS. F.: Yes, of course. Are there any direct flights from Stuttgart?

YOU: _____

(Sage, dass es immer mittwochs und samstags Direktflüge von Stuttgart nach Birmingham gibt.)

MRS. F.: I'd rather travel during the week. Maybe it's not too busy then.

YOU: _____

(Gib ihr Recht und sage, dass der Flug am Mittwoch aber schon um 7 Uhr morgens ist.)

MRS. F.: Oh, I don't mind getting up early. How much is a return flight to Birmingham?

YOU: _____

_____

(Sage, dass es 475 € kostet und sie bar oder mit Kreditkarte bezahlen kann.)

MRS. F.: Unfortunately I haven't got my card with me now. I think I'll come back later today.

YOU: _____

_____

(Sage, dass das in Ordnung geht und du den Platz schon mal reservieren wirst.)

MRS. F.: That's very kind of you. Thank you very much.

Part 3 – E-mail

8 pts

You got this e-mail from a friend.

> **Sorry mate!**
> I couldn't make it to your party last Saturday.
> Did you have a good time? What did you do at the party? Who was there? What presents did you get?
> I really want to know. Please write back soon!
> Paul

Bild: © cofkocof. Shutterstock

- Write an e-mail to your friend Paul
- Answer his questions

Write at least 60 words.

From:	To:
Subject:	

_____
_____
_____
_____
_____
_____
_____

Now please count your words: _____

Hauptschulabschlussprüfung in Baden-Württemberg
Englisch 2015

2015-1

I. Listening Comprehension

Part 1

You will hear five short conversations. You will hear each conversation twice. There is one question for each conversation. For questions 1–5 mark A, B or C.

1. Which costume is Nola going to wear at the party?

   A ☐   B ☐   C ☐

2. Where did the girl leave the keys?

   A ☐   B ☐   C ☐

3. What was the weather like at the last barbecue?

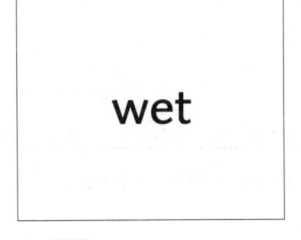

   | warm | frosty | wet |

   A ☐   B ☐   C ☐

4. How much is the concert ticket for Joe?

   | £15 | £18 | £20 |

   A ☐   B ☐   C ☐

5. What time did Bob probably leave the house?

| shortly before 8 o'clock | around 7 o'clock | at 10 o'clock |

A ☐   B ☐   C ☐

Part 2

You will hear a customer leaving a phone message on a voice mailbox.
You will hear the phone message twice. Listen and complete questions 6 to 10.

Champs' Sport Store

name of the customer:		Joseph Bailey
date of the order:	6	_____
instructions written in:	7	_____ / _____
missing equipment:	8	_____
price of the football table:	9	_____
order number:	10	_____

Part 3

You will hear a woman, Ruth Hiley, talking to a receptionist in a hotel.
You will hear the conversation twice. For questions 11 to 15 mark A, B or C.

11. Ruth Hiley booked
    A ☐ a single room for three nights.
    B ☐ a double room for four nights.
    C ☐ a single room for four nights.

12. The reserved room
    A ☐ will be free the next day.
    B ☐ will be free in a few hours.
    C ☐ won't be free for the next couple of days.

13. Ruth
    A ☐ is on a business conference in the hotel.
    B ☐ will get a double room instead.
    C ☐ wants to speak to the hotel manager.

14. The double room
    A ☐ is more expensive than the reserved single room.
    B ☐ is the same price as a single room for Ruth.
    C ☐ is free for Ruth.

15. While waiting for the room to be cleaned,
    A ☐ Ruth decides to go to the hotel lounge.
    B ☐ Ruth wants to visit some sights in town.
    C ☐ Ruth wants to drink a cup of tea in town.

Part 4

You will hear a radio interview with Nancy Clark who is arranging an activity course for the summer holidays. You will hear the interview twice.
For questions 16 to 20 mark 'true' or 'false'.

	true	false
16. Nancy was lucky with the weather last year.	☐	☐
17. They offer adventure sports like rock climbing and rafting.	☐	☐
18. Circus arts will be a class at the summer course too.	☐	☐
19. Children and teens take part in the same course.	☐	☐
20. You can find the application form online.	☐	☐

Part 5

Listen to Carol and Peter talking about part-time jobs. What are Peter's arguments <u>against</u> each job? You will hear this conversation twice.
For questions 21 to 25 write a letter, A–H, next to each person.

21. shop assistant ☐
22. swim coach ☐
23. gardener ☐
24. call center ☐
25. yoga instructor ☐

A low pay
B working outdoors
C talking to customers
D no fitness
E dirty hands
F poor swimmer
G far away
H working hours

Listening – Answer Sheet

Part 1: Mark A, B or C.
Part 2: Fill in the correct answer.
Part 3: Mark A, B or C.
Part 4: Mark 'true' or 'false'.
Part 5: Fill in the correct letter.

Part 1

Number	A	B	C
1			
2			
3			
4			
5			/5

Part 2

Number	
6	
7	/
8	
9	
10	/5

Part 3

Number	A	B	C
11			
12			
13			
14			
15			/5

Part 4

Number	true	false
16		
17		
18		
19		
20		/5

Part 5

Number	Letter
21	
22	
23	
24	
25	/5

___/25

II. Reading Comprehension

Part 1 – Signs

Where can you see these notices? Mark A, B or C on the answer sheet.

Example

Return books here
- A ☐ in a post office
- B ☐ in a bank
- C ☒ in a library

1. **Risk of ice**
   - A ☐ in a fridge
   - B ☐ on a road
   - C ☐ in a café

2. **Out of stock**
   - A ☐ in a forest
   - B ☐ in a library
   - C ☐ in a shoe shop

3. **Baggage reclaim**
   - A ☐ at school
   - B ☐ at the airport
   - C ☐ at the doctor's

4. **Read manual first**
   - A ☐ on a book cover
   - B ☐ on a pencil case
   - C ☐ on a PC cardboard box

5. **Pedestrians have priority**
   - A ☐ on a motorway
   - B ☐ in a football stadium
   - C ☐ on a public footpath

6. **Please take shower curtain inside bath before taking a shower. Thank you!**
   - A ☐ in a hotel room
   - B ☐ in a public toilet
   - C ☐ in a car wash

Part 2 – Signs

What information do these signs give you?
Mark A, B, C or D on the answer sheet.

7.

Reserved parking permit only

Violators will be fined $30

- A ☐ Reserving a parking space here costs $30.
- B ☐ Parkers could be violated here.
- C ☐ You have to pay a fine when parking without permission.
- D ☐ This car park is open to the public.

8.

Medical Centre Waiting Room

Please leave all the magazines in this room

- A ☐ Take the magazines with you before you leave.
- B ☐ Please don't take any magazines out of this room.
- C ☐ You have to leave the waiting room to read magazines.
- D ☐ You can bring your own magazines while waiting.

9.

Music Library

Increased charges for borrowing CDs from 1st September

- A ☐ Please return all borrowed CDs before 1st September.
- B ☐ No CDs available from 1st September.
- C ☐ There will be additional CDs to borrow from 1st September.
- D ☐ You will have to pay more to borrow CDs after 31st August.

10.

Joe's hair salon

Customers please note:

Salon will not open until 11 am on Monday because of staff training

- A ☐ The salon is going to open later than normal on Monday.
- B ☐ The salon closes from 11 am for staff training.
- C ☐ The manager will interview new staff on Monday morning.
- D ☐ Customers are invited to attend the staff training.

Part 3 – Text

Are the statements 'true' or 'false' or 'not in the text'? Mark the correct answer on your answer sheet.

A Town with no Sun

1. Giant mirrors were installed on top of the hills surrounding the town centre of Rjukan, a small town in Norway. These mirrors beam light into the
5. town during the dark winter months. That means at least some sunlight for the residents.
The sides of the valley are so steep and the mountain is so high that the town was in shadow for almost half the year
10. until the new invention was added.
"It's important to have the sun in wintertime, and in this town we didn't have the sun for six months in wintertime. The people up here want to have the sun. First, we used a cable car to take people quickly up the mountains towards the sun, but now we have made a 100 year-old idea real. We built
15. the mirror and it now reflects the sun down to us." This new invention has become so popular that other places are planning to follow the idea.
The mirrors are controlled by a computer that follows the path of the sun, adjusts them to the best angle to catch the rays and reflect them onto the town centre.

Adapted from: http://www.newsinlevels.com/products/town-with-no-sun-level-3/
Photo: picture alliance/dpa

Statements – 'true' or 'false' or 'not in the text'

	true	false	not in the text
11. Big lights were installed to illuminate the centre of Rjukan.	☐	☐	☐
12. In winter, rays of sunlight weren't able to reach the valley.	☐	☐	☐
13. The tickets for the cable cars were quite expensive.	☐	☐	☐
14. The new installation has not attracted much attention.	☐	☐	☐
15. The movable mirrors can follow the course of the sun.	☐	☐	☐

Part 4 – Text

Read the text and fill in the gaps. Mark A, B, C or D on the answer sheet.

Facebook Rally to Show Noah that Glasses are Cool

1 Lots of people _____ (16) glasses to make their vision better or even just for fashion. But when Noah, 4, found out he needed glasses, he wasn't happy about it. _____ (17), he was downright sad.

5 His mother asked him why he was so sad about wearing glasses. Noah told her he was worried that _____ (18) would laugh at him. Noah's mother started a Facebook page called "Glasses for Noah" to show Noah that wearing glasses is cool.

She asked people to post pictures of themselves and their kids wearing glasses.
10 That way, Noah could see how many people love wearing glasses and perhaps feel better _____ (19) his own glasses. And it worked.

More than 65,000 people from more than 30 countries "Liked" Noah's Facebook page, and many of them posted photos of themselves wearing glasses or left notes of encouragement for Noah. People even posted pictures of su-
15 perheroes in glasses like Superman and the Hulk. Noah's mum has shown him all the pictures and messages people posted on the Facebook page.

She said they've _____ (20) Noah very happy and he is feeling a lot better about his glasses.

Adapted from: Joyce Grant: Thousands Of People Rally On Facebook To Show Noah That Glasses Are Cool. In: Teaching Kids News, December 8, 2013
Photo: Dima Sobko. Shutterstock

	A	B	C	D
16	wear	where	we're	were
17	In spite	In time	In fact	In case
18	nobody	everyone	anyone	something
19	about	at	without	over
20	makes	make	making	made

Part 5 – Article

Complete the sentences by choosing the correct ending to each sentence.
Mark A, B or C on the answer sheet.

Think Before you Drink

1. The Irish are well known for loving alcohol. But when some pupils from Moyne Community School in County Longford saw how many other kids were drinking, they decided to do something about it.

5. The 14 teenagers spent about six months working on a project called *"Don't Drink 'Til You Drop, Think and Stop!"*. The pupils won two national awards, did TV and radio interviews about their work and spent a day talking about it at the home of the Irish president.

It is especially important for teenagers to know about the risks and conse-
10. quences of alcohol abuse. One aim of this project was to make people realize how dangerous alcohol can be. Therefore they carried out interviews and surveys in schools. In addition, the teenagers talked to doctors, pub owners and local politicians as well as alcoholics.

Last September the teens took part in a youth forum about alcohol and even
15. talked with the Irish government about their project.

In the summer, the teens were able to raise about 25,000 euros to open a youth club in Longford town in order to give teenagers a place to go – an alcohol-free zone as an alternative to pubs and clubs. In the meantime the club has been opened and now the kids have the opportunity to spend their
20. free time with various activities such as sports, playing music and acting in an environment suitable for their age.

Adapted from: Spot on, Spotlight Verlag, November 2006, S. 15.
Picture: Think Before You Drink/GGD West-Brabant

21. *"Don't Drink 'Til You Drop, Think and Stop!"* was started
    - A ☐ by alcohol addicted teenagers.
    - B ☐ by very enthusiastic teenagers.
    - C ☐ by teenagers who were homeless.

22. The aim of the group was
    - A ☐ to open a youth club in Longford town.
    - B ☐ to meet a lot of famous people.
    - C ☐ to show how dangerous alcohol is.

23. The group talked with
    - A ☐ a lot of different people.
    - B ☐ mainly other teenagers.
    - C ☐ some policemen.

24. Last September they took part
    A ☐ in a British talk show.
    B ☐ in a survey.
    C ☐ in discussions about alcohol among teenagers.

25. With the project they were able
    A ☐ to hire therapists.
    B ☐ to open a place for teenagers to go.
    C ☐ to earn money to make a good living.

Reading – Answer Sheet

Part 1: Mark A, B or C.
Part 2: Mark A, B, C or D.
Part 3: Mark the correct answer.
Part 4: Mark A, B, C or D.
Part 5: Mark A, B or C.

Part 1

Number	A	B	C
1			
2			
3			
4			
5			
6				/6

Part 2

Number	A	B	C	D
7				
8				
9				
10					/4

Part 3

Number	true	false	not in the text
11			
12			
13			
14			
15				/5

Part 4

Number	A	B	C	D
16				
17				
18				
19				
20					/5

Part 5

Number	A	B	C
21			
22			
23			
24			
25				/5

_____ /25

III. Writing

Part 1 – Letter

You write an application for the job as a secretary for computer software. Fill in the missing word.

Dear Mr. Hudgens,

I am writing to _____ for the job as a secretary in your computer software company published in the newspaper _____ 1st May 2015. As you will see from my CV, I am in my last _____ at secondary school in Aberdeen. My favourite _____ are Maths, ICT and English. I did my work experience at the Town Hall office in Aberdeen three months _____.

I'm good at working with computers and I'm also very interested _____ knowing more about different types of software. I like _____ in a team and I'm a motivated and organized _____.

I am available for an _____ at any time. I'm looking _____ to hearing from you and remain

yours sincerely,

Sandra Mason

Enclosed: CV

Part 2 – Dialogue

7 pts

On a visit to England you want to buy a sweatshirt as a present for a friend. You are now in a London shop for hip-hop fashion.
Complete the dialogue. Fill in the missing questions.

ASSISTANT: Good morning. Can I help you?

YOU: _____

(Erwidere den Gruß und sage, dass du gerne ein Sweatshirt kaufen möchtest.)

ASSISTANT: If you tell me what exactly you're looking for, perhaps I can help you.

YOU: _____

(Sage, dass das Sweatshirt ein Geschenk für eine/n Freund/in ist und dass er/sie ein echter HipHop Fan ist.)

ASSISTANT: Oh, I think you are in luck. This morning we got a new collection of hip-hop clothing in. What size is your friend?

YOU: _____

(Sage, dass du das nicht weißt. Dein/e Freund/in ist 16 Jahre alt und ziemlich groß.)

ASSISTANT: Well, let me see, then. A sweatshirt size L should be right, I think. Now, what about the colour?

YOU: _____

(Frage, ob sie Sweatshirts in verschiedenen Farben haben.)

ASSISTANT: Of course. What about these? We've got them in almost every colour.

YOU: _____

(Sage, dass dir das dunkelblaue Sweatshirt mit der Kapuze sehr gut gefällt.)

ASSISTANT: Brilliant. Well, that's £35. Is that all right?

You: _____

(Sage, dass es recht teuer ist, aber dass dein/e Freund/in sich sehr darüber freuen wird.)

Hauptschulabschlussprüfung in Baden-Württemberg
Englisch 2016

2016-1

I. Listening Comprehension

Part 1
You will hear five short conversations. You will hear each conversation twice. There is one question for each conversation. For questions 1–5 mark A, B or C.

1. What time are they going to meet?

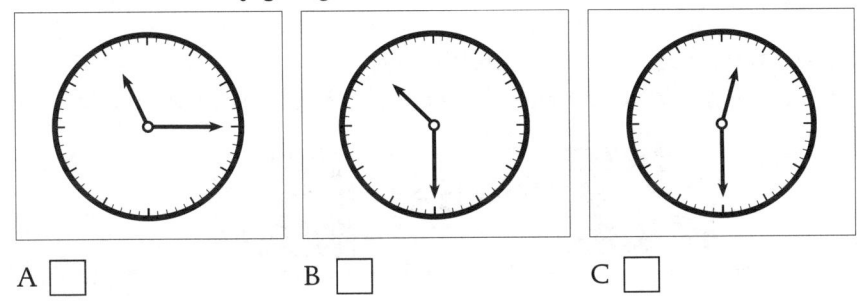

    A ☐   B ☐   C ☐

2. How much is the coat?

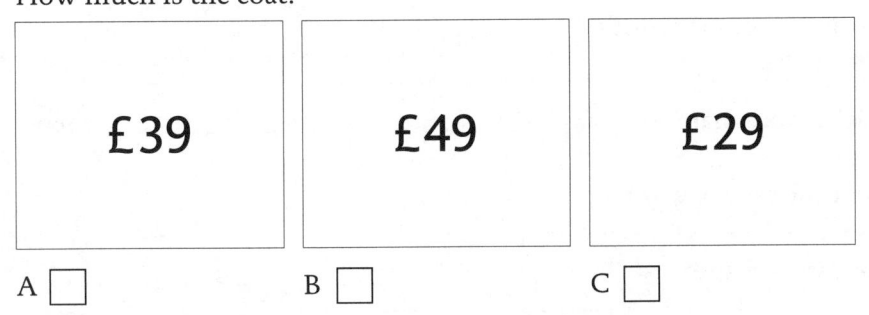

    | £39 | £49 | £29 |

    A ☐   B ☐   C ☐

3. Where is the next car boot sale going to take place?

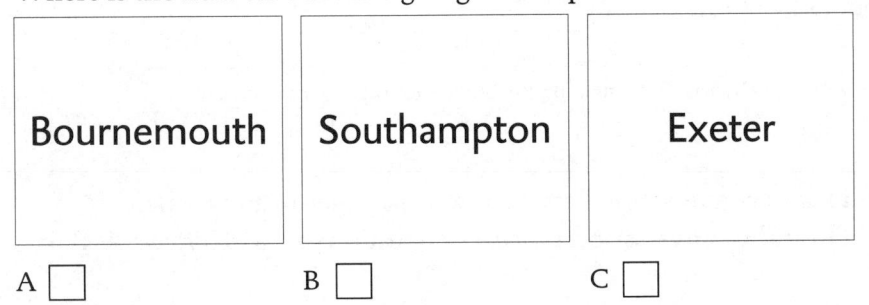

    | Bournemouth | Southampton | Exeter |

    A ☐   B ☐   C ☐

4. Who is going to the cinema?

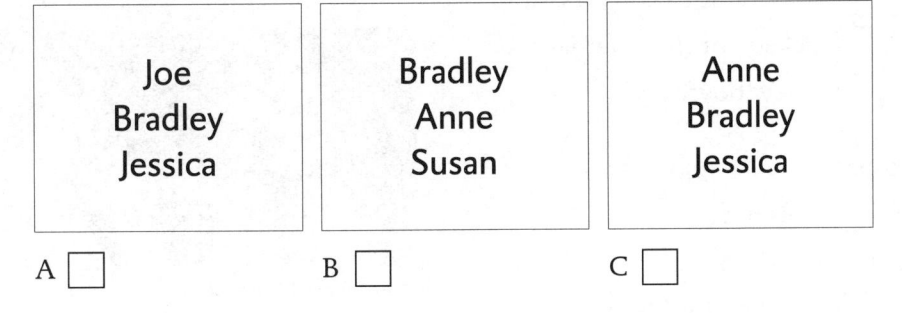

    | Joe | Bradley | Anne |
    | Bradley | Anne | Bradley |
    | Jessica | Susan | Jessica |

    A ☐   B ☐   C ☐

5. Which team is Pauline cheerleading for?

A ☐   B ☐   C ☐

Illustrationen: © Pearson Education, Inc.

Part 2

You will hear some information about Big Ben.
You will hear the information twice. Listen and complete questions 6 to 10.

Big Ben		
Big Ben is in:		London
struck the hour for the first time in (year):	6	_____
weighs more than:	7	_____ tons
about the same weight as:	8	_____
interesting shape:	9	_____ than _____
voted number one British landmark in (year):	10	_____

Big Ben Turm: © PeterSVETphoto. Shutterstock, Big Ben Glocke: author unknown, public domain

Part 3

You will hear a conversation between two girls, Megan and Fiona.
You will hear the conversation twice. For questions 11 to 15 mark A, B or C.

11. Megan has got
    A ☐ no time for a conversation.
    B ☐ tickets for the cinema.
    C ☐ a new boyfriend.

12. Fiona
    A ☐ feels bad.
    B ☐ is in love.
    C ☐ is happy for Megan.

© arek_malang. Shutterstock

13. When Megan had a date with Jake he
    A ☐ did not come.
    B ☐ took her to the cinema.
    C ☐ told a funny story.

14. After the film Andrew
    A ☐ bought concert tickets for the evening.
    B ☐ looked sad and lonely.
    C ☐ asked Megan out.

15. Megan thinks that Fiona is
    A ☐ not good-looking at all.
    B ☐ attractive.
    C ☐ intelligent.

Part 4

You will hear a radio interview with a health expert about the dangers of eating too much sugar. You will hear the interview twice.
For questions 16 to 20 mark 'true' or 'false'.

	true	false
16. More and more people in Britain have weight problems.	☐	☐
17. By 2050 there will be 50 % of men and 60 % of women overweight.	☐	☐
18. Obesity can cause serious health problems.	☐	☐
19. The expert says that low-fat products help to lose weight.	☐	☐
20. Replacing fat with sugar doesn't solve health problems.	☐	☐

Zuckerstreuer © Can Stock Photo Inc./LanaLanglois

Part 5

You will hear a radio interview about clothes and style. Which clothing style do people prefer? You will hear this interview twice.
For questions 21 to 25 write a letter, A–H, next to each person.

21. Liam ☐
22. Alexandra ☐
23. Mickey ☐
24. Aditi ☐
25. Presenter ☐

A multi-coloured T-shirts
B blue jeans
C sporty clothes
D punk style
E second-hand clothes
F skater style
G gothic style
H self-made trousers

Listening – Answer Sheet

Part 1: Mark A, B or C.
Part 2: Fill in the correct answer.
Part 3: Mark A, B or C.
Part 4: Mark 'true' or 'false'.
Part 5: Fill in the correct letter.

Part 1

Number	A	B	C
1			
2			
3			
4			
5				/5

Part 2

Number	
6	
7	tons
8	
9	than
10		/5

Part 3

Number	A	B	C
11			
12			
13			
14			
15				/5

Part 4

Number	true	false
16		
17		
18		
19		
20			/5

Part 5

Number	Letter
21	
22	
23	
24	
25		/5

_____/25

II. Reading Comprehension

Part 1 – Signs

Where can you see these notices? Mark A, B or C on the answer sheet.

Example

Return books here
- A ☐ in a post office
- B ☐ in a bank
- C ☒ in a library

1. **Wise drivers drive sober**
   - A ☐ at a motorway
   - B ☐ at university
   - C ☐ at a public toilet

2. **BULLY FREE ZONE**
   - A ☐ on a farm
   - B ☐ in a classroom
   - C ☐ at a butcher's

3. **Please tell us how we can improve our service**
   - A ☐ at the hairdresser's
   - B ☐ in a courtroom
   - C ☐ in a classroom

4. **Please** This is your lunch area Keep it clean
   - A ☐ in a bakery
   - B ☐ in a restaurant
   - C ☐ at a resting place

5. **Caution! Steep slope**
   - A ☐ in a skiing region
   - B ☐ at an indoor swimming pool
   - C ☐ in a church

6. **East stand:** use stairs 1–8
   North / upper stand: use stairs 9–14
   - A ☐ at a football stadium
   - B ☐ in a skyscraper
   - C ☐ on a ferry

Part 2 – Signs

What information do these signs give you?
Mark A, B, C or D on the answer sheet.

7.

Safety advice for our rollercoaster rides

no smoking
no food
no bare feet
no pregnancy

- A ☐ To be safe on this ride you have to wear shoes.
- B ☐ Women shouldn't go on this ride.
- C ☐ Children are not allowed on this rollercoaster.
- D ☐ People over 60 years can't go on this ride.

8.

Dog relief area

Use free poop bags from dispenser

- A ☐ Beware of dogs.
- B ☐ Dogs are not allowed here.
- C ☐ Your dog can be left here while you go shopping.
- D ☐ This place is a dog toilet. Please clean up after your dog.

9.

It's a Subway Car, Not a Dining Car
It may be take-out, but please, don't eat here.

- A ☐ You shouldn't eat take-out food too fast.
- B ☐ You're asked not to eat on the underground.
- C ☐ You may take out your food on the underground.
- D ☐ Don't eat in cars for safety reasons.

10.

STOP Extreme Heat Danger
Walking after 10 AM not recommended

- A ☐ You can't walk through Death Valley after 10 am.
- B ☐ You shouldn't walk through Death Valley at any time.
- C ☐ You shouldn't walk through Death Valley after 10 am.
- D ☐ Because of extreme heat, walking isn't allowed here.

Achterbahn © Marcio Jose Bastos Silva. Shutterstock;
Text und Bild „Subway Car": Courtesy Counts © MTA, Metropolitan Transportation Authority;
Stop-Schild © Forestangels

Part 3 – Text

Are the statements 'true' or 'false' or 'not in the text'? Mark the correct answer on your answer sheet.

Parliament Needs a Mouse Catcher

1. The Palace of Westminster is a beautiful building, but like many old buildings it has a few problems and one of them is mice.
5. After Christmas, one MP (Member of Parliament) came back to her office and found mouse droppings all over her papers. She told reporters: "I spoke to my staff and one of them saw three mice on my desk. It is so disgusting!"
About 40 mice per month are seen at the Houses of Parliament and, besides leaving their droppings, they also nibble on official documents. At the moment, about £ 6,000 per month are spent on pest control and some politicians are thinking of a better solution: getting a cat.
The *Battersea Dogs and Cats Home*, which rescues unwanted animals, has offered three of these expert mouse catchers to the politicians. One MP said: "They do a fantastic job and I would like to have one of their cats come and
15. take care of the mouse problem in my office too."
The home has been looking after cats for 130 years and looks after around 190 cats at a time. Larry, the cat at 10 Downing Street, also came from the Battersea Dogs and Cats Home and is the proud Chief Mouser to the Cabinet Office.

Adapted from: Read on, March 2014
Photo: © Can Stock Photo Inc./bloodua; Logo: Battersea Dogs & Cats Home

Statements – 'true' or 'false' or 'not in the text'

11. Mice have always lived in Westminster Palace.
12. The only mice traces in the buildings are their droppings.
13. They spent 6,000 pounds per month on cats.
14. One MP wants the Cats Home's employees to work in his office.
15. Larry is the chief of the Battersea Dogs and Cats Home.

Part 4 – Text

Read the text and fill in the gaps. Mark A, B, C or D on the answer sheet.

African Lions in Trouble

1 The world's most famous cat is in trouble. In 2014, the *U.S. Fish and Wildlife Service* (USFWS) asked if African lions could be listed as 'threatened' under the Endangered
5 Species Act. This would help to protect _____ (16) from dying out, because their number has gone down an lot.
"If things don't get better, lions _____ (17) soon die out," said Daniel Ashe, director of the USFWS. He said that the worst dangers for the big cats
10 were loss of territory, lack of prey and more conflicts with humans. Over the years more humans have moved into areas where lions live. Experts believe human population in Africa will double _____ (18) 2050, making the problem worse.
Ashe said they want to protect these animals as much as possible. "It _____
15 _____ (19) on all of us, not just the people of Africa, to help that wild populations of lions live there for the next generations," he said.
Wildlife expert Jane Goodall called the listing 'excellent news'. She said people _____ (20) not aware of the danger because they still see the animals in parks: "How terrible to lose the 'king of beasts' from the African
20 scene."

Adapted from: Dan Ashe: The African Lion Needs Our Help. In: U.S. Fish and Wildlife Service Home Page, fws.gov, Oct 27, 2014
Photo: © Corbis

	A	B	C	D
16	there	they	them	their
17	will	won't	would	are
18	from	to	into	by
19	depended	deepen	depend	depends
20	was	were	wear	where

Part 5 – Article

Complete the sentences by choosing the correct ending to each sentence.
Mark A, B or C on the answer sheet.

Blackout in New York

1 It was half past nine one hot evening in July 1977. Passengers on a plane flying into New York's Kennedy Airport
5 were enjoying the sight of Manhattan when suddenly the city disappeared. The sea of lights turned into darkness.
At the same time subways and elevators stopped, traffic lights went out,
10 water pumps failed and left the kitchens, bathrooms and toilets without water. Neither the Empire State Building nor the Chrysler Building could be seen anymore.
The blackout lasted for 25 terrible hours. During the time almost nothing worked in New York except telephones and radios. Buses and cars moved as
15 long as they had gas. Cabs charged five times the normal fare. Banks, offices and stores remained closed. Water became a luxury and air-conditioning a happy memory.
In the ghettos, plundering and burning started. Ten minutes after the lights went out, some citizens were already breaking into stores in order to steal
20 goods. All in all, store owners lost about a billion dollars during the blackout. But this was not the only incident. In August 2003 the lights went out once more. Not only in New York, but also in other big US and Canadian cities.

Adapted from: Lorenz Derungs, in: http://www.englischlehrer.in/contentLD/EN/T265Blackout.pdf
Photo: © Bettmann/Getty Images

21. Suddenly, the lights went out
    A ☐ on the plane.
    B ☐ in the city.
    C ☐ on the sea.

22. Vehicles stopped when
    A ☐ the lights went out.
    B ☐ water flooded the streets.
    C ☐ their fuel tanks were empty.

23. You had to pay
    A ☐ the same price for taxis.
    B ☐ a higher price for taxis.
    C ☐ a lower price for taxis.

24. Water was a luxury because
    A ☐ the price for water has risen.
    B ☐ the pumps were out of order.
    C ☐ there were no bottles in the shops.

25. Breaking into stores caused
    A ☐ bad injuries.
    B ☐ burning houses.
    C ☐ immense costs.

Reading – Answer Sheet

Part 1: Mark A, B or C.
Part 2: Mark A, B, C or D.
Part 3: Mark the correct answer.
Part 4: Mark A, B, C or D.
Part 5: Mark A, B or C.

Part 1

Number	A	B	C
1			
2			
3			
4			
5			
6			/6

Part 2

Number	A	B	C	D
7				
8				
9				
10				/4

Part 3

Number	true	false	not in the text
11			
12			
13			
14			
15			/5

Part 4

Number	A	B	C	D
16				
17				
18				
19				
20				/5

Part 5

Number	A	B	C
21			
22			
23			
24			
25			/5

_____ /25

III. Writing

Part 1 – Letter

Declan is writing an e-mail to his German friend Sascha. Fill in the missing word.

Hi Sascha,

Thanks for _____ me the photos of your birthday party. My friends and I had a good laugh looking through the pictures. Now we are really looking forward to your _____ to Dublin.

My father and I will pick you up from the airport _____ Wednesday. What time does your _____ arrive? I think you _____ like Dublin. We live about 6 km from the city centre but there _____ a regular bus service into town.

When you are here, we can go cycling around Phoenix Park and, of course, you'll meet all my friends and we can _____ football together. If you like horror stories, we _____ visit Dracula's Castle, woooh ... or go to the cinema.

Please don't _____ to bring a jumper and a jacket. The weather here is usually cold and rainy.

See _____ on Wednesday,

Declan

Part 2 – Dialogue

7 pts

You are doing a part-time job at your local cinema.
A group of young English-speaking people wants to see a film.
Complete the dialogue. Fill in the missing sentences.

YOU: Hallo zusammen.

YOUNG MAN: Hi. We would like to see "Cucumbers & Pumpkins". Are there still tickets available?

YOU: _____

_____

(Sage ja und frage, ob sie den Film im Originalton sehen wollen.)

YOUNG MAN: Yes, that would be great. When is the next show?

YOU: _____

_____

(Sage, dass der Film um 12.45 Uhr und um 16.15 Uhr läuft.)

YOUNG MAN: I think we'll take the later show then, so we have some time to go into town first.

YOU: _____

_____

(Sage, dass du die Karten reservieren kannst und frage, wie viele sie brauchen.)

YOUNG MAN: We need five tickets. We're all students. Is there a special price for students?

YOU: _____

_____

(Sage, dass Studenten heute nur den halben Preis bezahlen. Das sind € 4.)

YOUNG MAN: Excellent. I'll pay for my friends and me.

YOU: _____

_____

(Sage, dass es € 20 zusammen macht und der Film in Raum 3 läuft.)

YOUNG MAN: OK, we'll be back in time. Any idea what we could to in town until the film starts?

YOU: _____

_____

(Sage, dass es gleich um die Ecke ein nettes Café mit selbstgemachten Kuchen gibt.)

YOUNG MAN: Sounds good. Thanks for the tip and see you later.

Part 3 – E-mail

8 pts

You and your friend are organizing the farewell party for your class at the end of term. Write an e-mail to one of your classmates and tell her/him about the event and your plans.

Include the following points:
- date and place of the party
- what she/he should bring
- confirmation of attendance

Write at least 60 words.

From:	To:
Subject:	

_____
_____
_____
_____
_____
_____
_____
_____
_____
_____
_____
_____

Now please count your words: _____

Hauptschulabschlussprüfung in Baden-Württemberg
Englisch 2017

2017-1

I. Listening Comprehension

Part 1
You will hear five short conversations. You will hear each conversation twice. There is one question for each conversation. For questions 1–5 mark A, B or C.

1. In which colour would Taira like to paint her room?

| white | red | pink |
| A ☐ | B ☐ | C ☐ |

2. Why can't Raheem go to school today?

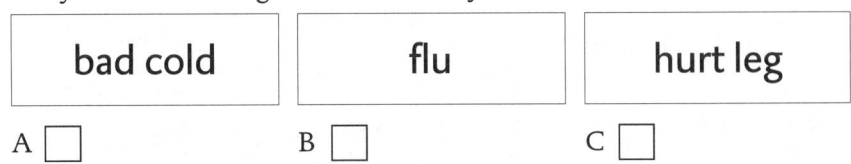

| bad cold | flu | hurt leg |
| A ☐ | B ☐ | C ☐ |

3. Which shuttle bus are they going to take?

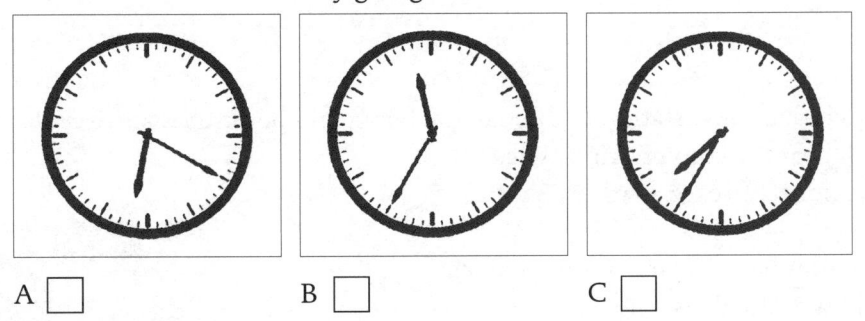

A ☐   B ☐   C ☐

4. What presents did Lucy get?

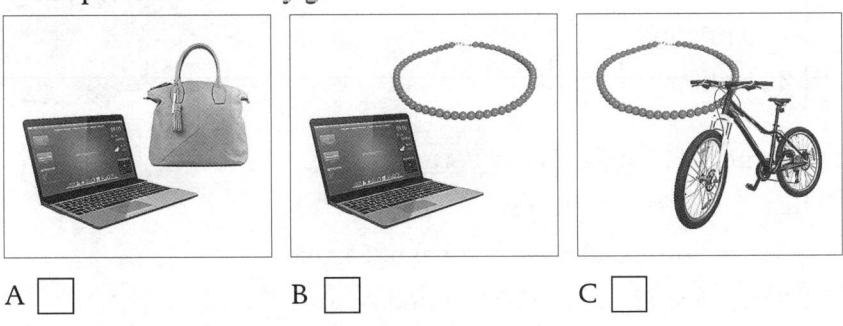

A ☐   B ☐   C ☐

5. Where is the party going to take place?

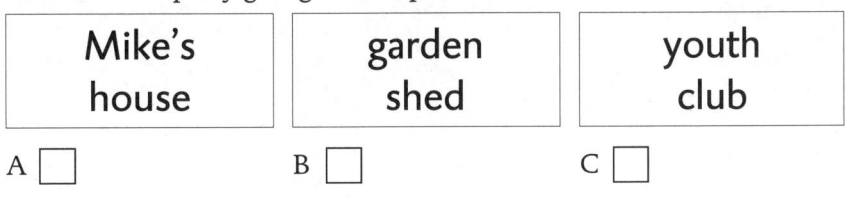

| Mike's house | garden shed | youth club |
| A ☐ | B ☐ | C ☐ |

Laptop: © You can more. Shutterstock, Tasche: © Nadiia Korol. Shutterstock, Kette: © MindStudio. Pearson Education Ltd, Fahrrad: © Angelika Smile. Shutterstock

Part 2

You will hear the captain's announcement on board an airplane.
You will hear the announcement twice.
Listen and complete questions 6 to 10.

captain's announcement

Flight going to:		London
Flight number:	6	BJ _____
Current altitude:	7	_____ ft.
Plane expected to land in London at:	8	_____ pm
The weather in London is	9	_____ and _____
The cabin crew sells:	10	light _____ and _____

Part 3

You will hear a conversation in a bookshop between a bookseller and a customer.
You will hear the conversation twice.
For questions 11 to 15 mark A, B or C.

11. The number of 'Harry Potter' copies sold worldwide is over
    - A ☐ 540 million.
    - B ☐ 450 million.
    - C ☐ 45 million.

    © Dan Gerber. Shutterstock

12. The customer's favourite 'Harry Potter' book is
    - A ☐ the complete collection.
    - B ☐ 'Harry Potter and the Chamber of Secrets'.
    - C ☐ 'Harry Potter and the Half-Blood Prince'.

13. The customer is looking for a book for
    - A ☐ adults.
    - B ☐ his cousin.
    - C ☐ children.

14. The computer system says that
    A ☐ the book is set in a small English town.
    B ☐ the book cannot be ordered.
    C ☐ the last copy has already been sold.

15. The customer spells his last name
    A ☐ L-A-M-B-U-R-T.
    B ☐ L-A-M-B-E-R-T.
    C ☐ L-A-M-B-I-R-T.

Part 4
You will hear Bethany talking about vegan food. You will hear the report twice. For questions 16 to 20 mark 'true' or 'false'.

	true	false
16. Bethany used to enjoy food with lots of meat and cheese.	☐	☐
17. Bethany thought her first vegan sandwich tasted boring.	☐	☐
18. Her first cooked vegan dinner was tofu with vegetables.	☐	☐
19. The only meat Bethany still loves is chicken.	☐	☐
20. She can't concentrate better being a vegan.	☐	☐

Part 5
You will hear a presenter on a TV show talking about selfies. Which selfies did the teenagers take? You will hear this report twice.
For questions 21 to 25 write a letter, A–H, next to each person.

21. Theresa ☐
22. Emily ☐
23. Wesley ☐
24. Ashley ☐
25. Danny ☐

A fun selfie
B mirror selfie
C shy selfie
D filtered selfie
E headless selfie
F snapshot selfie
G dark room selfie
H fashion selfie

Listening – Answer Sheet

Part 1: Mark A, B or C.
Part 2: Fill in the correct answer.
Part 3: Mark A, B or C.
Part 4: Mark 'true' or 'false'.
Part 5: Fill in the correct letter.

Part 1

Number	A	B	C
1			
2			
3			
4			
5			

/5

Part 2

Number		
6	BJ	
7		ft.
8		pm
9		/
10	light	/

/5

Part 3

Number	A	B	C
11			
12			
13			
14			
15			

/5

Part 4

Number	true	false
16		
17		
18		
19		
20		

/5

Part 5

Number	Letter
21	
22	
23	
24	
25	

/5

_____/25

II. Reading Comprehension

Part 1 – Signs

Where can you see these notices? Mark A, B or C on the answer sheet.

Example

Return books here
- A ☐ in a post office
- B ☐ in a bank
- C ☒ in a library

1. **Stay in your car**
   - A ☐ in a car park
   - B ☐ in a rest area
   - C ☐ in a national park

2. **easy-iron**
   - A ☐ on the label of a shirt
   - B ☐ on a mountain bike
   - C ☐ at a steel company

3. **Mechanic needed! Interested in the job? Call our manager: 213-435**
   - A ☐ at a car dealer
   - B ☐ at a bus station
   - C ☐ at a parking place

4. **Recommended by: THE MALTA TOURIST AUTHORITY**
   - A ☐ in a holiday brochure
   - B ☐ in a book shop
   - C ☐ on a bottle of malt beer

5. **Please report any unattended items or suspicious activity to a member of staff or the police.**
   - A ☐ at an underground station
   - B ☐ at the police station
   - C ☐ in the attic

6. **Please buy your ticket before you travel Minimum penalty fare £ 20**
   - A ☐ on the tube
   - B ☐ on a plane
   - C ☐ in an outdoor shop

Part 2 – Signs

What information do these signs give you?
Mark A, B, C or D on the answer sheet.

7. **Jane's Jeans**
No more than 3 pairs in the changing room

- A ☐ You must take 3 articles with you.
- B ☐ You can try on 3 pairs or less at one time.
- C ☐ You shouldn't leave more than 3 pairs in the room.
- D ☐ You mustn't take more than one pair with you.

8. **Sarah's Kitchen**
Our dishes are freshly prepared, please be patient.

- A ☐ Everything is freshly made so the dishes can take a while.
- B ☐ The dishes are for patients only.
- C ☐ There is fresh food for vegetarians as well.
- D ☐ The preparation of the dishes is made with patience.

9. **Ben's laundry**
Special offer
Cleans clothes in 24 h
Monday half price

- A ☐ You can have your shirts washed cheaper at the weekend.
- B ☐ You should wash your shirt within the next 24 hours.
- C ☐ You can have your shirt washed cheaper on Monday.
- D ☐ The special offer starts next Saturday.

10. **Hand Baggage Allowance**
Passengers travelling from or to London may only take one piece of hand baggage.
Maximum weight: 8 kg

- A ☐ Your hand baggage can weigh up to 8 kg.
- B ☐ You're allowed more than 8 kg when departing from London.
- C ☐ You can have more than one piece of hand baggage in May.
- D ☐ The hand baggage rules are only valid for Londoners.

Part 3 – Text

Are the statements 'true' or 'false' or 'not in the text'?
Mark the correct answer on your answer sheet.

Crows Caught on Camera Using Tools

1 Crows are well known for their clever tricks. Now they have been caught on camera making and using hooks like tools. Ecologists fitted
5 special tiny tail cameras that can see beneath the birds' bellies to find out how the wild New Caledonian crows behave. Christian Rutz from the University of St Andrews in the
10 UK said: "Why do New Caledonian crows use tools but other crows and birds don't? I think it's because they know how important tool use is in their everyday lives."
The crows spend most of their time looking for food with their beaks. "But every now and then, they use tools," Dr Rutz said.
15 They noticed two different crows making and using hooks. The birds had made these hooks by breaking off pieces of branches from a tree. These hooks were used to pick and pull out insects.
The crow cams have got a new design now to make recording easier. These new devices store the films on a micro SD card. They're full after about a week
20 and the gadgets fall off the birds.

http://www.bbc.co.uk/newsround/35174710, 24.12.2015
Photo: © stockphoto mania-fotolia.de

Statements – 'true' or 'false' or 'not in the text'

11. Crows are the most intelligent birds in the world.
12. Some of these clever birds get cameras fixed to their tails for research.
13. All crows make and use tools like hooks.
14. Parts of branches are used to make hooks.
15. Researchers catch the birds to take the cameras off again.

Part 4 – Text

Read the text and fill in the gaps. Mark A, B, C or D on the answer sheet.

Cleaning up Mount Everest

1 Imagine climbing all the way to the top of Mount Everest – the _____ (16) mountain in the world – and
5 when you get there, the summit is littered with garbage. Over the years, exhausted climbers _____ (17) left things like empty oxygen tanks, tent poles and food containers at the sum-
10 mit. There are even parts from a helicopter that crashed on the mountain in 1974. Experts say there are about 50 tons of garbage on the mountain. Nepal's government wants the mountain cleaned up _____ (18) five years. So starting in April, every climber who goes up Everest will have to bring back down at least eight kilograms of garbage. And that's in addition to
15 his or her _____ (19) trash. When climbers come down the mountain, they have to hand over their garbage to be weighed to make sure they've brought enough back. In 2011 and 2012, people brought eight tons of trash down from the mountain and gave some of it to _____ (20), who created sculptures with it. The garbage-sculptures were put on display, to help
20 bring awareness to the mountain's trash problem.

Adapted from: Joyce Grant, http://teachingkidsnews.com/2014/03/04/1-3/, March 4, 2014
Photo: Namgyal Sherpa / AFP / Getty Images

	A	B	C	D
16	high	heighten	higher	highest
17	have	are	been	will
18	since	within	at	by
19	only	self	own	owned
20	pilots	climbers	artists	workers

Part 5 – Article

Complete the sentences by choosing the correct ending to each sentence.
Mark A, B or C on the answer sheet.

Afghan Boy's Dream Came True

1 Murtaza Ahmadi, an Afghan boy, who captured the Internet's heart for changing a plastic bag into a Lionel Messi shirt, had his dreams
5 come true after the footballer sent him the real shirt personalised with his signature!
Now he proudly wears his new football jersey with Messi's famous number 10 on the back. From a poor family in Ghazni and unable to afford a real
10 Messi shirt, the 5 year-old got creative. He loves football and he loves one of the best footballers ever, Lionel Messi. When Murtaza asked his father for a Messi jersey he explained "that we are living in a poor village under bad conditions and it is impossible for me to get you the shirt."
The innovative use of a blue and white striped plastic bag to represent the
15 Argentinian national team shirt affected the heart of a lot of people all over the world and made the little boy an online hit.
Messi, who represents UNICEF, sent a package to Murtaza containing his two teams' soccer jerseys – Argentina and Barcelona – and a ball, to symbolise a child's right to play. Murtaza's father said that this was the happiest moment
20 in the five-year-old's life. Murtaza said: "I love Messi and my shirt says Messi loves me." From that day on Murtaza has worn the shirt every single day.

Adapted from: http://edition.cnn.com/2016/02/25/football/messi-boy-murtaza-ahmadi-barcelona-argentina-shirt/
Photo: picture alliance / dpa

21. Lionel Messi sent Murtaza Ahmadi
    A ☐ a shirt made from plastic.
    B ☐ signed shirts.
    C ☐ an Afghan shirt.

22. Murtaza had to create his own Messi shirt because
    A ☐ there are no sport shops nearby.
    B ☐ the Messi shirts were sold out.
    C ☐ the family was poor.

23. Lionel Messi is Murtaza's
    A ☐ favourite football player.
    B ☐ best friend.
    C ☐ favourite shirt.

24. A lot of people across the world
    A ☐ were curious about Murtaza's action.
    B ☐ were touched by Murtaza's action.
    C ☐ became creative after Murtaza's action.

25. UNICEF thinks that every child
    A ☐ should know Lionel Messi.
    B ☐ has the right to play.
    C ☐ should get a ball and a shirt.

Hauptschulabschlussprüfung Baden-Württemberg Englisch 2017 — 2017-11

Reading – Answer Sheet

Part 1: Mark A, B or C.
Part 2: Mark A, B, C or D.
Part 3: Mark the correct answer.
Part 4: Mark A, B, C or D.
Part 5: Mark A, B or C.

Part 1

Number	A	B	C
1			
2			
3			
4			
5			
6				/6

Part 2

Number	A	B	C	D
7				
8				
9				
10					/4

Part 3

Number	true	false	not in the text
11			
12			
13			
14			
15				/5

Part 4

Number	A	B	C	D
16				
17				
18				
19				
20					/5

Part 5

Number	A	B	C
21			
22			
23			
24			
25				/5

_____/25

III. Writing

Part 1 – Letter

Ronda is writing a letter of complaint about a computer game.
Fill in the missing words.

Dear Sir or _____,

I'm writing to _____ about the computer game that I've recently purchased from your online shop. To begin with, I had to wait for 6 weeks _____ the order arrived by post. The packaging was damaged and at first I wanted to _____ it back immediately.

When I opened the cover, I saw that the _____ was scratched. Then I put it in my computer but the game didn't _____.

Now I'm sending the computer game back and hope to _____ the money back, since I have already _____ € 49 for a game that doesn't work.

I have ordered a lot of things online so far, but this is the _____ time that something's just not right.

I hope to hear _____ you soon.

Yours,

Ronda Walker

Part 2 – Dialogue

You are in an Internet café in Italy. Dario who works there can speak English.
Complete the dialogue. Fill in the missing sentences.

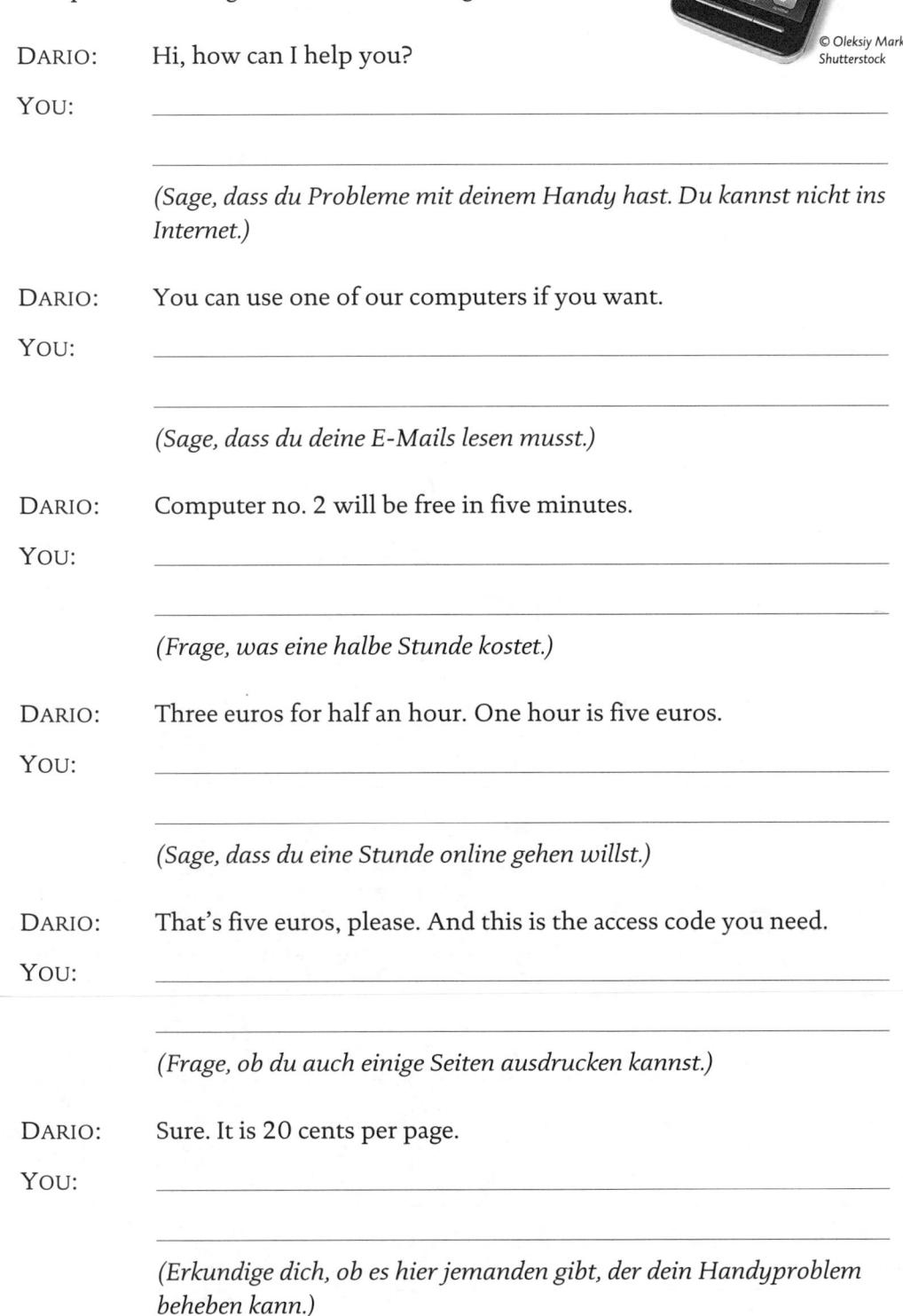

7 pts

DARIO: Hi, how can I help you?

YOU: _____

(Sage, dass du Probleme mit deinem Handy hast. Du kannst nicht ins Internet.)

DARIO: You can use one of our computers if you want.

YOU: _____

(Sage, dass du deine E-Mails lesen musst.)

DARIO: Computer no. 2 will be free in five minutes.

YOU: _____

(Frage, was eine halbe Stunde kostet.)

DARIO: Three euros for half an hour. One hour is five euros.

YOU: _____

(Sage, dass du eine Stunde online gehen willst.)

DARIO: That's five euros, please. And this is the access code you need.

YOU: _____

(Frage, ob du auch einige Seiten ausdrucken kannst.)

DARIO: Sure. It is 20 cents per page.

YOU: _____

(Erkundige dich, ob es hier jemanden gibt, der dein Handyproblem beheben kann.)

DARIO: Don't worry, my boss will have a look at it in a minute.

YOU: _____

_____

(Bedanke dich und bestelle eine Flasche Limonade.)

Part 3 – E-mail

8 pts

At the moment you are staying at a high school, the North Liverpool Academy, in Liverpool. Write an e-mail to your English teacher and tell him or her about your experiences so far.

Include the following points:
- school/classmates
- host family
- free-time activities

Write at least 60 words.

From:	To:
Subject:	

_____
_____
_____
_____
_____
_____
_____
_____
_____
_____
_____
_____
_____
_____

Now please count your words: _____

Lösungsvorschläge

Kompetenzbereich: Hörverstehen

Allgemeiner Hinweis: Zum Lösen aller folgenden Aufgaben zum Kapitel „Hörverstehen" musst du dir den Text genau anhören. Wenn du ihn nach dem ersten Hören noch nicht verstanden hast, kannst du ihn dir natürlich auch öfter anhören. Lies dir den Hörverstehenstext nur durch, wenn du mit den Lösungen ganz unsicher bist und gar nicht weiterkommst.

Hörverstehen Test 1: The football game

(telephone ringing)
TIM STONE: Hello, this is Tim Stone, Manchester Ticket Office, how can I help you?
MRS WARDEN: Hello, this is Cecily Warden speaking. I would like to order a ticket for next Saturday, please.
TIM STONE: OK, that's Manchester United against Arsenal, is that right?
MRS WARDEN: Yes, that's right. Are there still tickets available?
TIM STONE: Yes, you're lucky. Where does your husband want to sit?
MRS WARDEN: My husband? At home, I suppose. He doesn't like football at all. The ticket is for me. Normally I have a season ticket, but I gave it to my grandson while I was ill. But now I'm feeling better, he won't give it back to me, and I definitely want to see the game!
TIM STONE: I'm awfully sorry, Mrs Warden, it's just not that usual for a woman of your age to enjoy football so much! I do apologise. Where would you like to sit?
MRS WARDEN: Oh, you young people nowadays, it's incredible. If it were not such an interesting game, I would put the phone down this minute. Anyway, I usually sit in Block D. It would be lovely if there were still room for me there.
(sound of computer keyboard)
TIM STONE: Ah, I'm so sorry, Mrs Warden, but as you probably know, those are the best seats in the stadium and there aren't any left. This is such a popular match that we have almost sold out completely as it is. But, do you know what? As I was so rude to you, I'd like to give you my own ticket. Would that be all right with you?
MRS WARDEN: Well, that is very kind of you, I must say, and thank you very much for the offer … but I think I would prefer to watch it on television rather than sit next to young men who might be as old-fashioned as you are. I will never give away my season ticket so thoughtlessly again. Really. But I do appreciate your offer, and enjoy the game on Saturday. Goodbye.
TIM STONE: Goodbye, Mrs Warden!

Aufgabe 1
A

Aufgabe 2
a) wrong
   Hinweis: "Cecily Warden speaking." (Z. 4 f.)
b) wrong
   Hinweis: "Manchester United against Arsenal," (Z. 7 f.)
c) right
   Hinweis: "My husband? At home, I suppose. He doesn't like football at all." (Z. 13 f.)
d) wrong
   Hinweis: "The ticket is for me." (Z. 14 f.)
e) right
   Hinweis: "Normally I have a season ticket" (Z. 15)
f) wrong
   Hinweis: "we have almost sold out completely" (Z. 32 f.)
g) wrong
   Hinweis: "As I was so rude to you, I'd like to give you my own ticket." (Z. 33 ff.)
h) wrong
   Hinweis: "I would prefer to watch it on television" (Z. 38)
i) right
   Hinweis: "I would prefer to watch it on television" (Z. 38)

Aufgabe 3

A

Hinweis: Z. 5 ff.

Aufgabe 4

ticket: Tim Stone has a ticket for <u>the game on Saturday</u>.
Mrs Warden normally has a <u>season ticket</u>.

game on Saturday: He will watch it <u>in the stadium</u>.
She will watch it <u>at home</u>.

Aufgabe 5

Mrs Warden <u>calls</u> the ticket hotline because she wants to buy a ticket for the <u>Manchester United</u> game on Saturday. Normally she has a season ticket but she gave it to her <u>grandson</u> as she was ill. Tim Stone, who <u>works</u> for Manchester Ticket Office, thinks she wants to buy a ticket for her <u>husband</u>. Mrs Warden is <u>angry</u> about this misunderstanding. Tim Stone offers her <u>his</u> ticket for the <u>game</u> on Saturday as an apology. Mrs Warden refuses his offer and says she prefers to <u>watch</u> the game on TV.

Hörverstehen Test 2: Hit Radio 100.50

1 Hello! My name is Marc Bent, I'm your presenter for the afternoon show and you're listening to 100.50 – your Hit Radio. We play the latest hits and keep you up to date on what's going on in your home town.
5 Now we're presenting the best tips on what to do on Friday night. Stay tuned! All right, "Four Top" are giving a concert at Chamberlain's Hall at 9 o'clock tonight. There are still tickets available through our hotline – just call 01–1005010050.
10 There is a special event happening in every cocktail bar in town tonight: Hawaiian night! If you dress up as if you were in Hawaii, you'll get one cocktail for free and the second one will only cost you £ 3! But the most exciting event on tonight is the 100.50 Hit
15 Radio Party at the Bluebird with top DJ Tom X. There are no more tickets on sale, but we've still got 10 tickets left as a special treat for our listeners. Just call our hotline now – it's first come, first served – so get on the phone and call me. I'll see you there!

Aufgabe 1

a) B Marc Bent
   Hinweis: "My name is Marc Bent" (Z. 1)
b) A Hit Radio
   Hinweis: "you're listening to 100.50 – your Hit Radio" (Z. 2 f.)
c) C at 9 o'clock in the evening
   Hinweis: "All right, "Four Top" are giving a concert at Chamberlain's Hall at 9 o'clock tonight." (Z. 6 ff.)
d) A Hawaiian night
   Hinweis: "dress up as if you were in Hawaii" (Z. 11 f.)
e) A at the Bluebird
   Hinweis: "100.50 Hit Radio Party at the Bluebird" (Z. 14 f.)
f) C 10
   Hinweis: "we've still got 10 tickets" (Z. 16 f.)

Aufgabe 2

a) wrong
   Hinweis: "There is a special event happening in every cocktail bar in town tonight" (Z. 10 ff.)
b) right
   Hinweis: "If you dress up as if you were in Hawaii, you'll get one cocktail for free and the second one will only cost you £ 3!" (Z. 11 ff.)
c) wrong
   Hinweis: "But the most exciting event on tonight is the 100.50 Hit Radio Party at the Bluebird with top DJ Tom X." (Z. 13 ff.)
d) wrong
   Hinweis: "There are no more tickets on sale" (Z. 16)
e) wrong
   Hinweis: "Just call our hotline now – it's first come, first served – so get on the phone and call me." (Z. 17 ff.)

Aufgabe 3

Marc Bent is a <u>presenter</u>. His radio station arranges a <u>party</u>. There are no more tickets <u>on sale</u> for the party, but you can <u>call</u> the hotline and get tickets <u>for free</u>. You don't have to answer any questions – it's <u>first come, first served</u>. Marc also announces a <u>concert</u> by "Four Top". It will take place at 9 o'clock in the evening at <u>Chamberlain's Hall</u>.

Hörverstehen Test 3: Flight 175

Good morning, ladies and gentlemen. This is your captain speaking. My name is Sandy Brown and I'd like to welcome you aboard on flight 175 from Hannover to London Heathrow.
I'm sorry to tell you that our flight will start 20 minutes later than scheduled, as the airspace over southern Britain is overcrowded at the moment. Our flight will take one hour, so we will land at Heathrow Airport at about three thirty. We will be flying at an altitude of 35,000 feet and our average speed will be 600 miles per hour. We should be crossing the Channel at about ten past three. The weather in London is nice and sunny, with temperatures at about 25 degrees Celsius.
I hope you have a pleasant flight and that you enjoy your stay in London. Thank you for flying with British Airways. I'm looking forward to seeing you again on board one of our flights.

Aufgabe 1

a) B Sandy Brown
   Hinweis: "This is your captain speaking. My name is Sandy Brown" (Z. 1 f.)
b) A London Heathrow
   Hinweis: "I'd like to welcome you aboard on flight 175 from Hannover to London Heathrow." (Z. 2 ff.)
c) C 20 minutes later.
   Hinweis: "our flight will start 20 minutes later than scheduled" (Z. 5 f.)
d) B It is overcrowded.
   Hinweis: "the airspace over southern Britain is overcrowded" (Z. 6 f.)
e) A One hour.
   Hinweis: "Our flight will take one hour" (Z. 8)
f) B 35,000 feet
   Hinweis: "We will be flying at an altitude of 35,000 feet" (Z. 9 f.)
g) B 600 miles per hour
   Hinweis: "our average speed will be 600 miles per hour." (Z. 10 f.)
h) A nice and sunny.
   Hinweis: "The weather in London is nice and sunny" (Z. 12 f.)
i) C 25 degrees Celsius.
   Hinweis: "with temperatures at about 25 degrees Celsius" (Z. 13 f.)

Aufgabe 2

It is an announcement by a flight captain.

Aufgabe 3

numbers: We will be flying with an altitude of 35,000 feet.
Our flight will start 20 minutes later than scheduled,
names: This is your captain speaking. My name is Sandy Brown.
We will land at Heathrow Airport.
towns: I'd like to welcome you aboard on flight 175 from Hannover to London Heathrow.
I hope you have a pleasant flight and that you enjoy your stay in London.

Aufgabe 4

D
Hinweis: Die „Tower Bridge" ist eine berühmte Sehenswürdigkeit in London und der Zielort des Fluges ist London.

Hörverstehen Test 4: At the shopping centre

Ladies and Gentlemen, this is a short announcement to all our customers. I would like to ask for your attention for a moment, please. We have two urgent announcements. Sarah has lost her mum and dad. She's 4 years old, has long, brown hair, and is wearing a blue dress with red stripes and is carrying a yellow bag. Sarah's waiting at the information desk near the main entrance for her parents to pick her up.
The driver of the car with the number plate R 467 NXG should please move it immediately as it is standing in the no-parking zone.
I would also like to point your attention to our summer festival, which will be taking place in the last week of July. It will be an exciting week with a lot of surprises in store for our customers. Don't miss it!
Unfortunately, I must remind you to be on your guard against pickpockets, and ask you not to leave your bags unattended at any time. Have a nice day at our shopping centre! Thank you.

Aufgabe 1

a) wrong
   Hinweis: "Sarah has lost her mum and dad." (Z. 4)

b) wrong
   Hinweis: "Sarah has lost her mum and dad." (Z. 4)

c) right
   Hinweis: "wearing a blue dress with red stripes" (Z. 5 f.)

d) right
   Hinweis: "at the information desk near the main entrance" (Z. 7 f.)

e) wrong
   Hinweis: "is standing in the no-parking zone" (Z. 10 f.)

f) right
   Hinweis: "in the last week of July." (Z. 13 f.)

g) right
   Hinweis: "It will be an exciting week with a lot of surprises in store for our customers.." (Z. 14 f.)

h) wrong
   Hinweis: "an exciting week" (Z. 14)

i) right
   Hinweis: "I must remind you to be on your guard against pickpockets" (Z. 16 f.)

j) wrong
   Hinweis: "Have a nice day at our shopping centre! Thank you." (Z. 18 f.)

Aufgabe 2

The speaker asks the <u>customers</u> in the shopping centre for their <u>attention</u>. A little girl has <u>lost</u> her parents. They can pick her up at the <u>information desk</u>. The speaker also calls for the <u>driver</u> of the car identified to move it <u>immediately</u>. In the end he mentions the <u>summer festival</u>, which will <u>take place</u> at the shopping centre soon.

Aufgabe 3

A	B	C
	X	

Aufgabe 4

A	B	C
X		

Kompetenzbereich: Leseverstehen

Allgemeiner Hinweis: In diesem Kapitel wird dein Leseverständnis überprüft. Da du hier die Möglichkeit hast, dir den Text noch einmal durchzulesen, werden genauere Details abgefragt als in den Aufgaben zum Hörverstehen. Du solltest die Texte also besonders aufmerksam lesen.

Leseverstehen Test 1: Signs

Aufgabe 1
Hinweis: Sieh dir die Schilder genau an und überlege, wo du ein solches Schild finden könntest.
a) A
b) A
c) C

Aufgabe 2
Hinweis: Sieh dir auch hier wieder die Schilder genau an und überlege diesmal genau, was der Text auf den Schildern aussagt.
a) C
b) B
c) D

Aufgabe 3
Hinweis: Sieh dir wieder die Schilder genau an und überlege genau, was der Text auf den Schildern aussagt.
a) D
b) B
c) C

Leseverstehen Test 2: London attractions

Aufgabe 1

Hinweis: Bei dieser Aufgabe sollst du jeder Person bzw. Personengruppe jeweils eine Londoner Sehenswürdigkeit zuordnen. Hier ist es hilfreich, wenn du dir überlegst, was die einzelnen Personen auszeichnet und welche Sehenswürdigkeit am besten zu diesen Merkmalen passt.

London Planetarium: b

Phantom of the Opera: d

Tate Modern: a

Legoland Windsor: c

Aufgabe 2

Hinweis: Auch hier sollst du wieder zuordnen. Jetzt musst du dir überlegen, welches Foto zu welcher Sehenswürdigkeit passt. Vielleicht hilft es dir, wenn du dir die Texte zu den Sehenswürdigkeiten noch einmal durchliest.

The London Planetarium	Phantom of the Opera	Tate Modern	Legoland Windsor
6	4	2	5

Aufgabe 3

Hinweis: In den vorangegangenen Aufgaben solltest du dir bereits überlegen, was die verschiedenen Sehenswürdigkeiten auszeichnet. So sollte es dir jetzt nicht schwerfallen kurz zusammenzufassen, was die einzelnen Sehenswürdigkeiten zu bieten haben.

The London Planetarium

In „The London Planetarium" you can watch shows about the stars and you can also use the interactive areas.

Phantom of the Opera

The Musical is based on a novel that is about the life underneath the stage of the Paris Opera. It tells the love story between the mysterious masked man and the singer Christine.

Tate Modern

Tate Modern is Great Britain's latest gallery of modern art. There you can find pieces of art dated from 1900 up to now.

Legoland Windsor

This is an amusement park for the whole family. You can find detailed reproductions of cities, beautiful premises and a lot of restaurants.

Aufgabe 4

Hinweis: Alle Informationen, die du zum Ankreuzen der richtigen Antworten brauchst, findest du in den Texten zu den einzelnen Sehenswürdigkeiten.

a) wrong
   Hinweis: siehe Annonce 1
b) right
   Hinweis: siehe Annonce 1
c) not in the text
d) right
   Hinweis: siehe Annonce 2
e) wrong
   Hinweis: siehe Annonce 3
f) not in the text
g) right
   Hinweis: siehe Annonce 4

Aufgabe 5

where	what to do
theatre	see a play
amusement park	ride a roller coaster
gym	make different sports courses
movies	see a film
concert hall	listen to a concert

Leseverstehen Test 3: Cinema

Aufgabe 1

Hinweis: In dieser Aufgabe musst du die Bedürfnisse und Wünsche der Zuschauer genau erkennen und ihnen dann den passenden Film zuordnen. Dabei hilft es, wenn du dir die Werbung des Kinos noch einmal sorgfältig durchliest.

a) D – Lord of the Rings
   Hinweis: Lord of the Rings ist ein Fantasyfilm.
b) A – Finding Nemo
   Hinweis: Finding Nemo ist für die ganze Familie.
c) C – Titanic
   Hinweis: Titanic ist ein Liebesfilm.
d) B – The Matrix
   Hinweis: The Matrix ist ein Actionfilm.
e) A – Finding Nemo
   Hinweis: Finding Nemo ist ein kindgerechter Film mit Tieren.
f) C – Titanic
   Hinweis: Titanic ist ein romantischer Film.

g) D – Lord of the Rings
   Hinweis: Lord of the Rings wurde in Neuseeland gedreht.
h) A or C – Finding Nemo or Titanic
   Hinweis: Diese beiden Filme laufen nachmittags.
i) D – Lord of the Rings
   Hinweis: J. R. R. Tolkien hat Lord of the Rings geschrieben.

Aufgabe 2

Hinweis: In dieser Aufgabe wird nach Details aus der Kinowerbung gefragt. Überlege gründlich, bevor du die Antworten ankreuzt.

a) B James Cameron
b) C Hall 2
c) A popcorn and a 0.3 l soft drink
d) A The Matrix
e) A Lord of the Rings I–III
f) B Keanu Reeves
g) C a clown fish

Aufgabe 3

Hinweis: Es ist wichtig, dass du die Aufgabenstellungen immer sorgfältig durchliest. Sie enthalten alle wichtigen Informationen zum Lösen der Aufgabe.

a) right
b) wrong
c) right
d) not in the text
e) right
f) right

Leseverstehen Test 4: Very trendy

Aufgabe 1

a) wrong
   Hinweis: siehe 1. Seite der Homepage
b) wrong
   Hinweis: siehe 1. Seite der Homepage
c) wrong
   Hinweis: siehe 1. und 2. Seite der Homepage
d) right
   Hinweis: siehe 3. Seite der Homepage
e) not in the text
f) right
   Hinweis: siehe alle Seiten der Homepage
g) wrong
   Hinweis: siehe 1. Seite der Homepage
h) wrong
   Hinweis: siehe 3. Seite der Homepage
i) not in the text
j) wrong
   Hinweis: siehe 1. Seite der Homepage
k) right
   Hinweis: siehe 1. Seite der Homepage

Aufgabe 2

a) B
   Hinweis: siehe 1. Seite der Homepage
b) A
   Hinweis: siehe 1. Seite der Homepage
c) C
   Hinweis: siehe 2. Seite der Homepage
d) A
   Hinweis: siehe 1. Seite der Homepage
e) B
   Hinweis: siehe 2. Seite der Homepage

Aufgabe 3

Hinweis: Die Begriffe, die du einsetzen sollst, findest du alle im Text. Wenn dir die Vokabeln nicht bekannt sind, schlage sie im Wörterbuch nach und nimm sie in deine Vokabelkartei auf. Lass dich nicht abschrecken, wenn dir der Begriff nicht sofort einfällt, sondern schau noch einmal in den Text.

a) An invoice is something you <u>receive</u> when a company wants you to <u>pay</u> for a service you have received, for example. The <u>invoice</u> shows <u>exactly</u> what you have to pay.

b) A newsletter <u>informs</u> you about the latest <u>news</u> of a company or an institution. Normally you have to <u>sign up</u> in order to get a <u>newsletter</u>.

c) Free delivery <u>means</u> that you don't have to <u>pay</u> shipping fees when you have <u>ordered</u> something. to be sent to your <u>house</u>.

Aufgabe 4

trendshoes.com

ORDER FORM

- NAME: LUKAS STARK
- ADDRESS: KÖNIGSTR 63, 53113 BONN
- TEL.: 0049-228-31995843
- E-MAIL: lukas.stark@mail.de
- DATE OF BIRTH: 07.12.1990
- ARTICLE NUMBER: 4317
- COLOUR: BLACK

Leseverstehen Test 5: A dream come true

Aufgabe 1

a) wrong
   Hinweis: "After I had finished school," (Z. 3 f.)

b) wrong
   Hinweis: "I asked everyone to give me money" (Z. 8 f.); "together with my savings from the job I took the summer before" (Z. 10 f.)

c) not in the text

d) wrong
   Hinweis: "book a flight to Sydney" (Z. 12 f.)

e) not in the text

f) right
   Hinweis: "a special offer" (Z. 13 f.)

g) right
   Hinweis: "beautiful, sunny day." (Z. 32 f.)

h) right
   Hinweis: "I chose a youth hostel in Sydney which was especially for backpackers," (Z. 35 ff.)

i) not in the text

j) wrong
   Hinweis: "The backpackers were from all over the world" (Z. 44 f.)

k) wrong
   Hinweis: "chose to do the rest of our journey together –" (Z. 50 f.)

l) right
   Hinweis: "the best idea I ever had" (Z. 56 f.); "wouldn't have missed it for the world." (Z. 57 f.)

m) right
   Hinweis: "spend one year of my apprenticeship down under" (Z. 63 ff.)

Aufgabe 2

B	O	N	D	I	B	E	A	C	H
A	R	U	E	T	F	H	J	L	J
Y	F	R	K	S	J	Z	T	S	R
S	G	A	H	Y	G	U	N	B	F
F	G	J	R	D	W	Q	E	R	G
A	Z	Q	F	N	T	R	D	K	U
T	V	A	P	E	R	T	H	E	I
K	B	N	M	Y	F	G	T	U	H
R	Z	U	J	F	V	R	P	K	P
M	E	L	B	O	U	R	N	E	U

Aufgabe 3

a) B
b) A
c) D
d) C

Kompetenzbereich: Schreiben

Allgemeiner Hinweis: Für das gesamte Kapitel „Schreiben" ist es wichtig, dass du dir die Arbeitsschritte zum Verfassen eines Aufsatzes auf Seite 30 f. genau durchliest und dementsprechend arbeitest. Wenn du nach diesen Schritten vorgehst, wird dir bestimmt ein gut strukturierter Aufsatz nicht mehr schwerfallen.

Aufgabe 1

Hinweis: Hier musst du die fehlenden Wörter ergänzen. Einzufügen sind Attribute, durch die Wörter näher erklärt werden. Mit dieser Aufgabe sollst du für deine eigenen Aufsätze trainieren.

The <u>beautiful</u> (1) house at the end of the street belongs to my parents.

Grandma told me to throw the <u>old</u> (2) carpet away.

James loves sitting in his room and listening to <u>loud</u> (3) music.

Take off your <u>dirty</u> (4) shoes!

I live in a <u>small</u> (5) village.

I got a <u>dark</u> (6) blue coat for my birthday.

We travelled a lot during our <u>summer</u> (7) holidays.

Aufgabe 2

Hinweis: Konjunktionen helfen dir, Sätze elegant zu verknüpfen und nicht nur aneinanderzureihen. Es ist bestimmt hilfreich, wenn du sie mit Beispielsätzen in deine Vokabelkartei aufnimmst.

I took an umbrella with me this morning <u>because</u> (1) it was raining.

<u>When/As soon as</u> (2) I'm 18 years old I will leave home.

I'd love to visit New York, <u>but</u> (3) I don't have enough money.

Jack moved to another town <u>in order to</u> (4) become independent.

Clara washes the dishes <u>while</u> (5) she's talking to her best friend on the phone.

Aufgabe 3

On Saturday morning Kelly and Sara met in town to do <u>some</u> (1) shopping. They were invited to a birthday party <u>in the evening</u> (2) and wanted to buy a present. At first they couldn't <u>really</u> (3) decide <u>what</u> (4) to buy, but <u>then</u> (5) they saw the new Pink CD and were sure that that <u>would</u> (6) be the right present for Tina. Now they could take a look <u>around</u> (7) for some cheap and trendy clothes for the party. Kelly <u>bought</u> (8) a new T-shirt, but Sara didn't find anything. Afterwards they went home to <u>get dressed</u> (9) for the party.

Aufgabe 4

Hinweis: Dieser Text ist eine Musterlösung. Dein Text muss nicht exakt so aussehen; vielmehr soll die Lösung dir als Orientierung dienen, welche Elemente in den Text gehören und wie man solch einen Text formulieren kann. Zu den Bildern musst du einen Dialog schreiben. Sieh dir also die Bilder genau an und überlege, was die Personen in der jeweiligen Situation sagen könnten. Denke daran, dass du hier gesprochene Sprache wiedergibst. Du kannst also verkürzte Formen und Umgangssprache verwenden.

Bild 1
MUM: Ann, since you've been going out with Kevin you haven't spent enough time on your homework or on studying for your final exams. It can't go on like this.

DAD: We are worried about you and your future! That's why we've decided that you either stop seeing Kevin or you leave school. It's up to you now! You always want to be treated like an adult – so this is your chance.

Bild 2
KEVIN: What's up? You look upset.

ANN: My parents said I either have to stop seeing you or I have to leave school. They think that ever since I started going out with you I don't spend enough time on my homework or studying for my exams. But I don't want to stop seeing you. They are so cruel!

Bild 3
KEVIN: Oh no, that's such a hard decision. But it's true – you don't want to risk your future, do you? We have so many plans together. We want to go to Italy to study. That won't be possible if you don't finish school. We only have to stop seeing each other until you've finished school

and then we will have so much time together. Don't you think?

ANN: Oh no, Kevin. I don't know how I'll be able to bear it. But you're right. I have to finish school and I will show my parents that they're right to treat me like an adult. And afterwards we can do anything we want together.

Aufgabe 5

Hinweis: Hier musst du eine Geschichte zu den Bildern schreiben. Zu den einzelnen Bildern hast du deutsche Stichworte, die dir helfen, eine kleine Geschichte zu schreiben. Deine Geschichte sollte nachvollziehbar sein, auch wenn man die Bilder nicht gesehen hat. Auch dieser Text ist wieder eine Musterlösung zu deiner Orientierung.

A sample answer:
Mr Smith wants to eat some biscuits. He takes the box out of the cupboard but the box is empty. At once he goes to the cat with the empty box and screams at it furiously. Afterwards, he leaves the room, still very angry that he cannot eat biscuits that day. He goes into the kitchen to tell his wife about the biscuits. Mrs Smith is preparing some tea and biscuits. Suddenly, Mr Smith realizes that it wasn't the cat who ate the biscuits but that his wife had emptied the box to prepare the biscuits for tea. Mr Smith feels very guilty about how he treated the cat so he gives it a cake to apologise.

Aufgabe 6

a) No, I don't like maths. My favourite subject is Geography.
b) Yes, please. I'd like five sausages, please.
c) My name is Paul. How are you?
d) No, I don't. I prefer going to the cinema.
e) Yes, I do. It's my favourite sport.

Aufgabe 7

Hinweis: Die Wendungen auf Seite 31 f. helfen dir, diese Aufgabe zu lösen. Es ist hilfreich, wenn du die Wendungen auswendig lernst.

a) Dear (Aunt) Mary — Best wishes (Love)
b) Dear Mrs Smith — Yours sincerely
c) Dear Sir or Madam — Yours faithfully
d) Dear Luke — Best wishes (Love)
e) Dear Mr O'Brien — Yours sincerely
f) Dear Grandma and Granddad — Best wishes (Love)
g) Dear Sir or Madam — Yours faithfully
h) Dear Madam — Yours faithfully

Aufgabe 8

Hinweis: Bei dieser Aufgabe sind einige Wörter und Wendungen vorgegeben, die dir bei der Orientierung und Strukturierung deines Briefes helfen. Auf Seite 31 f. findest du außerdem Wendungen für eine angemessene Begrüßung und einen angemessenen Briefschluss. Beim Schreiben eines Briefes musst du immer an den Empfänger denken: Ist es ein Freund oder guter Bekannter? Oder handelt es sich um einen geschäftlichen/offiziellen Brief? Was ist der Zweck dieses Briefes? Der Adressat des Briefes entscheidet darüber, welchen Ton, welche Wortwahl du benutzt. Lies dir die Aufgabenstellung immer genau durch. Sie enthält alle wichtigen Informationen, die du als Grundlage für einen guten Brief benötigst.

Dear Anne,

How are you? Last weekend we went to see the musical "West Side Story" with our English class. As you know, the theatre is in Liverpool and we went there by bus. "West Side Story" is an old musical and I wasn't sure whether I would like the music. But it was great. The whole class enjoyed it a lot. The tickets weren't that expensive. We got them cheaper because we went there with the whole class. Our teacher told us that this musical is very famous. If you want to go there as well, you have to be very quick to buy tickets.

I'll give you a call.

Best wishes,

(your name)

Aufgabe 9

/ **Hinweis:** Bei diesem Brief ist es besonders wichtig, dass du
/ alle Fragen aufführst, damit du als Antwort auch alle benötig-
/ ten Informationen erhältst. Natürlich sollte der Brief beson-
/ ders höflich verfasst sein, denn du möchtest detaillierte Aus-
/ künfte über die Arbeit im Hotel haben und du kennst die Per-
/ son nicht, der du diesen Brief schreibst.

(address)
(date)

Hotel Bellevue
63 London Road
St Albans
Herfordshire
AL5 6 PH

Dear Mr Leary,

I am interested in working at Hotel Bellevue over the summer and I would like some more information.
My name is _____ and I live in Germany. In the summer holidays I would like to improve my English and earn some money. The job at your hotel would be a great opportunity for me to combine these two goals. After finishing school I want to work in a hotel and I would like to gain some experience before I start work next year.
Could you give me some detailed information about the job you are offering? How long would I have to work every day? How much would I be paid? As I come from Regensburg it is important for me to know if you have got staff rooms in the hotel I could stay in or whether I would need to search for other accommodation.

I look forward to hearing from you.

Yours sincerely,

(signature)

(your name)

Aufgabe 10

Hi Julian,

How are you? Thanks a lot for your e-mail. I got a job at a hotel in Cambridge for the holidays. That's great, isn't it? I will stay there for four weeks. I will have to clean the rooms or support the staff at reception. Afterwards I will still have one week left of my holidays and I would love to spend it in Dublin with you. I would love to come the last week of August and I'm looking forward to the festival you told me about. I will check the flights and tell you the details soon.

Best wishes,

(your name)

Kompetenzbereich: Sprechen

/ **Allgemeiner Hinweis:** Du findest Aufgaben zu allen Bereichen der mündlichen Prüfung. Lies die Aufgabenstellungen genau
/ durch aber beachte, dass du sie in der Prüfung nicht vorgelegt bekommst.

Aufgabe 1

a) It's on the coast.
b) Behind the boat, there is a beach and a house. You can also see some people standing behind the boat.
c) A man with a child is standing in front of the boat.
d) He is standing in the water and looking down. He is probably holding the child's hand.

Aufgabe 2

a) The man is playing some musical instruments.
b) The man is standing in front of a shop in a town.
c) He is playing the guitar, a drum set and a harmonica.
d) There are some children standing behind the man. They are enjoying the music. One little girl is clapping her hands.
e) The man is wearing socks with the Union Jack on them. That is the British flag, so either he is from Great Britain or he just likes the socks.

Aufgabe 3

Hinweis: In der Prüfung könnten folgende Fragen gestellt werden: *Why do you think that so many people around the world are Harry Potter fans? What do you like about J. K. Rowling? You like reading. What other hobbies do you have? What does it mean when you have to "raise a child on your own"?* Gliedere dein Referat in Einleitung, Hauptteil und Schluss.
Einleitung: Gib an, worüber du dein Referat hältst und warum du dieses Thema gewählt hast. Zur Veranschaulichung kannst du z. B. ein Harry-Potter-Buch, ein Filmplakat oder ein Foto von J. K. Rowling mitbringen.
Hauptteil: Unterteile dein Referat in Sinnabschnitte, z. B. Leben von J. K. Rowling vor dem Erfolg, Der Erfolg der Harry-Potter-Bücher, Leben von J. K. Rowling mit dem Erfolg. Dein Referat sollte alle wichtigen Informationen zu J. K. Rowling enthalten. Die Angaben müssen richtig sein, informiere dich deshalb z. B. im Internet.
Schluss: Am Ende des Referats kannst du nochmals deine eigene Meinung nennen. Der Schluss kann auch ein Fazit eine Zusammenfassung des Gesagten in einem Satz enthalten.

Like many people, I am a great fan of Harry Potter. I have read all of the Harry Potter books and seen the films in the cinema. Today I would like to tell you a few things about the person who invented Harry Potter, the British author Joanne Kathleen Rowling. Better known as J. K. Rowling, she was born in Chipping Sodbury, England in 1965. She grew up in a town called Chepstow and then went to study French at Exeter University. As a student, she also spent a year in Paris. Later, J. K. Rowling moved to London to work for the human rights organization[1] Amnesty International.
J. K. Rowling had the idea of Harry Potter while she was riding on a train from Manchester to London in 1990 and started to write the first book. Because she did not earn any money as an author at that time, she could only write in her free time. J. K. Rowling studied to become a teacher and moved to Portugal, where she taught English. She got married and had a baby. But later she had to raise[2] the child by herself. Sometimes she was only able to write the Harry Potter book when her little daughter was sleeping.
Before publishing[3] the first book, J. K. Rowling had very little money. While she was still studying to become a teacher, she and her baby had to live on 70 pounds a week. She was very glad when a female friend helped her and lent[4] her 4 000 pounds. After she became rich, J. K. Rowling bought that friend a flat in Edinburgh.
"Harry Potter and the Philosopher's Stone" was finally published in 1997 and was a great success[5]. Before that, most children had only been interested in television or computer games, but then they started to read again. But it was not just children, who liked Harry Potter – their parents did too. The next Harry Potter books followed quickly, and the films came into the cinemas. J. K. Rowling became one of the best-selling authors in the world. The third book, "Harry Potter and the Goblet of Fire", was sold three million times in the first 48 hours after the sales[6] started. It is the "fastest selling book in history". You can buy Harry Potter books in 200 countries and in 61 languages.
J. K. Rowling has won many international prizes for her books and become very rich. In 2004, she had over 500 million pounds. Today she lives in Scotland with her husband and two children. I hope that she will continue to write Harry Potter books!

1 human rights organization: *Menschenrechtsorganisation*
2 to raise: *aufziehen*
3 to publish: *veröffentlichen*
4 to lend: *leihen*
5 success: *Erfolg*
6 sale: *Verkauf*

Aufgabe 4

Hinweis: In der Prüfung könnten folgende Fragen gestellt werden: *What activity did you like best and why? How old is your sister and what did she enjoy? What souvenirs did you and your sister get at the flea market? Why did you like the Epcot Center?* Gliedere dein Referat in Einleitung, Hauptteil und Schluss.
Einleitung: Nenne das Thema deines Referates und begründe, warum du es gewählt hast.
Hauptteil: Wenn du über einen Urlaub berichtest, kannst du wie hier der Reihe nach erzählen, was passiert ist, oder du suchst dir nur bestimmte wichtige Ereignisse aus, von denen du berichtest. Wenn du Fachbegriffe verwendest oder die Namen bestimmter Attraktionen nennst, solltest du erklären, was sie bedeuten bzw. was es dort zu sehen gibt. Bringe zur Veranschaulichung Fotos oder Souvenirs mit oder erstelle ein Plakat zum Referat.
Schluss: Fasse den Inhalt deines Referats kurz zusammen oder finde einen Schluss, der das Referat abrundet.

I would like to tell you about the fantastic holiday I spent with my family this summer. My parents, my sister and I spent three weeks in Florida, which is a very exciting place to see.
In the middle of August, we flew to Miami. Because we had to change planes in Chicago, the trip was 15 hours long, and we were very tired when we arrived. My parents rented[1] a car at the airport, and we drove to a holiday flat[2] in Fort Lauderdale, where we all fell into bed. The next day, we all wanted to go to the beach first, so we drove to Miami Beach,

where we had a beach picnic for lunch. But it was too hot! It was 36 to 38 degrees and you had to wear sandals when walking in the sand because it was so hot! But my sister and I ran into the sea, and it was great!

For the first week we stayed in Fort Lauderdale. We went to the beach, and sometimes we went on a trip. In Miami we saw the Seaquarium, where they do shows with killer whales and dolphins. We also went to a parrot park, where we saw thousands of colourful birds. Some birds even sit down on the visitors, and we took a lot of photos there. Once, we also went to a big flea market in Fort Lauderdale, where we stayed for the whole afternoon. My sister and I bought some souvenirs there.

In the second week, we first drove to Orlando, which is in the middle of Florida, where we stayed in a motel for a couple of days. We went to different fun parks like Disney World and the MGM Studios. But I liked Epcot Center the best. It is a big park where you can go on different rides but also see a lot of interesting films or shows about other cultures, nature or animals. The next time I go to Florida, I will go to Epcot Center again, for sure! After Orlando, we drove to the Lyndon B. Johnson Space Center, where we lost my sister and had to look for her for 2 hours before we found her again. So we didn't see all of the spaceships. We then spent a few more days at the beach.

At the end of our holiday, my father wanted to drive to Key West. We drove for a whole day, and at the end of the trip we crossed a lot of bridges which go right over the ocean. In Key West we went to the spot which is the southernmost tip of the USA. We bought more souvenirs and went to see a museum about treasure hunting[3] in the sea. We also saw the house of Ernest Hemingway, the famous author.

We were all sad when we had to drive back to the airport in Miami. But my parents promised that we will travel to Florida again soon!

1 to rent: *mieten*
2 flat: *Appartment*
3 treasure hunting: *Schatzsuchen*

Aufgabe 5

Hinweis: In der Prüfung müsst ihr einen kleinen Dialog führen. Einer von euch stellt die Fragen, entsprechend seiner Karte, der andere hat die Karte mit den Informationen und beantwortet die Fragen. Versucht, das Gespräch so natürlich und flüssig wie möglich zu führen.

CANDIDATE B: Where exactly is the company where you can rent bikes?
CANDIDATE A: It is in Bristol.
CANDIDATE B: Do they recommend special occasions to rent bikes for?
CANDIDATE A: In the advert it says "for the summer holidays". It's a good idea to spend your holidays in a different way than usual.
CANDIDATE B: How much is it?
CANDIDATE A: It ist 9 pounds per day per person.
CANDIDATE B: Do they have special prices for groups, for example?
CANDIDATE A: They offer special family rates. You pay only 60 pounds for four persons for two weeks.
CANDIDATE B: What about an insurance?
CANDIDATE A: Insurance is included in the price and it covers damage of the bike and the case of thievery.
CANDIDATE B: Do they give any further information?
CANDIDATE A: They offer for example, to give you the adresses of "bike friendly" hostels where there are storage places for the bikes.
CANDIDATE B: Do they also offer completely organised tours?
CANDIDATE A: Yes, on demand they organise your bike trip completely.

Aufgabe 6

Hinweis: Im zweiten Dialog in der Prüfung tauscht ihr die Rollen: wer zuerst die Fragen gestellt hat, antwortet nun und umgekehrt. Achtet wieder darauf, dass euer Gespräch so echt und natürlich wie möglich ist.

CANDIDATE B: Is there something special about the cinema?
CANDIDATE A: It is new in town.
CANDIDATE B: Which new film is being shown there?
CANDIDATE A: Harry Potter.
CANDIDATE B: How many auditoriums does the cinema have?
CANDIDATE A: There are 8 auditoriums.
CANDIDATE B: Do they offer special prices for pupils?
CANDIDATE A: Yes, they do. You pay only 4 pounds per ticket as a pupil.
CANDIDATE B: Can you buy snacks and drinks there?
CANDIDATE A: Yes you can buy soft drinks, popcorn and several other snacks.

CANDIDATE B: Do they sell posters?
CANDIDATE A: Yes you can buy posters of all the films that are being shown there at the moment.
CANDIDATE B: Do they have any special offers?
CANDIDATE A: On Tuesdays you get a ticket, a soft drink and a snack for 9 pounds. I think that's a very good offer.

Aufgabe 7

Hinweis: Versuche, möglichst englische Wendungen zu benutzen und nicht nur Wort für Wort zu übersetzen.

TRAVEL AGENT: Hello, how can I help you?
YOU: **Hello. I would like some information on bike tours in Ireland. Do you have any brochures about tours like that?**
TRAVEL AGENT: When would you like to go?
YOU: **In the summer holidays.**
TRAVEL AGENT: Would you like to rent bikes there or are you going to take your own bikes?
YOU: **Could you give me some information for both possibilities? I'd like to compare prices at home and then decide.**
TRAVEL AGENT: No problem. Here you are. Don't hesitate to come back if you have any questions.
YOU: **Thank you very much. Bye.**

Aufgabe 8

Hinweis: Übertrage vom Englischen ins Deutsche und umgekehrt. Denke daran, dass du manchmal die Personalpronomen verändern musst, z. B. von „I" zu „he" oder „she".

RECEPTIONIST: Good afternoon. What can I do for you?
Guten Tag / Der Rezeptionist fragt, was er für Sie tun / wie er Ihnen helfen kann.
GERMAN TOURIST: Schmidt, guten Tag. Ich habe eine Reservierung.
Good afternoon. This is Mr. Schmidt. / He's Mr. Schmidt.[1] He's made a reservation.
RECEPTIONIST: Mr. Schmidt. Your reservation is from the fifteenth to the eighteenth of August. Could I have your passport and your credit card, please?
Mr. Schmidt. Sie haben vom 15. bis zum 18. August reserviert. Der Rezeptionist braucht Ihren Pass und Ihre Kreditkarte.
GERMAN TOURIST: Hier, bitte. Können Sie uns morgen um 6:00 Uhr aufwecken?
Here you are. Could you please wake them up at 6 o'clock tomorrow morning?
RECEPTIONIST: Sure! Here's your key. Your room is number 223. Breakfast is served from 6 to 10 a.m. The breakfast room is on the first floor[2].
Das macht er gerne! Hier ist Ihr Schlüssel. Ihr Zimmer hat die Nummer 223. Von 6 Uhr bis 10 Uhr gibt es Frühstück. Der Frühstücksraum befindet sich im Erdgeschoss.
GERMAN TOURIST: Können wir im Hotel auch Karten für das Musical „Lion King" kaufen?
Can Mr. Schmidt buy tickets for the musical "Lion King" at the hotel?
RECEPTIONIST: Sorry. We don't sell theatre tickets. You can buy them at the theatres on Broadway or at the ticket office on Times Square.
Es tut ihm leid, aber hier im Hotel werden keine Theaterkarten verkauft. Sie können sie aber in den Theatern am Broadway oder am Ticketstand am Times Square erwerben.
GERMAN TOURIST: Danke. Auf Wiedersehen.
Thank you. Goodbye.

1 Übertrage deutsche Nachnamen **nicht** ins Englische
2 First floor: *Erdgeschoss*

Aufgabe 9

Hinweis: Dolmetsche zwischen der deutschen Touristin und der Verkäuferin.

ASSISTANT: Hello, can I help you?
Die Verkäuferin fragt, ob sie Ihnen helfen kann?
GERMAN TOURIST: Ja, bitte. Ich hätte dieses T-Shirt gerne in Blau.
Yes, please. She would like to have this T-shirt in blue, please.
ASSISTANT: Here you are.
Hier, bitte schön.
GERMAN TOURIST: Wo kann ich es anprobieren?
Where can she try it on?
ASSISTANT: The changing rooms are over there.
Die Umkleidekabinen sind dort drüben.
GERMAN TOURIST: Dieses T-Shirt ist zu groß. Kann ich ein Kleineres haben?
This T-shirt is too large (for her). Could she have a smaller one, please?
(Nach dem Anprobieren:)
Jetzt passt es.
This one fits!
ASSISTANT: Would you like anything else?

Brauchen Sie sonst noch etwas? / Kann sie sonst noch etwas für Sie tun?
GERMAN TOURIST: Ich nehme auch diese beiden Postkarten. Verkaufen Sie auch Briefmarken?
These postcards, please. / She wants to have these postcards, too. Do you sell stamps?
ASSISTANT: No, I'm sorry. You have to buy them at the post office.
Nein, es tut ihr leid. Die können Sie nur im Postamt kaufen.
GERMAN TOURIST: Schade. Trotzdem Danke und auf Wiedersehen.
What a pity. Thanks for your help, anyway. Goodbye.

Abschlussprüfung 2012

I. Listening Comprehension

Allgemeiner Hinweis: Lies dir zuerst die Fragen genau durch, damit du weißt, worauf du beim Zuhören achten musst. Sieh erst in die Lösungen, wenn du die Aufgaben bearbeitet hast. Höre dir den Text noch einmal genau an, wenn deine Antwort nicht richtig war. Du kannst dir auch den Hörverstehenstext durchlesen, wenn du etwas nicht verstanden hast. Vergiss in der Prüfung auf keinen Fall, im *Listening* und im *Reading*-Teil deine Antworten richtig in das *Answer Sheet* zu übertragen!

Part 1

You will hear five short conversations. You will hear each conversation twice. There is one question for each conversation.

For questions 1 to 5 mark A, B or C.

[pause]

Question 1
When will Bob Hudson go to the restaurant?

WOMAN: Good afternoon. Shore Restaurant. What can I do for you?

BOB: Hello. My name is Bob Hudson. I booked a table for Tuesday evening. I would like to change my booking to Thursday evening. The booking was for 8.30.

WOMAN: Ah, yes sir. I've found it. I've made a note.

BOB: Thank you very much. Bye.

[pause]

Question 2
How did Judy get to her appointment?

JUDY: Sorry for being late but the traffic is terrible today.

PETER: Yes, it took me almost 45 minutes by bus.

JUDY: Well, I drove and it took me an hour.

PETER: So let's travel by bike next time! It will probably be quicker.

[pause]

Question 3
What type of vegetable isn't growing well this year?

JIM: Hey, Leslie. Look at your garden! Everything is growing so well, especially the tomatoes. You have a green thumb, just like your mother.

LESLIE: But look at the cucumbers! I haven't got a clue what's wrong with them.

JIM: You're right. Next to those enormous pumpkins they look quite small.

LESLIE: But at least they taste delicious.

[pause]

Question 4
When will the girl be able to play volleyball again?

DOCTOR: I'm sorry young lady, but I'm afraid to tell you that you've broken your arm. We are going to have to put it in plaster.

GIRL: A plaster cast? Oh dear, that means I won't be able to play volleyball for ages!

DOCTOR: Well, you'll have to keep the cast on for six weeks and have to be careful for another two. After that there is no reason why you won't be able to play volleyball again.

GIRL: So, I'll miss the finals taking place in a month. I can't believe this is happening...

[pause]

Question 5
Which train is the man going to take?

MAN: Excuse me, can you tell me where the 2 o'clock train to Newcastle leaves from? It said platform 3 on the departures board.

GUARD: Sorry sir, but the 2 o'clock to Newcastle has just left. You can either take the 2.15 to Darlington and change trains there or you'll have to wait for the 3.30 to Newcastle direct.

MAN: Impossible, I can't wait. I've got an important meeting. So I'll come back to your first suggestion. Same platform?

GUARD: Yes, sir!

[pause]

1. B
   Hinweis: "I booked ... for Tuesday ... I would like to change my booking to Thursday ..." (Z. 3 ff.)
2. C
   Hinweis: "... I drove ..." (Z. 12)
3. A
   Hinweis: "... cucumbers! I haven't got a clue what's wrong with them." (Z. 18 f.)
4. C
   Hinweis: "... keep the cast on for six weeks and have to be careful for another two." (Z. 28 f.)

5. B
   Hinweis: "…take the 2.15 to Darlington … or you'll have to wait for the 3.30…"; "…I'll come back to your first suggestion …" (Z. 38 ff.)

Part 2

You will hear a radio presenter giving a preview of today's programmes. You will hear the preview twice. Listen and complete questions 6 to 10.
[pause]

1 PRESENTER: "And now for a look at some of today's programmes on PURE RADIO.
   At 2.15 this afternoon in 'Hip Hop Football' Luke Harvey will be giving us the latest scores. In
5 addition he will be presenting hip-hop at its best. So, everyone who loves sport and a steady beat just switch on your radio at 2.15.
   Amanda Carter introduces 'News Watch' at 5 p.m. with all of today's local and national news.
10 At 6 o'clock it's time for 'The 80's Hour' with Paul Smith. You will be listening to nothing but great 80's tunes. Just ask for the songs and we'll play them.
   Enjoy yourselves at the 'Pure Classic Rock Party'
15 at 7 o'clock. Neil Skinner will be playing all of your favourite classic rock tracks from the old masters like Dylan to the metal heroes like Whitesnake.
   And 'Night Theatre' this evening at 10.15 fea-
20 tures a new radio play. It's a thriller called 'The Clock'. That's the day's information and entertainment here on PURE RADIO. We give you the no-repeat guarantee. You won't hear the same song twice during your working day. So
25 tune in and have fun!"
[pause]

6. 2.15
   Hinweis: "At 2.15 … will be giving us the latest scores. … who loves sport and a steady beat just switch on your radio at 2.15" (Z. 3 ff.)

7. local / national
   Hinweis: "…with all of today's local and national news." (Z. 9)

8. Paul Smith
   Hinweis: "…'The 80's Hour' with Paul Smith." (Z. 10 f.)

9. (classic) rock
   Hinweis: "…'Pure Classic Rock party' at 7 o'clock." (Z. 14 f.)

10. 'The Clock'
    Hinweis: "…a new radio play. It's a thriller called 'The Clock'." (Z. 20 f.)

Part 3

Listen to Chad Green who is having a job interview at a hotel at the moment. You will hear the interview twice. For questions 11 to 15 mark A, B or C. Look at questions 11 to 15 now.
You have 20 seconds.
[pause]
Now listen to the conversation.

MRS JONES: Good afternoon, Chad. My name is Debbie Jones. I'm the hotel manager. Please take a seat.
CHAD: Thank you, Mrs Jones. I'm really happy to have this interview for a job in your hotel. Its reputation is one of the best in town.
MRS JONES: Well, that's because our staff is one of the best! Tell me, Chad, why do you want to work in a hotel?
CHAD: My grandma owned a small bed and breakfast place in the countryside and I always enjoyed helping out. I took care of the guests' luggage, helped in the kitchen and did lots of other things to support her.
MRS JONES: That sounds nice, but do you think this can be compared to the great variety of things you will have to cope with when working in a hotel like this? Our guests are important businessmen and celebrities from all over the world. Now, what about your work experience?
CHAD: I did a two-week work experience in an old people's home last October and a three-week work experience in a restaurant in April this year.
MRS JONES: Tell me about the work you did in the restaurant, please.
CHAD: It was a very busy place. I served customers, worked at the bar and helped in the kitchen. The chef there was very pleased with me. What I liked in particular was working in a team. I could never imagine working on my own, like in an office.
MRS JONES: You seem to have the right attitude, Chad. In this job you have to be a team-worker, stress-resistant and always polite and friendly – even when the customers are difficult, grumpy or have unusual wishes.
CHAD: I think I can handle that. Being friendly and polite are two of my strong points.
MRS JONES: Well then, thanks for coming, Chad. We'll be in touch by the end of the week.
[pause]

11. C
   Hinweis: "My name is Debbie Jones. I'm the hotel manager." (Z. 1 f.)
12. C
   Hinweis: "... a small bed and breakfast ... I always enjoyed helping out." (Z. 9 ff.)
13. B
   Hinweis: "... a three-week work experience in a restaurant in April ..." (Z. 21 f.)
14. A
   Hinweis: "What I liked in particular was working in a team." (Z. 27 f.)
15. C
   Hinweis: "... always polite and friendly – even when the customers are difficult, grumpy or have unusual wishes." (Z. 32 ff.)

Part 4

You will hear an interview with a professional female skateboarder. You will hear the interview twice. For questions 16 to 20 mark 'true' or 'false'.
Look at questions 16 to 20 now.
You have 20 seconds.
[pause]
Now listen to the conversation.

1 INTERVIEWER: Ashley, you've become one of the world's top skateboarding queens. You began skateboarding as a little girl and you've shown outstanding talent ever since your professional
5 debut at the age of 14.
   Ashley, did you grow up skating with the boys or were you on your own?
ASHLEY: Female skateboarders and male skateboarders have a lot in common. Women who skate-
10 board basically dress like men who skateboard. We use the same ramps and try the same difficult tricks. We listen to the same music and above all, we can't imagine a life without skateboarding.
INTERVIEWER: Are you a female skateboarder or just
15 a skateboarder?
ASHLEY: I consider myself a female skateboarder. I think men are afraid that women are going to dominate the sport some day. They are worried and they should be. I keep on trying to do better
20 than the guys.
   Unfortunately, like most other professional sportswomen, female skateboarders don't get the same support as the guys do. The men's first place win is still worth more dollars than the women's
25 first place.
INTERVIEWER: You don't seem to care about what anyone says, do you?
ASHLEY: Well, I do count on my friends. If people who are close to you respect, support and like what you're doing, that's all you need. So, I'm 30 very grateful for their support.
INTERVIEWER: What do you say to girls trying to get into this male-dominated sport?
ASHLEY: You can pick up a lot from the boys. But you have to develop your own style and tricks. If 35 you want to be successful you have to put your heart and soul into it. It's all about having a great time and a lot of people forget that.
INTERVIEWER: Thank you for the interview, Ashley, and all the best for your career. 40
[pause]

16. false
   Hinweis: "You began skateboarding as a little girl ..." (Z. 2 f.)
17. false
   Hinweis: "Female skateboarders and male skateboarders have a lot in common." (Z. 8 f.)
18. true
   Hinweis: "The men's first place win is still worth more dollars than the women's first place." (Z. 23 ff.)
19. false
   Hinweis: "If people ... respect, support and like what you're doing, that's all you need." (Z. 28 ff.)
20. true
   Hinweis: "If you want to be successful you have to put your heart and soul into it." (Z. 35 ff.)

Part 5

You will hear a young couple talking about holiday plans. Where are the people going to spend their next summer holidays? You will hear this conversation twice. For questions 21 to 25 write a letter, A–H, next to each person.

1 MONA: Bill, do you know where I would love to go on holiday this summer?
BILL: Nope, no idea, Mona!
MONA: Come on, have a guess! It's the same place that Jenny wants to go to. 5
BILL: Right, let me think – is it the Canary Islands?
MONA: No, not this time. She's been there for the last six years and now she doesn't want to know anything about it. This time she's off to China. Could you imagine us going there, too? 10
BILL: Naa, you'll never get me there! My friend Ian went to China last year and came back with a really upset stomach. I'm sure I told you. That's

why he decided to go somewhere else this year. He thought about Norway but finally he has decided to visit his relatives in Austria instead. And anyway, you know I don't like Chinese food.

MONA: Oh sorry, I forgot. But talking about Norway reminds me: that's where Paul is going to go in June. He loves Scandinavia. I wouldn't be surprised if he settled there one day. So what about going to the USA?

BILL: Too expensive, Mona. Our neighbour, Mrs Stewart, is Australian, and she told me how much money she had spent on her last holiday in the USA. Which is why she's going to visit her home country this year. I think that entering the US has become so complicated: you have to fill in forms online, they collect your fingerprints, you are checked twice at the airport and so on and so on. Any other suggestions?

MONA: With you moaning all the time I'd be better off going on my own this year. Or I could join Mr and Mrs Brown and go to the south of France. After all, I could brush up on my French. I haven't been to France for 10 years, you know.

BILL: Sorry to put you off again but hot countries are just no good for me. Remember my getting sun stroke when we went to Spain three years ago? Tell you what: I'd really prefer going to Germany this summer. Good food, not too far away, decent prices, and not too much sun ...

MONA: Oh stop it! Let's discuss this another time, shall we. I definitely need a break now!

[pause]

21. E – China
    Hinweis: "This time she's off to China." (Z. 9)
22. C – Austria
    Hinweis: "My friend Ian ... he has decided to visit his relatives in Austria instead." (Z. 11 ff.)
23. H – Norway
    Hinweis: "... Norway ... that's where Paul is going to go in June." (Z. 18 ff.)
24. F – Australia
    Hinweis: "Our neighbour, Mrs Stewart, is Australian, ... she's going to visit her home country this year." (Z. 23 ff.)
25. D – France
    Hinweis: "... Mr and Mrs Brown ... go to the south of France." (Z. 33 f.)

II. Reading Comprehension

Part 1

1. B
2. C
3. A
   Hinweis: *to rinse* = spülen (mit klarem Wasser)
4. C
   Hinweis: *to buckle up* = anschnallen
5. A
6. B

Part 2

7. C
8. B
   Hinweis: *unwanted gift – box unopened*
9. D
10. A

Part 3

11. true
    Hinweis: (Z. 1 f.)
12. true
    Hinweis: "Golfers ... not afraid of him." (Z. 4 f.)
13. true
    Hinweis: "... someone walks by, he hops back in the water." (Z. 7)
14. false
    Hinweis: "... someone walks by, he hops back in the water." (Z. 7)
15. true
    Hinweis: "Freshwater crocodiles are shy and not as aggressive as their saltwater brothers." (Z. 8 f.)
16. not in the text
17. false
    Hinweis: "Crocodiles regularly visit Australia's golf courses, but unlike Steve they don't usually stay." (Z. 13 f.)
18. not in the text

Part 4

19. B
20. A
21. D

22. B
23. C
24. B

Part 5

25. A
    Hinweis: "... France presented the United States with an incredible birthday gift: the Statue of Liberty!" (Z. 1 f.)
26. B
    Hinweis: "... taken apart, shipped ... in crates and rebuilt ..." (Z. 7 f.)
27. A
    Hinweis: "It all started at dinner one night ... in 1865." (Z. 10 f.)
28. B
    Hinweis: "... a crown with seven rays, one for each continent and ocean." (Z. 17 f.)
29. C
    Hinweis: "French supporters raised money ... and the Americans only had to pay for the pedestal ..." (Z. 19 f.)

III. Writing

Part 1

sending/delivering – ordered/wanted/need – big/large – with/about – hard/stiff – send/return/give – refund/give back – as – by/before/until – contact/call/inform/tell/write

Part 2

Hinweis: Beachte, dass du hier nur den Anfang deiner Präsentation schreiben und nicht alle Stichworte aus der Mindmap verwenden musst.

Lösungsbeispiel:

Facts and highlights in his/her career:	The way your star looks/dresses:
• Grammy Awards in 2010 and 2011 • World Music Awards in 2010 • MTV EMA in 2008 and 2010	He's got long, blond hair. He often wears sunglasses and jeans.

David Guetta

Additional information (at least 2):	What do you like best about your star? Why?
• gender: male • age: 44 • nationality: French • martial status: married	He is the most important and successful DJ in the world.

This is how you can start your presentation:
Good morning everybody, today I'd like to tell you something about David Guetta who is the world's most important and successful DJ. He won two Grammy Awards, one in 2010 and another in 2011. He also won two World Music Awards in 2010, the MTV EMA in 2008 and 2010 and many other prizes. David Guetta is 44 years old and married. ...

Part 3

Hinweis: Dies ist ein förmlicher Brief. Achte deshalb auch auf Absender, Adresse, Datum, Anrede und Schluss. Kurzformen wie „I'd" oder „don't" solltest du nicht verwenden. Deine Fähigkeiten, von denen du berichtest, müssen natürlich zu der Arbeit passen.

(your address)

Mrs Zoe Bricks
City Gardens
101 Park Lane
Dublin

(date)

Dear Mrs Bricks,

My name is ..., I am ... years old and I will finish school this summer. The gardener's job you offered on the internet would suit me and I would like to apply for it.

I always help my parents with our garden and during my holidays I often visit my uncle on his farm where I help him to do the farmwork. So I don't mind dirt or bad weather.

I would be very happy to meet you for a job interview. I am looking forward to hearing from you.

Yours sincerely
(your name)   (94 words)

(your address)

Mr Sam Doe
BASIC ELECTRONICS
77 Masons Road
London

(date)

Dear Mr Doe,

My name is..., I am... years old and I will finish school this summer. Your offer on the internet sounds very interesting. That is why I would like to apply for the job as sales assistant.

I am a reliable person and I have already worked in customer services. Last year I did a work experience at an electronics shop where I did customer service at the counter and on the phone as well as back office tasks. I have a lot of experience with all Microsoft Office components and with database design.

I would be happy to meet you for a job interview. I am looking forward to hearing from you.

Yours sincerely

(your name)   *(119 words)*

Abschlussprüfung 2013

I. Listening Comprehension

Allgemeiner Hinweis: Lies dir zuerst die Fragen genau durch, damit du weißt, worauf du beim Zuhören achten musst. Sieh erst in die Lösungen, wenn du die Aufgaben bearbeitet hast. Höre dir den Text noch einmal genau an, wenn deine Antwort nicht richtig war. Du kannst dir den Hörverstehenstext auch durchlesen, wenn du etwas nicht verstanden hast. Vergiss in der Prüfung auf keinen Fall, im *Listening* und im *Reading*-Teil deine Antworten richtig in das *Answer Sheet* zu übertragen!

Part 1

You will hear five short conversations. You will hear each conversation twice. There is one question for each conversation.

For questions 1 to 5 mark A, B or C.

[pause]

Question 1
What music will they have at the birthday party?

DEBBIE: Paul, are you going to bring your guitar to my birthday party next Friday? You know I love to hear you playing.
PAUL: I'm afraid not. It's being repaired at the moment. But you can play the piano for us.
DEBBIE: Well, I really don't think I'm good enough and any way I'm too shy to play in front of so many people.
PAUL: So it's only CDs this time?
DEBBIE: Why not! I've just bought a couple of really good ones. I'll bring them.
PAUL: Right and I'll bring my guitar another time.

[pause]

Question 2
What is the daughter complaining about?

FATHER: Time to eat!
DAUGHTER: Coming. Oh yuck! What's that smell?
FATHER: It's pizza. I just followed an old family recipe and added some shredded carrot. Watch out! It's hot!
DAUGHTER: But you can't put carrot on top of a pizza. And you've added too much cheese.

[pause]

Question 3
Where does Georgia find her biology notes?

LIAM: Hi Georgia, why are you looking so desperate?
GEORGIA: Oh, Liam, I can't find my notes from biology class anywhere. I've already looked in my bag and on my desk.
LIAM: Maybe you should check behind it. The notes might have fallen off the desk. Sometimes that happens to me, especially when there is a pyramid of papers on top of the desk.
GEORGIA: Hooray, here they are! You were right! Perhaps I should start organizing my desk.

[pause]

Question 4
What does Finley say about his new job?

LAUREN: Congratulations, Finley. I heard about your new job.
FINLEY: Thanks. You know, it's nearly perfect for me. It's really interesting and I don't normally have to work long hours.
LAUREN: Sounds great. How long does it take to get to the office?
FINLEY: It's only a short walk from home. That's another plus point. The thing is, the pay could be better.

[pause]

Question 5
How much does the customer pay for one ticket?

CUSTOMER: Excuse me, how much is a ticket for the football match next Saturday?
MAN: It depends on where you want a place. Our ticket prices are £28, £76 and £145. Students and seniors can get a discount of 20%.
CUSTOMER: Well, no discount for me then. I need a ticket for my friend, too, so I think I'm gonna take two of the cheapest tickets, please.
MAN: Certainly! That'll be £56, please.

[pause]

1. B
   Hinweis: "So it's only CDs this time?" – "Why not!" (Z. 9 f.)
2. B
   Hinweis: "But you can't put carrot on top of a pizza. And you've added too much cheese." (Z. 18 f.)
3. B
   Hinweis: "… check behind it (the desk)." – "Hooray, here they are!" (Z. 24, 28)

4. A
   Hinweis: "... the pay could be better." (Z. 38 f.)
5. B
   Hinweis: "Our ticket prices are £ 28, ..." (Z. 42 f.),
   "... two of the cheapest tickets, please." "... £ 56, please." (Z. 47 f.)

Part 2

You will hear a short biography of the singer Amy Winehouse. You will hear the biography twice. Listen and complete questions 6 to 10.
[pause]

1 Amy Winehouse
She was born Amy Jade Winehouse in London, England, on September 14, 1983, to a Jewish family. Her father, Mitchell Winehouse, was a taxi driver; her mother, 5 Janis Winehouse, was a pharmacist. Amy was brought up on jazz music and got her first own guitar at the age of 13.
She began her career at 16 with club gigs and low cost demos. At 19, she recorded her first album called 10 "Frank", which became a hit and earned her several award nominations. Her 2006 album "Back to Black" was an international hit, and "Rehab" made No. 9 on the US pop charts. Her big breakthrough came in 2008. Amy Winehouse became the first British female to win 15 five Grammy Awards on the same night including Best New Album. Winehouse also performed for Roman Abramovich's party in Moscow, where she earned $ 2 million for her one-hour gig.
Tragically her whole career was accompanied by huge 20 personal problems and the struggle with drug abuse. On July 23, 2011 Amy Winehouse died of alcohol poisoning at the age of 27 in her London home. There was considerable mourning worldwide.
[pause]
adapted from: http:/www.imdb.com/name/nm1561881/ bio; Stand: 25. 10. 2012

6. September 14, 1983
   Hinweis: "... on September 14, 1983 ..." (Z. 3)
7. jazz (music)
   Hinweis: "Amy was brought up on jazz music ..." (Z. 5 f.)
8. Back to Black
   Hinweis: "Her 2006 album 'Back to Black' ..." (Z. 11)
9. 2 million
   Hinweis: "... performed for Roman Abramovich's party in Moscow, where she earned $ 2 million ..." (Z. 16 ff.)
10. alcohol/poisoning/drug abuse
    Hinweis: "... and the struggle with drug abuse." (Z. 20),
    "... Amy Winehouse died of alcohol poisoning ..." (Z. 21 f.)

Part 3

You will hear a conversation between a cab driver and his passenger in New York. You will hear the conversation twice.
For questions 11 to 15 mark A, B or C.
Look at questions 11 to 15 now.
[pause]
Now listen to the conversation.

PASSENGER: Hey, cab! Ah, great.
CAB DRIVER: Hi, where to?
PASSENGER: Museum of Modern Art, please. How long will it take?
CAB DRIVER: Well, that depends on the traffic. Today is Friday – and traffic is usually quite heavy on Friday afternoons. Usually it takes more than twenty or twenty-five minutes, but I know some shortcuts. So we should make it in less than fifteen minutes.
PASSENGER: Great. Any idea what it will cost?
CAB DRIVER: Oh, not more than $ 18 – including a 15 % tip. It's your first visit to the city, right?
PASSENGER: Yeah, how do you know?
CAB DRIVER: Well, locals don't usually press their noses up against the window and stare with open mouths at the skyscrapers.
PASSENGER: Oh, is it that obvious? By the way, do you know what time the museum closes?
CAB DRIVER: Well, I would guess at 5.30. 6 o'clock at the latest. Oh, I forgot, the museum stays open until 8 in the evening on Fridays.
PASSENGER: That's good. It's half past four now so I've got plenty of time.
CAB DRIVER: But don't forget, you get hungry walking around the museum.
PASSENGER: That's a thought! Can you recommend any good restaurants in Chinatown that offer meals at fair prices?
CAB DRIVER: The Peking Duck Grill is fantastic and it's not as expensive as other places. The restaurant doesn't look that nice but the portions are large and the crispy duck is really yummy.
PASSENGER: Sounds great. How do I get there?
CAB DRIVER: You could take the subway and there are buses that run that way, but you would have to change a couple of times. Or I could pick you up if you want me to. Let's say 7.30?
PASSENGER: That's a good idea, thanks.
[pause]

11. B
   Hinweis: "... we should make it in less than fifteen minutes." (Z. 9 f.)
12. C
   Hinweis: "... not more than $ 18 ..." (Z. 12)
13. A
   Hinweis: "... open until 8 in the evening on Fridays." (Z. 21 f.)
14. C
   Hinweis: "... it's not as expensive as other places ... the portions are large ..." (Z. 31 ff.)
15. C
   Hinweis: "... I could pick you up ..." (Z. 37 f.)

Part 4

You will hear an interview with a songwriter and guitarist from Tahiti. You will hear the interview twice. For questions 16 to 20 mark 'true' or 'false'. Look at questions 16 to 20 now.
[pause]
Now listen to the conversation.

INTERVIEWER: Bob, you used to be one of the world's top surfers. You travelled around the world taking part in surfing competitions in Australia, Mexico, Costa Rica, South Africa and Brazil. Now you are on tour as a musician in countries like Germany and Austria. When did you decide to become a musician?
BOB: I started playing the guitar at the age of nine. Some years later, in September 1998, I surfed at Cloudbreak on the Fiji Islands. The waves there are really powerful. I fell off my surfboard and hurt myself badly. After this accident I had more time to practise the guitar and became much more serious about music, but, you know, I never quit surfing completely.
INTERVIEWER: And this is why you're never on tour long, right?
BOB: Got it. I can't wait to get back to the ocean – to think, to surf and to write new songs.
INTERVIEWER: Your songs are usually slow and sometimes they even sound sad.
BOB: If you listen to the lyrics carefully, you'll hear that I'm trying to give my listeners hope. Everybody has sad times. But if you keep moving it's possible to overcome a crisis. I perform joyful songs as well. I even used to play in a punk band. I like just about everything.
INTERVIEWER: Do you really play barefoot on stage?
BOB: Well, sometimes I do wear flip-flops, but never ever socks!
INTERVIEWER: Well, thanks a lot for the interview and the best of luck in whatever you do.
BOB: You're welcome.
[pause]

16. false
   Hinweis: "Now you are ... in countries like Germany ..." (Z. 4 f.)
17. false
   Hinweis: "I started playing the guitar at the age of nine." (Z. 8)
18. false
   Hinweis: "... I never quit surfing ..." (Z. 14 f.)
19. true
   Hinweis: "I perform joyful songs as well." (Z. 25 f.)
20. true
   Hinweis: "... sometimes I do wear flip-flops, but never ever socks!" (Z. 29 f.)

Part 5

You will hear Harry and Donna talking about New Year's Resolutions. What are the people going to do next year? You will hear this conversation twice.
For questions 21 to 25 write a letter, A–H, next to each person.
[pause]

HARRY: Hi Donna, hope you had a good New Year's Eve. Did you make any resolutions?
DONNA: Well, of course I did, Harry. Everybody does I guess. Take my brother Tony, for instance. 'Cause he's had a lot of clients from Spain recently, he's decided to learn a foreign language.
HARRY: Spanish? That's interesting. Actually, I was thinking the same, but now I've decided to lose five kilos over the next six months.
DONNA: So you're going to join a fitness club or go scuba diving in the Caribbean, are you?
HARRY: No, that's far too expensive. I think I'll do more sports like jogging, riding my bike and so on.
DONNA: Good idea. Hope you'll be successful! Next to stopping smoking, losing weight is the most common New Year's Resolution, I guess.
HARRY: You're probably right. Anyway, I'm really glad that my wife Nelly agrees with my resolution. She is going to cook and eat healthier food from now on, so we'll hopefully fight the flab together.
DONNA: Wish you all the best then. But I hope not everybody will stick to their resolutions. My

neighbour Mr Stuart told me yesterday he was going to learn to play an instrument.

HARRY: At his age? That's amazing. But when you think about it, why shouldn't he play an instrument?

DONNA: Because he's going to play the drums! What a nightmare!

HARRY: You haven't told me about your New Year's resolution yet, Donna. Come on, what have you decided to do?

DONNA: I think you already know. I always wanted to go to Spain, but my boyfriend never liked the idea. So now that we've split up I can finally visit that beautiful country.

HARRY: Don't forget to send a postcard!

[pause]

21. B
   Hinweis: "... he's had a lot of clients from Spain recently, he's decided to learn a foreign language." (Z. 5 f.)
22. F
   Hinweis: "I think I'll do more sports ..." (Z. 12 f.)
23. C
   Hinweis: "She is going to cook and eat healthier food ..." (Z. 20)
24. D
   Hinweis: "... he was going to learn to play an instrument." (Z. 25 f.)
25. A
   Hinweis: "I always wanted to go to Spain ... I can finally visit that beautiful country." (Z. 35 ff.)

II. Reading Comprehension

Part 1

1. C
2. A
3. C
4. C
   Hinweis: *diverted* = umgeleitet
5. C
6. B
   Hinweis: *fabric* = Stoff

Part 2

7. D
8. C
9. A
10. B
    Hinweis: Es ist nur von *coins* (= Münzen) die Rede.

Part 3

11. true
    Hinweis: "The animal got into a shed ... and sprayed them with its terrible scent." (Z. 2 ff.)
12. not in the text
13. not in the text
14. true
    Hinweis: "... they use it to defend themselves against other animals and enemies." (Z. 15 f.)
15. false
    Hinweis: "... very, very difficult to remove." (Z. 18)

Part 4

16. A
17. C
18. A
19. C
20. D

Part 5

21. A
    Hinweis: "But he also eats the chickens' food, sits on chicken eggs and likes to hang out with hens." (Z. 3 ff.)
22. C
    Hinweis: "... Otto came along as a bonus." (Z. 9)
23. C
    Hinweis: "... he jumped on the beam with the hens ..." (Z. 13)
24. B
    Hinweis: "... a breed of chickens well-known for its fluffy feathers ..." (Z. 16 f.)
25. A
    Hinweis: "He often sits on the perch between the hens and under their wings." (Z. 20 f.)

III. Writing

Part 1

/ **Hinweis:** Nachdem du die Lücken gefüllt hast, solltest du den
/ Text noch einmal durchlesen, um zu überprüfen, ob deine Lö-
/ sung Sinn ergibt. Falls dir etwas nicht richtig erscheint, solltest
/ du deine Lösung überdenken.

inform/tell – from – through/until/to/till – fee/
cost/price – excursions/trips/events/activities –
contact/e-mail/call – cancel – information/help/
details – me/us – meeting/seeing/welcoming

Part 2

1. Can I help you?/What can I do for you?
2. When did you lose it?/
   When did you notice that you had lost it?
3. Where were you then?/
   Where did you notice that you had lost it?
4. What does it look like?/
   Can you describe it, please?
5. What was in it?
6. Is this it?/Is this your wallet?/
   I think that could be your wallet.
7. Could you sign this form, please?

Part 3

/ **Hinweis:** Wie in formellen Briefen solltest du auch in einer /
/ E-Mail, die du an eine dir unbekannte Person schreibst, darauf /
/ achten, höflich zu sein und auch keine Kurzformen wie *don't* /
/ oder *I'm* zu verwenden. Gehe auch auf alle Punkte ein, die in /
/ der Angabe genannt werden. /

From: (your name)
To: Janet@ti-sportsandclothes
Subject: The $ 30,000 prize

Dear Janet,

My name is (your name) and I am ... years old. I am still at school, but in two years time I will graduate. After that I would like to go to Australia in order to improve my English and gain some work experience. Winning the prize would help to make my dream come true!

Maybe I could also treat my parents to a holiday in Florida. My mother has dreamed of going there for many years.

I look forward to hearing from you.

Yours sincerely,
(your name)

(89 words)

Abschlussprüfung 2014

I. Listening Comprehension

Allgemeiner Hinweis: Lies dir zuerst die Fragen genau durch, damit du weißt, worauf du beim Zuhören achten musst. Sieh erst in die Lösungen, wenn du die Aufgaben bearbeitet hast. Höre dir den Text noch einmal genau an, wenn deine Antwort nicht richtig war. Du kannst dir den Hörverstehenstext auch durchlesen, wenn du etwas nicht verstanden hast. Vergiss in der Prüfung auf keinen Fall, im *Listening* und im *Reading*-Teil deine Antworten richtig in das *Answer Sheet* zu übertragen!

Part 1

You will hear five short conversations. You will hear each conversation twice. There is one question for each conversation.
For questions 1 to 5 mark A, B or C.
[pause]

Question 1
What is the customer criticizing?

WAITER: How was your meal today?
CUSTOMER: Well, the food was as good as it always is and the drinks were nice and cold. I was a bit disappointed in the service, though.
WAITER: Oh, I'm sorry to hear that. Well, I'd like to make it up to you. Can I offer you a free drink?
CUSTOMER: That would be nice. I'll have a coffee, please.
WAITER: You're welcome.
[pause]

Question 2
What couldn't be found after Tony's party?

PIA: Tony, how was your birthday party last Saturday?
TONY: Really great, except my friend Mia couldn't find her jacket afterwards and Peter lost his scarf.
PIA: Oh dear, I don't understand how anyone can lose a jacket!
TONY: You'd be surprised. Don't you remember my winter coat was never found after Harry's party last year?
PIA: You're right, I remember that.
TONY: At least Peter found his scarf in the end.
[pause]

Question 3
What time are they going to watch the film?

ALISON: Hey, Robert, I thought we might go to the cinema on Sunday. The new James Bond film is on.
ROBERT: Good idea. What time does it start?
ALISON: There are four screenings, one at half past ten in the morning, one at quarter past two, one at quarter to six and then there is one at half past nine in the evening, but I think the last one is really too late for me. What about you?
ROBERT: You're right. I'd rather watch it a bit earlier. Let's take the screening at quarter to six, shall we?
ALISON: Fine, but please remind me to book the tickets in time. They must be ordered before quarter to five that day.
[pause]

Question 4
What is the man having for dinner?

WAITRESS: Would you like to order your food now, sir?
MAN: Yes, please. Can you offer anything special today?
WAITRESS: As a starter we have tomato soup, the main course is steak with potatoes and finally cheese cake or vanilla ice cream with raspberries as a dessert.
MAN: Oh dear, I'm a vegetarian. Is there another main course?
WAITRESS: We can also offer baked pancakes or fish and chips as main courses.
MAN: Right, so I'll have the fish as a main course and the cake afterwards but no starter.
WAITRESS: Fine, thank you, sir.
[pause]

Question 5
Which homework needs to be done by tomorrow?

TEACHER: Right guys, listen. You know that Mrs. Sanchez, your Spanish teacher, is not at school for the rest of the week. She has sent you a to-do list.
STUDENT: Oh, no! We still have to do our maths exercises, write an essay in English and prepare a presentation for geography by tomorrow.
TEACHER: Oh, stop complaining. Okay, I'll give you another three days for your English essay and Mrs. Sanchez told me you don't have to finish

your Spanish tasks before Monday.
[pause]

1. A
   Hinweis: "I was a bit disappointed in the service..." (Z. 3 f.)
2. B
   Hinweis: "... my friend Mia couldn't find her jacket..." (Z. 12 f.)
3. C
   Hinweis: "Let's take the screening at quarter to six..." (Z. 31)
4. C
   Hinweis: "... I'll have the fish as a main course and the cake..." (Z. 48 f.)
5. A
   Hinweis: "... I'll give you another three days for your English essay and Mrs. Sanchez told me you don't have to finish your Spanish tasks..." (Z. 58 ff.)

6. open-top
   Hinweis: "There's no better way... than on one of our open-top buses." (Z. 2 ff.)
7. Edinburgh Castle/Palace of Holyroodhouse/The Royal Mile/Edinburgh Dungeons/Scottish Parliament
   Hinweis: "Some of our tour highlights are Edinburgh Castle, the Palace of Holyroodhouse, The Royal Mile, the Edinburgh Dungeons and the Scottish Parliament." (Z. 6 ff.)
8. hop-on hop-off/24 hour (ticket)
   Hinweis: "... with our hop-on hop-of ticket. / ... the prices for a 24 hour ticket are..." (Z. 11 f.)
9. £ 11
   Hinweis: "... and 11 £ for seniors and students." (Z. 13)
10. 1 (one) hour
    Hinweis: "A complete tour takes about one hour." (Z. 18 f.)

Part 2

You will hear some information and highlights about a guided bus tour in Edinburgh. You will hear the information twice. Listen and complete questions 6 to 10.
[pause]

Welcome to the Edinburgh Tour.
There's no better way to experience Edinburgh, Scotland's great capital, than on one of our open-top buses. Each guide adds his own personal touch and knowledge to the tour so there's always something new to learn. Some of the tour highlights are Edinburgh Castle, the Palace of Holyroodhouse, The Royal Mile, the Edinburgh Dungeons and the Scottish Parliament. You can get on and off the bus as often as you like and visit many of Edinburgh's places of interest with our hop-on hop-off ticket. The prices for a 24 hour ticket are £ 12 for adults, and £ 11 for seniors and students. Children under six only have to pay £ 5. You can either buy your tickets from one of the ticket sellers in town or online at www.edinburghtour.com. In summer the first tour starts at 9.20 a.m. from Waverly Bridge. The last possible departure is at 7.10 p.m. A complete tour takes about one hour. So, stop wondering what to do today and experience Edinburgh's must-see attractions with one of our bus tours. Hop on!
[pause]

Adapted from: http://www.goscotlandtours.com/scotland-operator/edinburgh-bus-tours

Part 3

You will hear a father and his daughter talking about a car accident. You will hear the conversation twice. For questions 11 to 15 mark A, B or C.
Look at questions 11 to 15 now.
[pause]
Now listen to the conversation.

DAD: What? You crashed into the garage door? Are you okay? At least it wasn't the tree in the front yard. Ah, I bet you were texting your friends while driving.

DAUGHTER: It wasn't that at all. Just when I was turning into the driveway, something rolled from under the driver's seat and got stuck under the brake pedal. I couldn't stop the car.

DAD: Um, I forgot to put those tennis balls away. You know, the ones I left under the driver's seat the other day.

DAUGHTER: Plus, Dad, the windscreen and the windows are so smeared that I couldn't see very well in the rain.

DAD: Well, I've wanted to wash the car for weeks...

DAUGHTER: Dad, I was going to use the car this weekend to go camping with my friends. Now my plans are ruined. I'm sure my friends will hate me.

DAD: Sorry, young lady, the car has to be repaired. Why don't you just invite your friends over on Saturday and I'll order pizza for everyone? Afterwards you can rent a movie or I could drive you to the cinema.

DAUGHTER: Dad, we've been planning this weekend for months. I need a car. What I'm trying to say is that you could let me have your new Jeep.

DAD: Wait, not my new Jeep. It hasn't even got 500 miles on it.

DAUGHTER: You do love me, don't you?

DAD: Ask me after you've returned from the trip. Oh dear, what have I done now? Why can't your friends just visit you at the weekend?

DAUGHTER: Ah, Dad. Now we are right back where we started. I think I'll call my friends to tell them about the Jeep. Thanks, Dad, I knew I could count on you.

[pause]

11. B
   Hinweis: "At least it wasn't the tree in the front yard." (Z. 2 f.)

12. B
   Hinweis: "... the windscreen and the windows are so smeared ..." (Z. 12 f.)

13. A
   Hinweis: "Dad, I was going to use the car this weekend to go camping with my friends." (Z. 16 f.)

14. B
   Hinweis: "... invite your friends over on Saturday and I'll order pizza for everyone?" (Z. 21 f.)

15. B
   Hinweis: "I think I'll call my friends ..." (Z. 35)

Part 4

You will hear an interview with Roseanne who has successfully completed her apprenticeship as a hairstylist. You will hear the interview twice. For questions 16 to 20 mark 'true' or 'false'.
Look at questions 16 to 20 now.

[pause]

Now listen to the conversation.

INTERVIEWER: Hi, Roseanne, nice to have you here. My first question is: How did you find your job as a hairstylist?

ROSEANNE: Well, I've always wanted to work with people and be creative, I never really thought of becoming a hairstylist, my original idea was to become a social worker. But then I found the ad of this hairstyling salon in a paper. I applied for an apprenticeship and my boss hired me on the spot. I tried hairstyling and fell in love with the job.

INTERVIEWER: Do you use a computer in your daily work?

ROSEANNE: Of course. We have a company website and we use software to check how many customers we have each month, how many are new, how many colours we do and so on. A lot of appointments are made by email and some customers send me messages on Facebook. It's great because people who aren't customers of mine see that I get recognition for my work.

INTERVIEWER: Yes, that is really important. And just how important is life-long learning in your job, Roseanne?

ROSEANNE: Very! We go to courses all the time. Actually I just came back from one yesterday. I was at a class for new cutting techniques.

INTERVIEWER: Oh really? Why do you do so many courses?

ROSEANNE: It's basically because of the money. When I first started as a hairstylist, I didn't start making money immediately. The more courses I attend, the better I get and the more customers ask for me. That's how I am able to make more money.

INTERVIEWER: Thanks a lot for the interview and best of luck in whatever you do.

ROSEANNE: You're welcome.

[pause]

16. false
   Hinweis: "... I never really thought of becoming a hairstylist, my original idea was to become a social worker." (Z. 5 ff.)

17. false
   Hinweis: "I ... fell in love with the job." (Z. 10 f.)

18. true
   Hinweis: "A lot of appointments are made by email and some customers send me messages on Facebook." (Z. 17 ff.)

19. false
   Hinweis: "I was at a class for new cutting techniques." (Z. 26 f.)

20. false
   Hinweis: "I didn't start making money immediately." (Z. 31 f.)

Part 5

You will hear a teacher from a small school in Broadstairs talking to his students. He wants to know what the best and worst things about London are. What are the worst things in the students' opinion? You will hear this conversation twice.
For questions 21 to 25 write a letter, A–H, next to each person.

[pause]

1 TEACHER: Now we've been in London for five days. Bradley, what do you think? What are the best and the worst things about London in your opinion?

5 BRADLEY: Well, I think the best thing about London is that there are a lot of places to go. The worst thing is that everything is so expensive.

TEACHER: And Aileen, what about you? What do you think are the best and the worst things about 10 this city?

AILEEN: I enjoy meeting people from all over the world. But there are far too many people and everyone is just rushing off to go somewhere else. It's like go, go, go, all the time. That is the 15 worst thing. Life in London seems to be twice as fast as life in Broadstairs.

TEACHER: Alright, what about you, Gordon?

GORDON: Well, I think London is a beautiful city. It is lovely and the buildings are amazing. But peo-20 ple don't seem to be very friendly and it is even worse on the tube. People should talk rather than sit there and ignore each other. By the way, Judy told me she thinks the tube itself is the worst thing. Not only that it's too hot, she says it 25 doesn't work very well either.

TEACHER: Leona, you haven't told me what you think, yet. What's the best and the worst thing about being in London for you, Leona?

LEONA: Well, I like the food best.

TEACHER: Really? That's interesting. What kind of 30 food?

LEONA: Well, not traditional British dishes like bangers and mash or fish and chips. I love trying international food, like Mexican, African and Asian dishes. The worst thing about London is 35 that I never feel clean because of the pollution.

TEACHER: Alright. Thank you very much.

[pause]

21. D
    Hinweis: "… everything is so expensive." (Z. 7)
22. G
    Hinweis: "… everyone is just rushing off to somewhere else … go, go, go, all the time … Life in London seems to be twice as fast as life in Broadstairs." (Z. 13 ff.)
23. H
    Hinweis: "But people don't seem to be very friendly and it is even worse on the tube." (Z. 19 ff.)
24. B
    Hinweis: "By the way, Judy told me she thinks the tube itself is the worst thing." (Z. 22 ff.)
25. E
    Hinweis: "The worst thing about London is that I never feel clean because of the pollution." (Z. 35 f.)

II. Reading Comprehension

Part 1
1. A
2. B
3. C
   Hinweis: *gate* = Tor; *access* = Zugang
4. A
5. B
6. C

Part 2
7. C
   Hinweis: *bumper car* = Autoscooter
8. B
9. A
10. D

Part 3
11. true
    Hinweis: "… made it public for all users to see for about half an hour." (Z. 3 ff.)
12. false
    Hinweis: "… had planned 'the best party ever' for about 30 friends at his home" (Z. 6 ff.)
13. not in the text
14. true
    Hinweis: "The teen's father … came back when a neighbour phoned him …" (Z. 16 f.)
15. not in the text

Part 4
16. B
17. A
18. C

19. D
20. C

Part 5

21. B
    Hinweis: "… teams from 32 countries …" (Z. 4)
22. C
    Hinweis: "Brazil … Italy … Germany … Argentina … Uruguay … England … Spain … France …" (Z. 12 ff.)
23. C
    Hinweis: "After 1950, Brazil is hosting this tournament once again this year." (Z. 16)
24. A
    Hinweis: "India … withdrew when they found out …" (Z. 17 ff.)
25. C
    Hinweis: "Nevertheless they passed the qualification …" (Z. 23)

III. Writing

Part 1

Hinweis: Lies dir den Text zuerst mit den Lücken durch, damit du ungefähr weißt, wovon er handelt. Fülle dann die Lücken so aus, dass die vollständigen Sätze einen Sinn ergeben und grammatikalisch richtig sind. Lies dann noch einmal alles durch. Falls der Text keinen Sinn ergibt, solltest du deine Lösungen überdenken.

want/like – between – price – fill – number – by – information/details – as – possible – write/send

Part 2

1. When do you want/would you like to travel?
2. Oh, that's very soon. / That's rather soon.
3. Do you want/wish to travel alone/on your own? Are you travelling on your own?
4. There are direct flights (from Stuttgart to Birmingham) every Wednesday and Saturday.
5. You're right. But the flight on Wednesday is at 7 a.m./7 o'clock in the morning.
6. That'll be € 475. You can pay by cash or credit card.
7. No problem./That's fine. I'll reserve a seat for you.

Part 3

Hinweis: Da sich hier zwei Jugendliche schreiben, die Mails also nicht formell sind, kannst du hier auch Kurzformen wie *it's* oder *I'm* verwenden. Du solltest jedoch Internet-Slang und Abkürzungen wie *CU* vermeiden. Achte darauf, dass du auf alle Fragen eingehst, die Paul dir gestellt hat. Schreibe mindestens 60 Wörter.

From: (your name)
To: Paul
Subject: My birthday

Dear Paul,

Thanks for your e-mail. It's a pity you couldn't come to my party! It was so much fun.
Most of my classmates and some friends from the youth club came around. The weather was great, so we had the party in the garden. We could also swim in the pool!
I got many presents like CDs, clothes and money.

Hope to see you soon.

Yours,
(your name)

(67 words)

Abschlussprüfung 2015

I. Listening Comprehension

Allgemeiner Hinweis: Lies dir die Aufgaben auf jeden Fall zuerst genau durch, damit du weißt, worauf du beim Zuhören achten musst. Sieh erst in die Lösungen, wenn du die Aufgaben bearbeitet hast. Höre dir den Text noch einmal an, wenn deine Antwort nicht richtig war. Wenn du etwas nicht verstanden hast, kannst du dir den Hörverstehenstext auch durchlesen. Vergiss in der Prüfung auf keinen Fall, im *Listening*- und im *Reading*-Teil deine Antworten richtig in das *Answer Sheet* zu übertragen! Nur die dort eingetragenen Lösungen zählen in der Prüfung!

Part 1

You will hear five short conversations. You will hear each conversation twice. There is one question for each conversation.
For questions 1 to 5 mark A, B or C.
[pause]

Question 1
Which costume is Nola going to wear at the party?

ALEX: Nola, are you going to the Halloween party next Saturday?
NOLA: Yes, sure. But I don't know what to wear yet.
ALEX: Why don't you dress in that funny pumpkin costume like you did a couple of years ago?
NOLA: Actually I did think about it, but this time I think I'd rather go as a ghost or a witch.
ALEX: Well, Jenny told me that she wants to be a ghost too.
NOLA: Oh, so I'll have to go for the witch, right?
[pause]

Question 2
Where did the girl leave the keys?

PATSY: Mum, any idea where my keys are? I've looked for them everywhere.
MOTHER: No, dear. I haven't seen them. Have you had a look in your school bag?
PATSY: Yes, but they aren't in my school bag either.
MOTHER: What about your desk? It is so messy at the moment. I wouldn't be surprised if they were under a pile of books, magazines or any other stuff you keep there.
PATSY: I tidied my desk last night – no keys on the desk.
MOTHER: Oh, now I know: Have a look in your coat. They might be there after all.
PATSY: Mum, you're an ace! Got them! Thanks for the tip!
[pause]

Question 3
What was the weather like at the last barbecue?

ANGELA: This barbecue sure beats the last one we went to.
RITA: Yes, it certainly does. Last time, we had to spend the whole time inside. At least my tomatoes were happy about the rain.
ANGELA: Good thing the weather is fine today so we can enjoy this warm evening outside.
RITA: Yes, we couldn't ask for a better evening than this. Would you like a burger now?
[pause]

Question 4
How much is the concert ticket for Joe?

KIM: Ellie, have you bought the concert ticket for Joe's birthday?
ELLIE: Yes, and hear this: They are normally £18 each but because I bought three tickets I only had to pay £45 altogether.
KIM: £15 for one ticket? Oh, that's great Ellie. I'm glad we'll be able to join him at the concert. Listen, I've only got £20 with me at the moment. Can I give you the rest of the money at the party on Saturday?
ELLIE: Sure, no problem, Kim. See you Saturday then.
KIM: I'm really looking forward to the party. See you on Saturday, bye.
[pause]

Question 5
What time did Bob probably leave the house?

BOB: Hi Sarah, I didn't expect to see you studying here in the library so early in the morning. It's only 10 o'clock.
SARAH: Would you believe that I was up before eight this morning?
BOB: Before eight? Well, my first class starts at eight and it takes me about an hour to get here.
SARAH: It's the early bird that catches the worm, huh? *[pause]*

1. C
   Hinweis: "... I'll have to go for the witch, right?" (Z. 10)
2. B
   Hinweis: "Have a look in your coat." (Z. 22); "Got them." (Z. 24)
3. C
   Hinweis: "Last time we had to spend the whole time inside. (Z. 28 f.); "... the rain." (Z. 30)
4. A
   Hinweis: "£ 15 for one ticket?" (Z. 40)
5. B
   Hinweis: "Well, my first class <u>starts at eight</u> and it takes me <u>about an hour to get here</u>." (Z. 53 f.)

Part 2

You will hear a costumer leaving a phone message on a voice mailbox. You will hear the phone message twice. Listen and complete questions 6 to 10.
[pause]

1 CUSTOMER: Hello, my name is Joseph Bailey – that's B-A-I-L-E-Y. I bought a table football set from Champs Sports Store ten days ago. I ordered it on May 23rd and it arrived only five days later so I
5 was very happy about the speed of service. But then the problems started. I had to put the table together – which was quite difficult because the instruction booklet was only written in Chinese and Spanish, but not in English. This was not
10 very helpful. Anyway, I was able to follow the illustrations. Then there was another problem with the equipment. Once I had put the table together I noticed that the set of balls was missing. How can I play without a ball? So I went to the shop
15 and bought one. But when I started playing the ball kept rolling to the left. I'm not an expert but I just know I don't want to spend £ 275 for a table that can't be used.
  I would appreciate it if you could get in touch
20 with me as soon as possible. My name is Joseph Bailey. The order number is 17 CF 442. My phone number is 42637759.
  I do hope to hear from you soon. Bye.
[pause]

6. May 23rd
   Hinweis: "I ordered it on May 23rd ..." (Z. 3 f.)
7. Chinese/Spanish
   Hinweis: "... was only written in Chinese and Spanish, ..." (Z. 8 f.)
8. (set of) balls
   Hinweis: "... the set of balls was missing." (Z. 13)
9. £ 275
   Hinweis: "... spend £ 275 for a table ..." (Z. 17 f.)
10. 17 CF 442
    Hinweis: "The order number is 17 CF 442." (Z. 21)

Part 3

You will hear a woman, Ruth Hiley, talking to a receptionist in a hotel. You will hear the conversation twice.
For questions 11 to 15 mark A, B or C.
Look at questions 11 to 15 now.
[pause]
Now listen to the conversation.

1 RECEPTIONIST: Good morning. How can I help you?
RUTH: Good morning. I have a room booked. My name is Ruth Hiley.
5 RECEPTIONIST: Can I have a look at your booking confirmation, please?
RUTH: Of course, one single room for four nights from Saturday the 20th to Wednesday the 24th.
RECEPTIONIST: Right, ... oh, something has gone wrong here. The problem is that our single
10 rooms are fully booked and the room you reserved won't be free until tomorrow morning, I'm afraid.
RUTH: How annoying!
RECEPTIONIST: Let me see... At the moment we
15 have a business conference in our hotel and all of the rooms are occupied. But wait, one double room is being cleaned at the moment and will be free in about an hour.
RUTH: That's OK for me. What about the price for
20 the double room?
RECEPTIONIST: Since it's our fault, it will be the same price as a single room. Unfortunately, we can't give you the room for nothing.
RUTH: Right, thank you. Any idea what I could do
25 while waiting for my room?
RECEPTIONIST: Yes, sure. You could have a break in our hotel lounge, or if you fancy a trip to town, there is the famous old church to the right when you leave the hotel. Opposite the church there
30 are lots of lovely traditional coffee and tea shops.
RUTH: Sounds good. I think after all this, I definitely need some fresh air and a cup of tea. I'll be back in about an hour then.
RECEPTIONIST: Many apologies, madam. See you lat-
35 er! Enjoy yourself!
[pause]

11. C
   Hinweis: "… one single room for four nights …" (Z. 6)
12. A
   Hinweis: "… won't be free until tomorrow morning …" (Z. 11)
13. B
   Hinweis: "… one double room is being cleaned … and will be free …" (Z. 16 ff.)
14. B
   Hinweis: "… the same price as a single room." (Z. 21 f.)
15. C
   Hinweis: "… I … need … fresh air and a cup of tea." (Z. 31 f.)

Part 4

You will hear a radio interview with Nancy Clark who is arranging an activity course for the summer holidays. You will hear the interview twice. For questions 16 to 20 mark 'true' or 'false'.
Look at questions 16 to 20 now.
[pause]
Now listen to the conversation.

1 INTERVIEWER: Today we are lucky to have Nancy Clark in the studio. She is arranging an activity course for children in the summer holidays. Nancy, this is the second year of the course, isn't it?
5 NANCY: Yes, that's right. Because last year's course was such a success that we decided to keep to the same plan. Only the weather caused us some problems. There was so much rain that we couldn't go outside as often as we wanted to.
10 Fortunately we had prepared for that. We had art and music activities for the children to do indoors, so they weren't left with nothing to do. But I really do hope that we'll be luckier with the weather this time.
15 INTERVIEWER: So, what activities can the children look forward to this year?
NANCY: Well, once again art and music experts will lead creative classes for the kids. We thought about having adventure sports like rock climbing
20 and rafting but we decided not to in the end. It would make the course a lot more expensive. Instead, we've included some fun projects like a circus the kids will organize themselves.
INTERVIEWER: The course is for children aged eight
25 to twelve. Why aren't teenagers allowed to join the summer course?
NANCY: It's true that there really should be something for teenagers too but teens shouldn't be forced to spend their summer holidays with eight-year-olds. One day I'd like to organize a
30 summer course for teens too.
INTERVIEWER: So, if any listener is interested in your summer course, what should they do?
NANCY: They should go to my website, www.summerkids.co.uk, and print out an application form.
35 INTERVIEWER: Thank you very much for coming, Nancy. Hope you enjoy your summer course!
[pause]

16. false
   Hinweis: "Only the weather caused us some problems." (Z. 7 f.)
17. false
   Hinweis: "… adventure sports like rock climbing and rafting but we decided not to in the end." (Z. 19 f.)
18. true
   Hinweis: "… we've included … projects like a circus …" (Z. 22 f.)
19. false
   Hinweis: "Why aren't teenagers allowed to join the summer course?" (Z. 25 f.)
20. true
   Hinweis: "… go to my website … and print out an application form." (Z. 34 f.)

Part 5

Listen to Carol and Peter talking about part-time jobs. What are Peter's arguments against each job? You will hear this conversation twice.
For questions 21 to 25 write a letter, A–H, next to each person.
[pause]

1 CAROL: Hello, Peter. What are you reading?
PETER: Oh, I was just looking through the newspaper. I need a part time job.
CAROL: Oh, really. Me, too. Look, there's an advert
5 for a shop assistant in a boutique.
PETER: Naah, I'm no good at talking to customers. So I don't want to be a shop assistant. I'd like to be a swim coach because the pay is good: fifty dollars a week.
10 CAROL: Looks good, but do you really want to go 30 miles to Springfield?
PETER: Springfield? You're right, that's so out of the way. [pause] Wait, what's this? A gardener. You work outside for ten dollars an hour, fifteen
15 hours a week.
CAROL: But I know you like to keep your hands clean, don't you?

PETER: You're right. You sure know me well.
CAROL: Maybe you should go for an indoor job then. There's one at a call center.
PETER: Really? what is that about?
CAROL: Computer help. Twenty dollars an hour, but you have to work twenty hours a week.
PETER: Wow, that's a lot. I don't think I could do that, since I'm going to university. Oh, hey, what's this? A yoga instructor! I can't do that because I'm not so fit. But how about you, Carol? Didn't you take yoga classes once?
CAROL: Yeah, I love yoga. I haven't done it for a while, but I guess I could give it a go. Wow! Fifty dollars a class. That sounds pretty good.
PETER: Maybe you should go for that one then. I'll apply for the job in the student café next to the gym. It's a flexible schedule, ten dollars an hour, plus tips. *[pause]*

21. C
    Hinweis: "... I'm no good at talking to customers." (Z. 6)
22. G
    Hinweis: "... that's so out of the way." (Z. 12 f.)
23. E
    Hinweis: "... you like to keep your hands clean, ..." (Z. 16 f.)
24. H
    Hinweis: "... but you have to work twenty hours a week." (Z. 22 f.)
25. D
    Hinweis: "... I'm not so fit." (Z. 27)

II. Reading Comprehension

Part 1

1. B
2. C
   Hinweis: *stock* = Vorrat
3. B
   Hinweis: *baggage reclaim* = Gepäckausgabe
4. C
   Hinweis: *manual* = Bedienungsanleitung
5. C
   Hinweis: *priority* = Vorrang
6. A
   Hinweis: *shower curtain* = Duschvorhang

Part 2

7. C
   Hinweis: *violator* = jemand, der gegen eine Regel verstößt; *fine* = Geldstrafe
8. B
9. D
   Hinweis: *increased charges* = erhöhte Gebühren
10. A

Part 3

11. false
    Hinweis: "Giant mirrors were installed ..." (Z. 1)
12. true
    Hinweis: "... we didn't have the sun for six months in wintertime." (Z. 11 f.)
13. not in the text
14. false
    Hinweis: "... has become so popular that other places are planning to follow the idea." (Z. 15 f.)
15. true
    Hinweis: "The mirrors are controlled by a computer that follows the path of the sun, ..." (Z. 17)

Part 4

16. A
17. C
18. B
19. A
20. D

Part 5

21. B
    Hinweis: "The 14 teenagers spent about six months working on a project called ..." (Z. 5)
22. C
    Hinweis: "One aim of this project was to make people realize how dangerous alcohol can be." (Z. 10 f.)
23. A
    Hinweis: "... the teenagers talked to doctors, pub owners and local politicians as well as alcoholics." (Z. 12 f.)
24. C
    Hinweis: "Last September the teens took part in a youth forum about alcohol ..." (Z. 14)

25. B

Hinweis: "... the teens were able ... to open a youth club ... to give teenagers a place to go ..." (Z. 16 f.)

III. Writing

Part 1 – Letter

Hinweis: Nachdem du die Lücken gefüllt hast, solltest du den Text noch einmal durchlesen, um zu überprüfen, ob deine Lösung richtig ist. Überdenke deine Lösungen, falls der Text keinen Sinn ergibt.

apply/ask – from/on/dated – year/term/semester – subjects/courses – ago – in – working/being – person/worker/student/pupil/girl – interview – forward

Part 2 – Dialogue

1. Good morning./Hi. I'd like to buy a sweatshirt.
2. The sweatshirt is a present/souvenir/gift for a friend. He's/She's a real hip-hop fan.
3. I don't know. My friend is 16 and quite tall.
4. Have you got/Do you have/Are there sweatshirts in different/various colours?
5. I like the dark blue hoodie/the dark blue sweatshirt with the hood very much.
6. That's quite expensive, but I think my friend will be very happy about it/like it very much.
7. Thank you very much, bye!

Part 3 – E-mail

Hinweis: Deine Aufgabe ist es hier, eine Mail an eine Lehrerin zu schreiben. Achte deshalb darauf, Höflichkeitsformen zu verwenden und auch Abkürzungen wie *don't* oder *I'm* zu vermeiden. Zähle abschließend, wie viele Wörter du geschrieben hast – es müssen auf jeden Fall mindestens 60 Wörter sein.

From: (your name)
To: Mrs O'Neil
Subject: Activity for the project week

Dear Mrs O'Neil,

My name is (your name) and I am 15 years old. I am in class 9. For the project week, I would like to offer a dance workshop for about ten students. I will teach them some basic hip-hop steps. At the end of the week, the group will be able to present a short choreography of a popular hip-hop song.

I hope you like the idea and write back soon.

Yours sincerely,

(your name)

Abschlussprüfung 2016

I. Listening Comprehension

Allgemeiner Hinweis: Lies dir alle Aufgaben zuerst genau durch, damit du weißt, worauf du beim Zuhören achten musst. Sieh dir die Lösungen erst an, wenn du die Aufgaben bearbeitet hast. Höre dir einen Text noch einmal an, wenn deine Antwort nicht richtig war. Falls du etwas nicht verstanden hast, kannst du dir den Hörverstehenstext auch durchlesen. Vergiss in der Prüfung auf keinen Fall, im *Listening*- und im *Reading*-Teil deine Antworten richtig in das *Answer Sheet* zu übertragen! Nur die dort eingetragenen Lösungen zählen in der Prüfung!

Part 1

You will hear five short conversations. You will hear each conversation twice. There is one question for each conversation.

For questions 1 to 5 mark A, B or C. *[pause]*

Question 1
What time are they going to meet?

CINDY: Hey Tara, I don't have to work tomorrow. How about a shopping trip together?

TARA: Sure, sounds good. What time do you want to go?

CINDY: Well, I wanted to go for a run first, at about 9 o'clock. So we could meet at 10.30 if you like.

TARA: Actually, I'm expecting an important phone call at 11.15. Would you mind us going after lunch?

CINDY: Not at all. You find a time then.

TARA: I should be ready by 12.30. Do you want me to pick you up?

CINDY: Yes, great. I'll see you then. Bye.

[pause]

Question 2
How much is the coat?

JENNY: Excuse me, I'm looking for a winter coat and I saw that you have some things on sale at the moment.

ASSISTANT: That's right. We are offering a great variety of coats during the sale. They're all over there. Let me show you.

JENNY: Oh, I really like the red one with the fur collar. It says £49 on the price tag.

ASSISTANT: Well, that was the price before we reduced it. It's 20 % off now. That's £39.

JENNY: Perfect. And you know I've also got a gift voucher worth £10. Does that mean that I will only have to pay £29?

ASSISTANT: I'm afraid not. Gift vouchers can only be redeemed on non-sale articles.

JENNY: Right, £39 is still a good price for a winter coat. I think I'll take it.

[pause]

Question 3
Where is the next car boot sale going to take place?

WOMAN: Hello!

CLERK: Hello! How can I help you?

WOMAN: I wanted to ask when the car boot sale in Exeter is taking place. I want to sell some of my summer skirts.

CLERK: Exeter – let me have a look. It's on July 19th. That's a Saturday.

WOMAN: July 19th. Oh no! That's the day of my sister's wedding. Are there any other car boot sales taking place nearby this summer?

CLERK: Yes. There will be one in Bournemouth on August 23rd.

WOMAN: In August? Okay. I was hoping to sell my skirts at the beginning of summer, though.

CLERK: Well, just let me look again. Yes, it seems you're lucky. There'll be a car boot sale in June. In Southampton. That's just around the corner. You could sell your skirts there.

WOMAN: Sounds good. When will it be?

CLERK: On June 14th.

WOMAN: Fantastic. I'll be there!

[pause]

Question 4
Who is going to the cinema?

BRADLEY: Hi Anne, I just wanted to confirm our movie night at 8 pm. Are you still on?

ANNE: Yes, Bradley. I'm coming and my cousin Jessica is joining us. She's in town visiting at the moment.

BRADLEY: Great. I remember Jessica. The tall blonde girl who came over last Christmas.

ANNE: Oh no, that was her sister Susan. But Susan is not visiting this time, she's doing an internship in Oxford.

BRADLEY: Right, never mind. By the way, I asked my friend Joe to come and see the movie tonight but he's busy working night shift and can't take a day off.

ANNE: So it'll only be the three of us. I hope you like going out with two girls, Bradley.

[pause]

Question 5
Which team is <u>Pauline</u> cheerleading for?

DIANA: Hello, Pauline. I heard you are a cheerleader now?

PAULINE: Hi, Diana. Yes, that's right.

DIANA: Congratulations! Which team are you cheerleading for? The Falcons?

PAULINE: No, not the Falcons. They are a very good team as well but I decided for the Tigers.

DIANA: The Tigers! Good choice, Pauline. Maybe I should start cheerleading as well. Do you know if any of the teams are looking for new dancers?

PAULINE: Yes. I do. The Lions need three new girls.

DIANA: The Lions? Is that team any good?

PAULINE: I should think so! I watched their performance the other day. It was great, Diana!

DIANA: Okay. So maybe I'll become a lion.

1. C
   Hinweis: "I should be ready by 12.30." (Z. 11)
2. A
   Hinweis: "Right, £ 39 is still a good price ..." (Z. 29)
3. B
   Hinweis: "There'll be a car boot sale in June. In Southampton." (Z. 46 f.)
4. C
   Hinweis: "Yes, Bradley. I'm coming and my cousin Jessica is joining us." (Z. 54 f.)
5. A
   Hinweis: "... but I decided for the Tigers." (Z. 74)

Part 2

You will hear some information about Big Ben. You will hear the information twice. Listen and complete questions 6 to 10.

[pause]

If you think of Big Ben you might think of the huge tower at the Houses of Parliament. The truth is, Big Ben is the name of the giant bell in the clock tower at the Palace of Westminster in London. Although the bell is from 1858 it struck the hour for the first time the following year. So it was in 1859 that the people of Westminster eventually heard Big Ben's sound. The bell is very heavy. It weighs more than 12 ½ tons. Just imagine: that's about the same as two elephants weigh. The bell strikes every 15 minutes and can be heard for miles. The shape of Big Ben is also quite interesting. It is wider than it is tall. 7 feet and 6 inches, which is about 2.28 metres – that's how tall it is. But it is 2.75 metres wide. That's about 9 feet. Big Ben is so special that it has become a symbol of the United Kingdom. It was even voted the number one British landmark in a survey in 2008.

[pause]

6. 1859
   Hinweis: "Although the bell is from 1858 it struck the hour for the first time the following year." (Z. 4 ff.)
7. 12,5 / 12 ½ / twelve and a half
   Hinweis: "It weighs more than 12 ½ tons." (Z. 8 f.)
8. 2/two elephants
   Hinweis: "... that's about the same as two elephants weigh." (Z. 9 f.)
9. wider, tall
   Hinweis: "It is wider than it is tall." (Z. 12)
10. 2008
    Hinweis: "... in a survey in 2008 ..." (Z. 17 f.)

Part 3

You will hear a conversation between two girls, Megan and Fiona. You will hear the conversation twice. For questions 11 to 15 mark A, B or C. Look at questions 11 to 15 now.

[pause]

Now listen to the conversation.

MEGAN: Hi, Fiona!

FIONA: Hi, Megan! How are things going?

MEGAN: Not too bad!

FIONA: What do you mean: "Not too bad"? I heard you are a lucky girl. You're dating Andrew.

MEGAN: Where did you hear that?

FIONA: Jenna told me the other day. She saw you walking hand-in-hand through town when she was shopping.

MEGAN: Yes, it's true. Andrew and I have been a couple for about four weeks now.

FIONA: That's really great. Andrew is very attractive and soooo charming. He is such a good catch. How did you get together?

MEGAN: Oh, that's rather a funny story. To start with, I had a date with Jake. We wanted to go to the cinema but he didn't show up! Imagine that!

FIONA: How embarrassing! So you were standing there in the entrance hall, all alone.

MEGAN: Exactly. And then Andrew showed up, like, out of nowhere. He saw me standing there looking sad and lonely. He asked me if I was alright.

FIONA: And then?

MEGAN: Then he bought two tickets, invited me to see the film and asked me out afterwards. That's how things got going …

FIONA: That's so romantic! I wish I could meet a boy like Andrew. He is a perfect gentleman.

MEGAN: You will, Fiona. I'm sure about that.

FIONA: Do you really think so?

MEGAN: Of course! You're so pretty and you truly deserve it. All you need is a little patience.

[pause]

11. C
   Hinweis: "You're dating Andrew." (Z. 5)
12. C
   Hinweis: "That's really great." (Z. 12)
13. A
   Hinweis: "… but he didn't show up!" (Z. 17)
14. C
   Hinweis: "… invited me to see the film and asked me out afterwards." (Z. 24 f.)
15. B
   Hinweis: "You're so pretty …" (Z. 31)

Part 4

You will hear a radio interview with a health expert about the dangers of eating too much sugar. You will hear the interview twice. For questions 16 to 20 mark 'true' or 'false'.
Look at questions 16 to 20 now.
[pause]
Now listen to the conversation.

INTERVIEWER: Good morning, listeners. Today's guest in the show is Paul Miller, health expert and author of many articles about the dangers of consuming too much sugar. Welcome, Paul.

PAUL: Hi, good to be here today.

INTERVIEWER: Paul, you write about the increasing number of people in Britain whose weight is getting alarmingly high. Can you give our listeners some information on that?

PAUL: Well, according to official figures, a quarter of all adults in Britain are now obese, which means seriously overweight. If this trend continues, 60 % of the men and 50 % of the women in Britain could be obese by the year 2050.

INTERVIEWER: That is very alarming. What does this actually mean for these people – I imagine this could cause many health problems.

PAUL: You're absolutely right. There will be an increase in health problems such as diabetes, some types of cancer and heart disease.

INTERVIEWER: Is the government trying to do anything about it?

PAUL: Yes, it is. There are loads of brochures about healthy eating and getting more exercise. And industry brought low-fat foods on the market. Ironically, the effect was that people just gained more weight.

INTERVIEWER: What's wrong with these low-fat products that we can buy in the supermarkets?

PAUL: The problem with low-fat products is that less fat also means less taste. To make low-fat food tasty again you have to add sugar, for example. That's why the fat is reduced but the calories are still there, sometimes even more. Too much sugar is like poison. It's addictive and can be deadly. We should really try to reduce it to a low level.

INTERVIEWER: Thanks for the interview, Paul, and all the helpful information.

Adapted from: Moya Irvine, Obesity. Sugar not fat is the problem; in: Read on, Nov 2014

[pause]

16. true
   Hinweis: "… the increasing number of people in Britain whose weight is getting alarmingly high." (Z. 6 ff.)
17. false
   Hinweis: "… 60 % of the men and 50 % of the women …" (Z. 13)
18. true
   Hinweis: "… this could cause many health problems … You're absolutely right." (Z. 16 ff.)
19. false
   Hinweis: "… people just gained more weight …" (Z. 26 f.)
20. true
   Hinweis: "Too much sugar is like poison. It's addictive and can be deadly." (Z. 34 ff.)

Part 5

You will hear a radio interview about clothes and style. Which clothing style do people prefer? You will hear this interview twice.
For questions 21 to 25 write a letter, A–H, next to each person.
[pause]

1 PRESENTER: How do young people express their individual style these days? We interviewed some young Brits in different parts of the UK. Here is what Liam, a student from Leicester, told us.
5 LIAM: Young people in the UK have always been creative about their clothes. Punks cut them up and add zips and safety pins. Goths wear anything black. Personally, I like the skater-style: baggy pants, baseball caps and chains.
10 PRESENTER: Thank you, Liam. How about 22-year-old Alexandra from Portsmouth?
ALEXANDRA: I like multi-coloured T-shirts and I used to make some for my friends. They looked a bit messy but sort of cool. A couple of years
15 ago, I made a T-shirt with a picture of Obama dressed as Che Guevara. I still wear it in fact. It looks great!
PRESENTER: And now Mickey. He's an artist from London.
20 MICKEY: I used to make clothes sometimes when I was a student. Once I found a pair of trousers in a shop that I really liked but I couldn't afford them. So, I made a little sketch, bought some fabric in the same colour and copied the trou-
25 sers using my mum's sewing machine. In the end my trousers looked even better than the ones in the shop.
PRESENTER: And finally Aditi. 17 years old and from Birmingham.
30 ADITI: I buy stuff like jackets, trousers and dresses in second-hand shops. With second-hand clothes you can be sure you will always have something original as well as cheap. The other day I bought a second-hand T-shirt and skirt and dyed them black. Very cool. I also cut up an old pair of leg-
35 gings to make some long fingerless gloves.
PRESENTER: A dyed black skirt and fingerless gloves? Not for me! I think I'll just stick to my good old blue jeans and their pockets! That was our today's interview on clothes and style. Thanks for
40 tuning in.

Adapted from: http://learnenglishteens.britishcouncil.org/node/2332

[pause]

21. F
    Hinweis: "... I like the skater-style." (Z. 8)
22. A
    Hinweis: "I like multi-coloured T-shirts ..." (Z. 12)
23. H
    Hinweis: "I used to make clothes ..." (Z. 20)
24. E
    Hinweis: "I buy ... in second-hand shops." (Z. 30 f.)
25. B
    Hinweis: "... I'll just stick to my good old blue jeans ..." (Z. 38 f.)

II. Reading Comprehension

Part 1

1. A
   Hinweis: *sober* = nüchtern
2. B
   Hinweis: *(to) bully* = schikanieren, mobben
3. A
   Hinweis: *(to) improve* = verbessern
4. C
5. A
   Hinweis: *steep slope* = steiler Hang, steile Piste
6. A
   Hinweis: *stand* = hier: Tribüne

Part 2

7. A
   Hinweis: *no bare feet* = keine nackten Füße, nicht barfuß
8. D
   Hinweis: *dispenser* = hier: Spender
9. B
10. C
    Hinweis: *recommended* = empfohlen

Part 3

11. not in the text
12. false
    Hinweis: "... they also nibble on official documents." (Z. 9)
13. false
    Hinweis: "... about £ 6,000 per month are spent on pest control ..." (Z. 10)
14. false
    Hinweis: "... I would like to have one of their cats come ..." (Z. 14)

15. false
   Hinweis: "... is the proud Chief Mouser to the Cabinet Office." (Z. 18 f.)

Part 4

16. C
17. A
18. D
19. D
20. B

Part 5

21. B
   Hinweis: "... when suddenly the city disappeared." (Z. 6 f.)
22. C
   Hinweis: "Buses and cars moved as long as they had gas." (Z. 14 f.)
23. B
   Hinweis: "Cabs charged five times the normal fare." (Z. 15)
24. B
   Hinweis: "... water pumps failed ..." (Z. 10)
25. C
   Hinweis: "... store owners lost about a billion dollars during the blackout." (Z. 20)

III. Writing

Part 1 – Letter

Hinweis: Lies den gesamten Text noch einmal durch, nachdem du die Lücken gefüllt hast, um zu überprüfen, ob deine Lösungen richtig sind. Achte u. a. darauf, ob du jeweils die richtige Wortart eingesetzt hast. Beachte bei Verben auch die richtige (Zeit)form.

posting/sending – visit/journey/trip – on/next – plane/flight – will/'ll – is – play/watch – can/could/should/must/will – forget – you

Part 2 – Dialogue

1. Yes, there are. Do you want to see/Would you like to see/the film/movie in the original version/language?
2. The film runs/starts/is at 12.45 pm and at 4.15 pm.
3. I can reserve the tickets (for you). How many (tickets) do you need/want?
4. Today students only have to pay half price./Students only have to pay half price today. That's € 4.
5. That's/That'll be € 20 (together). The film runs/is playing/is shown in room/cinema 3.
6. There is/There's a nice café around the corner with home-made cakes.
   Hinweis: „Selbstgemacht" kann hier nur mit „home-made" und nicht mit „self-made" übersetzt werden, da „self-made" nur im Sinne von „es aus eigener Kraft zu Erfolg und Reichtum bringen" gebraucht wird.

Part 3 – E-mail

Hinweis: Verfasse eine E-Mail an einen Klassenkameraden deiner Wahl. Verwende hierfür eine persönliche Anrede und Grußformel. Deine E-Mail sollte eine kurze Einleitung oder Begrüßung sowie alle drei genannten Punkte der Aufgabenstellung beinhalten. Zähle abschließend, wie viele Wörter du geschrieben hast – es müssen mindestens 60 Wörter sein.

From: (your name)
To: David
Subject: Farewell party

Hi David,

How are you? As you know, Pia and I are organising the farewell party for our class. We decided that it would take place in the youth club in town on 15th July. It will start at 7 pm. We will order some pizzas. But maybe you can bring some snacks like crisps or popcorn?

Can you come to the party? Please send me an answer as soon as possible. The youth club needs to know the number of guests.

Hope to hear from you soon.

Yours,
(your name)

(90 words)

Abschlussprüfung 2017

I. Listening Comprehension

Allgemeiner Hinweis: Lies dir alle Aufgaben zuerst genau durch, damit du weißt, worauf du beim Zuhören achten musst. Sieh dir die Lösungen erst an, wenn du die Aufgaben bearbeitet hast. Höre dir einen Text noch einmal an, wenn deine Antwort nicht richtig war. Falls du etwas nicht verstanden hast, kannst du dir den Hörverstehenstext auch durchlesen. Vergiss in der Prüfung auf keinen Fall, im *Listening*- und im *Reading*-Teil deine Antworten richtig in das *Answer Sheet* zu übertragen. Nur die dort eingetragenen Lösungen zählen in der Prüfung!

Part 1

You will hear five short conversations. You will hear each conversation twice. There is one question for each conversation.
For questions 1 to 5 mark A, B or C.
[pause]

Question 1
In which colour would Taira like to paint her room?

TAIRA: Daddy! I would like to paint the walls in my room in a different colour.
DADDY: Oh, okay! Don't you like your white walls any longer?
TAIRA: No, not really. White just seems to be so boring …
DADDY: I see. And what colour would you like instead? Red, blue, green, pink?
TAIRA: Pink walls! Are you joking? I'm not a baby! I would like red.
DADDY: Yeah, why not. We can go and buy some paint tomorrow if you like.
TAIRA: Great! You're the best!
[pause]

Question 2
Why can't Raheem go to school today?

SECRETARY: Franklin D. Roosevelt Junior High School. You're talking to Morgan Miller. How can I help you?
MOTHER: Good morning, Ms Miller. This is Tanvi Ackerman, Raheem's mother.
SECRETARY: Good morning, Mrs Ackerman.
MOTHER: I just wanted to let you know that Raheem won't be coming to school today.
SECRETARY: Oh, dear. Another one. Quite a few parents have called this morning to excuse their children because they've got the flu.
MOTHER: Oh, sorry to hear that! But in Raheem's case it's not the flu. He has hurt his leg and has to give it some rest.
SECRETARY: I'm sorry to hear that. My son's at home as well. He's caught a bad cold. Tell Raheem to get well soon!
MOTHER: Thank you, Ms Miller. Bye!
[pause]

Question 3
Which shuttle bus are they going to take?

HARRY: Look, darling. There's a shuttle bus to Luton airport going at 6:20.
BELINDA: 6:20. That's very early. Our plane only takes off at 11:35.
HARRY: Yes. Maybe you're right.
BELINDA: Aren't there any shuttle buses going later? Then we could sleep a little longer.
HARRY: Let me have a look. Yes, there's one going at 7:35 and one at 8:50.
BELINDA: 8:50 might be a bit too late. So how about 7:35 then?
HARRY: Sounds good to me. Let's take that one. I'll call the bus company and book two seats.
[pause]

Question 4
What presents did Lucy get?

PETER: Hi Lucy. It was your birthday last week, wasn't it? Did you get any nice presents?
LUCY: Oh yes, I did. Although, it's strange. I didn't get a single thing I had wished for.
PETER: Really? So what did you get? I know you wanted a new mountain bike.
LUCY: That's right. But my parents bought me a laptop instead. I guess they thought it would be a good thing for my studies.
PETER: Well, there are worse presents than a laptop, Lucy.
LUCY: Fair enough. And the necklace I got from Tom was even better than the handbag I had seen in the shops and told him about.
PETER: So altogether a successful birthday!
LUCY: I'm not complaining.
[pause]

Question 5
Where is the party going to take place?

MIKE: Hey Sam, my parents said I could celebrate my birthday at home this year.

SAM: Wow, Mike. This is the first time that your parents will let you have a party in the house, right?

MIKE: Yes, that's right. At first I was so happy about it but now I'm not so sure. There'll be a lot of people around and my parents are so fussy about their furniture and their antiques. I don't want anything spoilt or broken.

SAM: I see. So why don't you rent a room in the local youth club?

MIKE: I had that idea as well, but Jenny told me that all the rooms are fully booked for the next couple of weeks.

SAM: Shame. Tell you what, my aunt and uncle have a garden shed nearby. It's a great place for a party. I could ask them.

MIKE: A garden shed in February? Thanks for the offer, Sam, but I think I'd rather celebrate at my place and get mum and dad to put the expensive stuff away for one night.

1. **B**
   Hinweis: "I would like red." (Z. 9 f.)
2. **C**
   Hinweis: "He has hurt his leg and has to give it some rest" (Z. 26 f.)
3. **C**
   Hinweis: "So how about 7:35 then? ... Let's take that one." (Z. 41 ff.)
4. **B**
   Hinweis: "But my parents bought me a <u>laptop</u> ..."; (Z. 51 f.), "And the <u>necklace</u> I got from Tom ..." (Z. 56)
5. **A**
   Hinweis: "... celebrate at my place ..." (Z. 80 f.)

Part 2

You will hear the captain's announcement on board an airplane. You will hear the announcement twice. Listen and complete questions 6 to 10.
[pause]

Good afternoon, ladies and gentlemen. This is your captain Ben Miller speaking. I would like to welcome you on board our BestJet Flight BJ 107-003 from Stuttgart to London. We are currently cruising at an altitude of 33,000 feet and our speed is 570 miles per hour. The time is 3:35 pm and we are on time. With the wind on our side we should land in London at 4:25 local time. London time is one hour behind CET. So don't forget to adjust your watches. The weather in London at the moment is clear and sunny, the temperature is a comfortable 22 degrees Celsius this afternoon. The cabin crew will be coming around in about 15 minutes to offer you light snacks and drinks. You can choose from a wide range, the prices are listed in the brochure in the seat pocket in front of you. Sit back, relax and enjoy the flight.

6. **BJ 107 003**
   Hinweis: "... Flight BJ 107-003 from Stuttgart to London." (Z. 3 f.)
7. **33,000**
   Hinweis: "... at an altitude of 33,000 feet ..." (Z. 4 f.)
8. **4:25**
   Hinweis: "... should land in London at 4:25 ..." (Z. 7 f.)
9. **clear** and **sunny**/**sunny** and **clear**
   Hinweis: "... weather in London at the moment is clear and sunny ..." (Z. 10)
10. **snacks** and **drinks**/**drinks** and **snacks**
    Hinweis: "... to offer you light snacks and drinks." (Z. 13 f.)

Part 3

You will hear a conversation in a bookshop between a bookseller and a customer. You will hear the conversation twice.
For questions 11 to 15 mark A, B or C.
Look at questions 11 to 15 now.
[pause]
Now listen to the conversation.

BOOKSELLER: Hello! What can I do for you?

CUSTOMER: Hi! I am looking for a book by Joanne K. Rowling. But I'm afraid I've forgotten what it's called.

BOOKSELLER: Right. Is it a book out of the Harry Potter series that you are looking for? The Harry Potter ones are her most famous and best sold books. Over 450 million copies have been sold worldwide.

CUSTOMER: No, it's not Harry Potter. I've read all the books and my favourite is the one where he misses the train to Hogwarts after the summer holidays. Wasn't it in 'Harry Potter and the Half-Blood Prince'?

BOOKSELLER: No, it wasn't. You mean 'Harry Potter and the Chamber of Secrets'.

CUSTOMER: That's the one! Fantastic book!

BOOKSELLER: But not the one you are actually looking for.

CUSTOMER: No. My cousin said it's a novel for adults, not for children.
BOOKSELLER: You mean 'The Casual Vacancy'. That's just brilliant, too.
CUSTOMER: Yes. 'The Casual Vacancy'. Do you have it?
BOOKSELLER: Let me have a look in our computer system. No ... unfortunately the last copy was sold yesterday. But I can order it if you like.
CUSTOMER: That would be great. How much is it?
BOOKSELLER: It costs £ 8.99 and should be here tomorrow. Shall I order it?
CUSTOMER: Yes, please.
BOOKSELLER: Can I have your name, please?
CUSTOMER: My name is Paul Lambert. That's L-A-M-B-E-R-T.
BOOKSELLER: Lambert, Paul ... Alright. I've ordered the book for you.
CUSTOMER: Cool. Then I'll come to fetch it tomorrow morning. See you then. Have a nice day.
BOOKSELLER: You too. Thanks, bye-bye.
[pause]

11. B
    Hinweis: "Over 450 million copies have been sold ..." (Z. 8)
12. B
    Hinweis: "... my favourite is the one ..." (Z. 11); "You mean 'Harry Potter and the Chamber of Secrets'." (Z. 15 f.)
13. A
    Hinweis: "... the one you are actually looking for. ... it's a novel for adults ..." (Z. 18 ff.)
14. C
    Hinweis: "... the last copy was sold yesterday." (Z. 27 f.)
15. B
    Hinweis: "That's L-A-M-B-E-R-T." (Z. 34 f.)

Part 4

You will hear Bethany talking about vegan food. You will hear the report twice. For questions 16 to 20 mark 'true' or 'false'.
Look at questions 16 to 20 now.
[pause]
Now listen to the report.

No meat, no problem

My favorite food used to be spaghetti and meatballs with lots of mozzarella cheese. I liked anything with lots of meat and cheese. So when my family decided to go vegan and live without meat, I was shocked. My first day as a vegan was terrible. For lunch I had a sandwich with lots of lettuce and tomatoes. But without ham, it tasted like paper. I went to our fridge looking for meat, but my parents had given all of it away. Our first cooked vegan dinner was rice and vegetables. Then my mum bought a vegan cookbook and learned how to prepare tofu. When she served dinner the next time, it was tofu which looked like scrambled eggs mixed with vegetables. And it tasted just like egg! After that, my mum's recipes got even better. Everything tasted just like non-vegan, so I didn't miss meat anymore. For lunch at school I took some fruit and a vegan sandwich. One day one of my friends asked me if I wanted some chicken. "No, I'm fine," I said. I didn't like chicken anymore. "Come on! You know you want some," he said, as he waved it in front of my face. "It's not going to work," I said, laughing. "You can't convince me!" A few years ago if you'd asked me to try being vegan, I would have called you crazy. But now I believe that this diet is great because it's made me feel healthier. I have more energy and I can concentrate in school better.

Adapted from: http://www.layouth.com/no-meat-no-problem
[pause]

16. true
    Hinweis: "I liked anything with lots of meat and cheese." (Z. 3 f.)
17. true
    Hinweis: "... it tasted like paper." (Z. 8)
18. false
    Hinweis: "... was rice and vegetables." (Z. 10 f.)
19. false
    Hinweis: "... I didn't miss meat anymore." (Z. 16 f.)
20. false
    Hinweis: "... I can concentrate in school better." (Z. 27 f.)

Part 5

You will hear a presenter on a TV show talking about selfies. Which selfies did the teenagers take? You will hear this report twice. For questions 21 to 25 write a letter, A–H, next to each person.
[pause]

PRESENTER: Hi folks, great that you are with me. Today's topic: what your mobile phone selfies say about you. Posting photos on social networks is basically a part of everyday life now. But, did you know that your selfies can say a lot more about you than you think? Last week I asked you to email some of your snapshots and here are five examples of your selfies and what they say about yourself.

Selfie number one was taken by Theresa. Her head is down, she has turned her eyes away and seems to be looking somewhere in the distance. These characteristics can indicate a shy and reserved personality. That's why I call it the 'shy selfie'.

Selfie number two is by a girl called Emily. As you can see, Emily loves expensive clothes. Her hobby is shopping and she takes selfies in the dressing room. That's why it is a 'fashion selfie'. This kind of selfie says that you are a fun person to hang out with.

Now here's selfie number three. I call it the 'headless selfie'. It is a snapshot of a body only. The headless selfie says that you're proud of your body and that you like some parts of it, but also that you're not happy with other parts. By the way: this selfie was taken by Wesley.

Selfie number four, taken by a girl named Ashley, is somehow strange. The picture is almost dark. So I want to label it the 'dark room selfie'. It's a shot you take so that only your face is in the light and the background is dark. The dark room selfie says that you want to get out and meet people but you're still holding back.

The fifth and last selfie was sent in by Danny. He's taken a selfie in his bathroom in front of a mirror. Sometimes these selfies are also edited with a photo programme so they become filtered selfies. But Danny's isn't. It's just the usual 'mirror selfie'. Now let's have a short music break and we'll be back with more information about selfies in a minute.

Adapted from: http://www.teenscene.com/life/what-your-selfies-say-about-you

[pause]

21. C
    Hinweis: "Selfie number one was taken by Theresa ... can indicate a shy and reserved personality." (Z. 10 ff.)

22. H
    Hinweis: "... Emily loves expensive clothes ... That's why it is a 'fashion selfie'." (Z. 16 ff.)

23. E
    Hinweis: "I call it the 'headless selfie' ... was taken by Wesley." (Z. 21 ff.)

24. G
    Hinweis: "... taken by a girl named Ashley ... to label it the 'dark room selfie'." (Z. 27 ff.)

25. B
    Hinweis: "... was sent in by Danny ... in front of a mirror." (Z. 34 f.)

II. Reading Comprehension

Part 1

1. C
   Hinweis: *stay* = bleiben
2. A
   Hinweis: *(to) iron* = bügeln
3. A
   Hinweis: *car dealer* = Autohändler
4. A
   Hinweis: *recommended* = empfohlen
5. A
   Hinweis: *unattended items* = unbeaufsichtigte Gegenstände
6. A
   Hinweis: *penalty fare* = Bußgeld; *tube* = Londoner U-Bahn

Part 2

7. B
8. A
   Hinweis: *dishes* = Gerichte, Speisen; *to be patient:* Geduld haben
9. C
10. A
    Hinweis: *maximum weight* = Höchstgewicht

Part 3

11. not in the text
12. true
    Hinweis: "Ecologists fitted special tiny tail cameras ..." (Z. 4 f.)
13. false
    Hinweis: "Why do New Caledonian crows use tools but other crows and birds don't?" (Z. 10 f.)
14. true
    Hinweis: "... made these hooks by breaking off pieces of branches from a tree." (Z. 16)
15. false
    Hinweis: "... the gadgets fall off the birds." (Z. 20)

Part 4

16. D
17. A
18. B
19. C
20. C

Part 5

21. B
    Hinweis: "… sent him the real shirt personalised with his signature!" (Z. 5 ff.)

22. C
    Hinweis: "From a poor family …" (Z. 9)
23. A
    Hinweis: "… and he loves one of the best footballers ever, Lionel Messi." (Z. 10 f.)
24. B
    Hinweis: "… affected the heart of a lot of people all over the world …" (Z. 15 f.)
25. B
    Hinweis: "Messi, who represents UNICEF, sent … a ball to symbolise a child's right to play." (Z. 17 ff.)

III. Writing

Part 1 – Letter

Hinweis: Nachdem du die Lücken gefüllt hast, solltest du den Text noch einmal durchlesen, um zu überprüfen, ob deine Lösungen Sinn ergeben.

Madam – complain/you – until/till/before – send/post/give – disc/DVD/CD/game – work/start/run – get – paid/spent/given/transferred – first – from

Part 2 – Dialogue

Hinweis: Wenn du statt Fragen Aussagesätze formulierst, werden diese als richtig gewertet, wenn sie den auf Deutsch formulierten Inhalt korrekt wiedergeben.

1. I've got problems with my mobile (phone)/smartphone. I can't go online/I can't use the Internet.
2. I have to/must read/check my e-mails.
3. How much is it/does it cost for half an hour?
4. I would like to go online for an hour.
5. Can I print a few/some pages, too?
6. Is there anyone here who can help me with my mobile phone/smartphone (problem)?
7. Thank you. Could/Can I have/get a bottle of lemonade, please?

Part 3 – E-mail

Hinweis: Deine Aufgabe ist es hier, deinem Englischlehrer/deiner Englischlehrerin eine E-Mail aus Liverpool zu schreiben, wo du gerade eine Austauschschule besuchst. Achte dabei auf Höflichkeitsformen bei Anrede und Schluss.
Beschreibe in wenigen Sätzen die Schule und deine Klassenkameraden, deine Gastfamilie und deine Freizeitgestaltung. Abschließend zählst du deine Wörter. Es müssen mindestens 60 Wörter sein. Die folgende Lösung ist ein Beispiel.

From: (your name)
To: (your English teacher's name)
Subject: My experiences at the North Liverpool Academy

Dear Mr Müller,

I am writing to tell you about my experiences in Liverpool. The school I attend is very good. The building is old but has big classrooms. The teachers are helpful and my classmates have become good friends of mine. My host family is nice, too. They have a daughter of my age and, luckily, she is in my class, too. Her mum is a great cook. She makes the best chocolate cake. In the afternoons, I play volleyball in the school club or I go out with my classmates. There are a lot of activities you can do. I am really enjoying my stay in Liverpool.

See you soon.

Yours,
(your name)

(113 words)